SOMEONE ELSE'S WAR

SOMEONE ELSE'S WAR

Mercenaries from 1960 to the present

ANTHONY ROGERS

HarperCollins*Publishers*

HarperCollins*Publishers*
77-85 Fulham Palace Road
Hammersmith
London W6 8JB

First published by HarperCollins*Publishers* 1998

1 3 5 7 9 8 6 4 2

© Anthony Rogers, 1998

Anthony Rogers asserts the moral right to be
identified as the author of this work.

ISBN 0 00 472077 6

Maps: Martin Brown

Printed and bound in Great Britain by
Caledonian International Book Manufacturing Ltd,
Glasgow, G64

CONTENTS

Acknowledgements   7
Preface   8
Introduction   9

1 A Call to Arms:
      The Congo and 5 Commando, 1960-68   11
2 Rhodesia, 1966-79   32
3 Angolan Fiasco:
      'Colonel Callan's' Mercenaries, 1975-76   56
4 From Rhodesia to South Africa:
      SADF, 1975-82   78
5 Coup and Counter Coup:
      Comoros, 1975-95   116
6 Comedy of Errors: Seychelles, 1981   127
7 Malta, 1984-85   148
8 Surinam, 1986-91   155
9 Operation Phoenix: Colombia, 1988-91   171
10 "Lovely People": Yugoslavia, 1991-95   186
11 Foreign Legions   209
12 Into the 21st Century   227

Notes   234
Bibliography   248
Index   250

ACKNOWLEDGEMENTS

This book could not have been written without the assistance and co-operation of many former and active mercenaries. For various reasons, several have asked not to be named, including some whose identities have been previously publicized and who are hoping to avoid further attention. As an additional safeguard of their anonymity, certain individuals have also been provided with a different pseudonym for each chapter in which they feature. My thanks and appreciation to them all and to the writers and journalists who gave freely of their time, as well as to those publishers and television production companies who kindly gave permission to quote from their works.

All men dream: but not equally. Those who dream by night in the dusty recesses of their minds wake in the day to find that it was vanity: but the dreamers of the day are dangerous men, for they may act their dream with open eyes, to make it possible.

T.E. Lawrence, *Seven Pillars of Wisdom*

INTRODUCTION

Traditionally, a mercenary is somebody who fights for a foreign power in return for financial or material gain. In ancient times, this may have been the case, but how appropriate is such a definition today? Throughout the 20th century, men continued to risk their lives fighting other people's wars, and not always for monetary reward. Consider, for example, the French Foreign Legion or the various nationalities who served on both sides during the Spanish Civil War (1936-39). What about the Americans who joined the Royal Air Force long before Pearl Harbor and their own nation's involvement in World War II? What were these men? Adventurers? Desperadoes? Ideologists? Opportunists? Whatever their motivation, all took up arms on behalf of another country or government, though few would have considered themselves true mercenaries.

Similarly, while those who volunteered to fight in the Congo in the 1960s were mercenaries in the accepted sense of the word, many who arrived in Rhodesia a decade later resented being labelled as such. It somehow mattered that they were part of a regular army, police or air force, serving under the same terms and conditions and for the same meagre wages as their Rhodesian colleagues.

The mercenaries of, say, Ancient Greece are really no different from those who have served in a foreign force during this century, for example in Africa, or more recently in the Middle East. But as society has changed, so has the perception of the warrior caste, which may explain why so many are reluctant to acknowledge their enjoyment of soldiering for its own sake.

But if the role of the 20th century mercenary is essentially still the same as that of his predecessor, the circumstances in which he is likely to serve are not. Article 47 of Protocol I Additional to the Geneva Convention of 1949 describes a mercenary as any person who:

a) is specially recruited locally or abroad in order to fight in an armed conflict;

b) does, in fact, take a direct part in the hostilities;

c) is motivated to take part in the hostilities essentially by the desire for private gain and, in fact is promised, by or on behalf of a Party to the conflict, material compensation substantially in excess of that promised or paid to combatants of similar ranks and functions in the armed forces of that Party;

d) is neither a national of a Party to the conflict nor a resident of territory controlled by a Party to the conflict;

e) is not a member of the armed forces of a Party to the conflict; and

f) has not been sent by a State which is not a Party to the conflict on official duty as a member of its armed forces.

But where does this leave foreigners who fought for little or no pay in the former Yugoslavia and similar conflicts? Few would argue that they, too, were mercenaries. They certainly would have been treated as such if captured by the enemy. Perhaps, therefore, it is time to clarify their status; for these soldiers and others prepared to fight for a foreign cause, irrespective of motive or reward, all fit the definition of the modern mercenary.

CHAPTER 1
A CALL TO ARMS: THE CONGO AND 5 COMMANDO, 1960-68

On 30 June 1960, the Belgian Congo celebrated its independence after 52 years of colonial rule. Within days, the new country was in turmoil, with President Joseph Kasavubu and Prime Minister Patrice Lumumba unable to control the diverse tribes of the huge nation. An uprising within the ranks of the Congolese National Army (ANC), until recently the colonial Public Force, led to military intervention by Belgium. The dissenters were quickly disarmed and disbanded, but in the southern province of Katanga troops loyal to Moise Tshombe were retained as the regional leader's own army – the *Gendarmerie*. On 11 July, Tshombe proclaimed the secession of Katanga and appointed Colonel Norbert Muké as Commander-in-Chief of the new force.

Two weeks after independence, the United Nations (UN) arrived in response to an appeal by Kasavubu and Lumumba, and began to take over from departing Belgian units. Confidence in the central government faded rapidly and Albert Kalonji, leader of Kasai province, also declared independence. Dissatisfied with the inability of the UN to restore order, Lumumba turned to the Russians for assistance. By September, his forces were sufficiently equipped to march on Kasai, but an attempt to take Katanga ended with the repulse of his troops at the border.

For Tshombe, the immediate threat came not so much from the UN or even central government, but from his own political and tribal rivals, the Baluba of North Katanga. Tshombe decided to seek the assistance of white mercenaries.

On 5 September, Lumumba was dismissed from office and placed

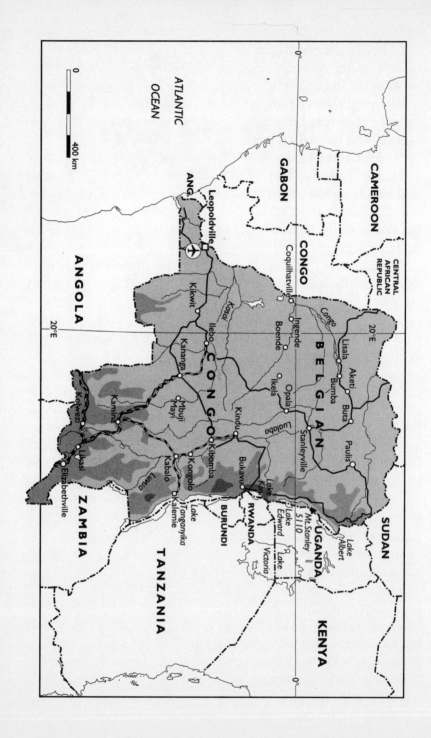

under house arrest. He was replaced with the more moderate Joseph Ilio. Shortly afterwards, the ANC Commander-in-Chief, Colonel Joseph Désiré Mobutu (see chapters 3 and 12) suspended the government in Léopoldville and declared that his administration would temporarily take over the running of the country. Led by Antoine Gizenga, Lumumba's supporters continued to oppose Mobutu and formed a rival government in Stanleyville.

Patrice Lumumba was assassinated in early 1961[1]. Although he had hardly endeared himself to Western leaders by his outspoken tirades during his brief period in office, nevertheless his death caused consternation in diplomatic circles and certainly affected the decision by hitherto sympathetic nations not to provide support to any of the political parties.

Tshombe was fortunate to escape death after being detained in Coquilhatville in April after a conference with opposition leaders. He was released in June. By August 1961 the governments in Léopoldville and Stanleyville had united under Cyrille Adoula, with key posts assigned to Gizenga and his political ally, Christopher Gbenye. Predictably, Tshombe refused to accept such an administration.

There were now many English-speaking and Belgian mercenaries in Katanga as well as Belgian officers on contract to the *Gendarmerie*. There was also a group of French mercenaries that included men from the regiments disbanded by President de Gaulle after the military revolt in French Algeria. The contrived image of many mercenaries soon earned them an apt sobriquet: *Les Affreux* (the dreadful ones)! The UN, however, was unimpressed by the estimated 512 'foreign military or paramilitary personnel' in Katanga, and at the end of August launched Operation Rumpunch, during which some 400 men were expelled. Nevertheless, according to South African mercenary Jerry Puren (see chapter 6), "Operation Rumpunch had, after its initial success, diminished the key mercenary population very little. Several prominent mercenaries had gone into hiding during the operation and had not been caught. A number who had jetted out at UN expense had jetted right back in at Tshombe's expense and found diverse means of getting back into service, while others still had not even been touched by the dragnet."[2]

On 13 September 1961, UN troops seized control of key points throughout Katanga, including the capital, Elizabethville. The next day a combined mercenary/Katangese force counterattacked. The UN Irish garrison at Jadotville, north-west of the capital, surrendered within days, prompting the UN secretary-general, Dag Hammarskjöld, to fly out to Northern Rhodesia to meet with Tshombe. Soon after, the aircraft carrying Hammarskjöld was reported to have mysteriously crashed: there was one survivor, who died a few days later.

Hostilities between the UN and Tshombe's forces were suspended until 5 December 1961 when the UN went on the offensive, ostensibly in response to their discovery of an aggressive mercenary battle plan in case of a UN/ANC attack. In two and a half weeks of action, the mercenaries, together with the Katangese, again showed themselves to be aggressive and courageous fighters. But in the end sheer weight of numbers and superior firepower resulted in a UN victory. Negotiations between Tshombe and Adoula failed to put a stop to the fighting between the *Gendarmes* and ANC, however, and a year later the UN firmly demanded an end to Katanga's secession. When the ultimatum was rejected, UN troops advanced in force against Elizabethville and other major towns, eventually forcing the mercenaries and several thousand Katangese *Gendarmes* across the border into the Portuguese colony of Angola.

Katanga saw the emergence of several notable mercenaries such as Roger Falques, a superb commander and tactician, formerly of the French Foreign Legion's 1st Foreign Parachute Regiment (1er REP); and Jerry Puren, an ex member of the South African Air Force and Royal Air Force, who served as a platoon officer and later as chief of the Katangese Air Force. Other infamous personalities included the Belgians Jean 'Black Jack' Schramme and Christian Tavernier (see chapter 12), Frenchman Bob Denard (see chapters 5 and 6) and Irishman Mike Hoare (see chapter 6).

On 30 June 1964, two important events took place in the Congo. The United Nations withdrew and Moise Tshombe replaced Cyrille Adoula as Prime Minister. Meanwhile, an uprising was underway in the eastern region of the Congo, instigated primarily by Pierre Mulele.[3] Notionally Communist, the revolt of the 'Simbas' (Lions) had spread rapidly, spearheaded by a savage force of teenage *Jeunesse*. It was believed by the Congolese that the rebels were bewitched: Mulele's followers had only to take their *dawa*, a specially prepared potion, and cry "*Mai* Mulele!" (*Mai* means 'water') as they went into battle to render an enemy and his weapons ineffective. When confronted by such powerful magic, ANC soldiers panicked and fled for their lives.

Moise Tshombe was invited by President Kasavubu to return from voluntary exile in Spain and take charge of the administration. Tshombe attempted to resolve the issue by debate, hoping to bring together the warring parties under a 'Government of Reconciliation'. However, by August the rebel leaders were in control of half the country, which they retitled the Popular Republic of the Congo. Tshombe's response was to follow the advice of his old friend Jerry Puren and recruit a force of white mercenaries. Puren was asked to organize an air force. Mike Hoare, brought in to command the ground troops, was authorized to recruit 200 volunteers to spearhead an offensive by Tshombe's *Gendarmes*, who were to be airlifted in from Angola courtesy of the United States' government.

Puren was soon in action, using T6 Harvards to strafe *Jeunesse* columns north-east of Luluabourg in Kasai Province. Two days later, he overflew the *Gendarmes* during their first major offensive.

From 350 metres above we took grandstand seats of the battle unfolding below us. The rebels, by now many strong, moved on foot and by truck. Densely packed, they surged down the road towards the approaching *Gendarme* column, a long snakelike movement of people, weapons and vehicles.

The lead jeep of the *Gendarme* column didn't even reduce speed as it approached. I held my breath as the two forces drew closer. The thin line of olive green vehicles was partially obscured by billows of dust; the black mass of Simba infantrymen equally obscured. It looked as if the lead *Gendarme* jeep was only metres away from the first ranks of rebels when the gunner began blasting furiously, almost at point blank range, at the surge of faces.

15

Battle hardened as I was, I felt sickened at the slaughter that followed. The lead jeeps clove a path through the chanting, swaying spearmen and, at almost arms length, mowed then down in swathes. I could imagine the drugged, sweating rebels desperately holding out their ampoules of *dawa*, the medicine that was to turn the ANC bullets to water.

The outcome was inevitable. Rebels scattered for cover, clawing each other to get away from the merciless hail of bullets. The rebels disappeared off the road and, over a long stretch of track the *Gendarmes'* jeeps moved slowly forward, sometimes over heaped bodies, as the sweating gunners raked the bush with belt after belt of .30 and .50 calibre bullets.

From the air bodies could be seen scattered astride the road and on either side right up to the bush wall as carelessly as shed clothing. The *Jeunesse* and rebels were never to threaten Luluabourg again. A turning point had been reached.[4]

Within weeks, the first of Hoare's mercenaries arrived at Kamina airfield. They were soon deployed on Operation Watch Chain to capture the airfield at Albertville, on the west bank of Lake Tanganyika, and to free any white hostages held in the town jail. According to Hoare's own account[5], not all the mercenaries were overly keen to fight. Of the 38 arrivals, nine allegedly refused to take part in the mission because they had not yet signed a contract; one Belgian volunteer opted out as the men prepared to negotiate the lake, and several others were ordered to stay behind as they were considered by Hoare to have "no stomach for the fight".[6]

The remainder boarded three boats and began the 160-km journey north to Albertville. When about a third of the way to their objective, the mercenaries encountered a priest in a small motor boat, who implored them to hurry to the jail where 60 white priests faced imminent death at rebel hands. Against his better judgement, Hoare decided to change his plan of attacking the airfield first, thereby jeopardizing a simultaneous assault by two ANC columns converging on the town from the south and west, and also putting at risk a plane-load of mercenary reinforcements scheduled to arrive at the airfield with Major Blume of the Belgian Air Force.

The first contact occurred at Malembe, just south of Albertville.

The rebels, equipped with a few old Mauser rifles and crude home-made weapons, stood no chance. Within 15 minutes it was all over, and 28 rebels lay dead in front of the mercenaries' positions. That night, as the mercenaries attempted a beach-landing at Albertville, they came under heavy fire and were forced to withdraw past Malembe. Hoare decided to revert to his original plan and dispatched a party under one of his officers, Pat Kirton, to Mpala from where they could radio Kamina airfield to request an air resupply. Unfortunately, engine trouble forced Kirton and his men to abandon their boat and continue the journey on foot. After waiting in vain for three days, Hoare decided to take Albertville airfield with his force alone, and at 0300 hours on 29 August landed his men on the beach alongside the objective. The attack was a disaster. Former Royal Marines Commando, Eric Bridge, was wounded by a spear and two Germans, Nestler and Köhtler, killed. The survivors pulled back to the relative safety of Mpala.

Subsequently, Albertville was relieved by the ANC, and hundreds of Belgian nationals, including some of the 60 priests, were saved. For Hoare and his fledgling 5 Commando, it was an ignominious beginning. Operation Watch Chain may explain what seems to have been a reluctance on Hoare's part to engage in future night work, a trait that would re-emerge years later in the Seychelles (see chapter 6).

★ ★ ★

After the recapture of Albertville the mercenaries retired to their main base at Kamina where more than 500 volunteers had assembled. Not all were considered suitable by Hoare, who soon reduced the number to just over 300. Officers, senior NCOs and NCOs were selected, the troops split into 40-man teams, or 'Commandos', and an intensive training programme begun. Responsibility for logistics and administration was taken over by the Belgians. When the mercenaries next deployed, they would be much better prepared.

★ ★ ★

5 Commando eventually comprised eight sub-units designated 51 to 58 Commandos, each consisting of about 30 to 40 men. The Commandos frequently operated independently of each other, relying on speed, surprise and superior firepower. Armed jeeps were used as the vanguard during attacks – a method not dissimilar to that employed by the Special Air Service in its raids against Axis installations in Libya during World War II. There, the enemy had been a well-equipped, heavily armed and combat-tried professional force. In the Congo, the enemy were usually inadequately equipped and poorly armed tribesmen, although their weaponry improved as sympathetic countries supplied arms and ammunition.

5 Commando's first major success was an attack on the Simbas at Lisala and Bumba, in the north of the country. The victory, by a company of ANC and 51 Commando under Second Lieutenant Gary Wilson, also took the pressure off Gemena, in the north-west, and stemmed the rebel advance on the capital, Léopoldville. Subsequently, Hoare's men were deployed throughout the Congo. After the rebels took Ingende, 52 Commando under Captain Siegfried Müller – who wore on his left breast pocket the Iron Cross First Class – was rushed up to nearby Coquilhatville, principal city of Equator Province. The mercenaries then advanced on Ingende before continuing eastwards towards Boende, 320 km further on. On the outskirts, unexpectedly heavy resistance forced Müller to withdraw to the village of Bikili, where the enemy succeeded in encircling his force.

Meanwhile, 54 Commando, led by Second Lieutenant Forsbrey, had been flown north, where the mercenaries joined the ANC in repelling the enemy from Yakoma. After this, Forsbrey was ordered to assist Müller. Soon after, Hoare arrived and learnt that the German intended to take Boende in a pincer movement, using the two Commandos at his disposal. He agreed to allow the plan to proceed, but appointed Lieutenant Ben Louw to lead 52 Commando. Müller, it seems, had made the cardinal error of becoming over-familiar with his men, and Hoare (who clearly intended to run his command in British Army fashion), saw a clear distinction between officers and other ranks. Notwithstanding the fact that the assault on Boende was accomplished without casualties, Müller was unceremoniously sent back to Kamina as Base Commander after the operation. 52 Commando was transferred north to replace 51 at Bumba, and 54 moved east to Ikela.

On 23 September, Jack Maiden's 53 Commando was ordered to bolster ANC defences at Bukavu, on the Congo-Rwanda border. After successful operations at Kabare and Uvira to the south, 53 Commando moved north, taking Lubero and Butembo. Maiden was then told to consolidate his position and await orders to advance on Stanleyville. According to Hoare:

> I presented Mr Tshombe with a plan to give him Stanleyville by the end of October. The plan was simple. 5 Commando should be concentrated forthwith at Lisala, with orders to advance on Stan via the axis Aketi-Buta-Banalia, as a highly mobile and armour-tipped column, supported by air. As each town fell, it must be garrisoned by troops of the ANC who would be flown in. Belgian mercenaries, who were now arriving in the Congo in large numbers, would accompany the ANC and would be used as military police. Finally, Belgian Technical Assistance would provide men to administer the captured towns, as we went forward.[7]

After being airlifted to Kongolo, 55, 56 and 57 Commandos headed towards Samba by road. The mercenaries formed part of 5 Mechanized Brigade, which also included two Ferret Scout Cars, three Swedish Scania Vabis APCs, as well as ANC infantry and engineers. A Belgian regular officer, Lieutenant Colonel Liegeois, commanded the column, although Hoare was responsible for overseeing his own men in action. Samba was seized after a brief skirmish. En route to Kibombo, their next objective, the mercenaries encountered heavier resistance when the rebels attacked with three improvized armoured vehicles. The first was destroyed with a rocket launcher, and the crews of the other two were cut down by machine-gun fire. Fifty km from Kindu the mercenaries shot up two bus-loads of Simba reinforcements on their way to Kimbombo. The column pushed on, reaching the town soon after and pausing only to allow an air-strike immediately before the mercenaries' assault. Kindu and the surrounding area was liberated, and the victors were treated to an emotional welcome by those European inhabitants who had survived the murderous onslaught of the Simbas.

Next to be liberated was Kamina, whose grateful European population was escorted back to Kindu and flown to Léopoldville. The column paused at Kindu, where it was joined by 51 Commando for a final drive on Stanleyville. Meanwhile, 52 Commando had been ordered to proceed to Aketi and Paulis; 53 was detailed to take Mambasa, in the north-east; while 54 would advance on Stanleyville via Ikela and Opela. The main column of at least 200 vehicles was to attack via Kindu, Punia and Lubutu. The air force, based at Kindu, was well within range of all fronts.

Punia was easily taken, but the mercenaries met with some resistance further on at Yumbi, where they were to cross the Lowa River. After the rebel defence had been dealt with, there was another delay as the long column was laboriously ferried across the river by pontoon. The five armoured cars and 5 Commando transport were the first across, and pushed on to Lubutu to await the arrival of the remaining vehicles. Further north, the ANC and mercenary units had reached Mambasa, Aketi and Ikela as planned. Another unexpected bonus was the arrival at Kamina of Belgian paratroopers for a proposed drop on Stanleyville, where rebel leader Christopher Gbenye had made hostages of the 1700 white inhabitants. Others, including the Mayor, had already been killed, together with numerous Africans opposed to the Popular Republic.

At last, the column was formed up ready for the assault on Stanleyville. The mercenaries (reinforced by a number of Cubans who would later form 58 Commando) were to launch a co-ordinated strike with the paratroopers who were scheduled to drop on the town at 0600 hours on 24 November. Hoare had hoped to reach his objective after an all-night race from Lubutu, but after taking fire from enemy positions and sustaining five casualties, including one mercenary and a CBS correspondent killed, he decided to wait until daylight before proceeding further. Another mercenary died later in hospital.

The advance continued at dawn, and by 0600 hours 5

Commando had reached Wanie Rukulu, 60 km from Stanleyville. At 0635 hours the Belgian paratroopers were dropped on the outskirts of the city, and after securing the airport they pushed on towards Stanleyville proper. By the time the first soldiers arrived it was already too late for many inhabitants, slaughtered in a frenzy of blood lust by the Simbas. It took 5 Commando more than three hours to reach their objective, by which time the battle for Stanleyville was effectively over. The surviving Europeans were evacuated and rebel sympathizers rounded up and executed. Then the looting began – carried out by both the ANC and mercenaries. The paratroopers, their job done, quietly withdrew in preparation for another drop on Paulis, scheduled for two days' time.

5 Commando was now tasked with clearing outlying areas and freeing isolated groups of Europeans. They were not always in time. At the Rive Gauche, near Stanleyville, at least two dozen Europeans were murdered just two days before the mercenaries arrived to find the sole surviving British missionary and her two children. Another rescue effort of British missionaries at nearby Yakusu succeeded when all nine were saved. In the meantime, Colonel Laurent's paratroopers descended on Paulis where some 250 hostages were freed but, as at Stanleyville, others had suffered brutal deaths at the hands of the rebels. In the preceding weeks, thousands of Congolese suspected of opposing the rebel regime were also murdered.

Mopping up operations in Stanleyville were carried out ruthlessly by the ANC, supported by 5 Commando and the new 6 Commando, formed from Belgian, French and Spanish mercenaries. Hoare's men then resumed their pursuit of the rebels, advancing as far as the Aruwimi River, 160 km north of Stanleyville. 54 Commando moved north with 57 Commando to relieve 52 at Paulis, from where 54 launched a successful strike on Wamba. In the meantime, 53 Commando took Mambasa, by way of Beni, before capturing Bunia early in December. The mercenaries' advance spared hundreds of white civilians, many of them priests and nuns, and thousands of Congolese from torture and death at the hands of the Simbas.

★   ★   ★

By January 1965, the men of 5 Commando were nearing the end of their six-month contracts. Hoare, promoted by General Mobutu to Lieutenant Colonel, was asked to raise a new 5 Commando to secure the rest of Orientale Province. To assist him were two of his original team: Englishmen Alastair Wicks, recently promoted to major, and Captain John Peters. A new base was established at Bunia, west of Lake Albert on the border with Uganda, and on 15 March, 5 Commando started operations in the north-east.

Mahagi and Port Mahagi were soon taken, allowing Hoare to begin phase one of Operation White Giant: to seize Aru, Aba and Faradje. The first task was to take Golu, just north of the start-line at Nioka-Ngote. Commandant Christian Tavernier and his mainly Katangese battalion was assigned the left flank from Nioka, with the main column of 5 Commando in the centre, and Force John-John, consisting of around 100 men under Peters, on the right flank. Within an hour, Force John-John had clashed with the enemy, killing twelve men and capturing two heavy machine guns. Golu was reached the following day and taken at a cost of one man wounded by a land-mine. Hoare then revised his plan of attack and struck at Djalasiga and Kerekere. The former fell to Major Wicks, and the latter to the aggressive Captain Peters, who pushed on to capture nearby Essebi. The next objective, Aru, the main staging area for Communist aid arriving for the Simbas via Uganda, was taken by Tavernier's 14 Commando. Force John-John remained in the forefront of the action during the advance on Aba – the location of rebel headquarters in Orientale and a channel for rebel aid from the Sudan – but by the time Aba was reached, the enemy had fled. Hoare ordered the destruction of a bridge linking the road from Aba to the Sudan, and early the following morning dispatched Wicks to Faradje. 14 Commando, less one company, also participated in the attack, and by dusk the town was securely in government hands.

Phase two of Hoare's operation targeted the remaining major towns in the province. Watsa, south of Faradje, was the first objective. Thirty-eight Belgian civilians had been murdered there the previous November, and hundreds of Congolese had also perished. The ANC had no sympathy for the perpetrators of such crimes, and frequently tortured and executed captured dissidents.

22

At Watsa, they avenged themselves by killing an estimated 50 to 60 wounded Simbas.

After capturing Dungu and Niangara, north-west of Watsa, Hoare returned to Stanleyville and met the ANC command to discuss the next stage of the campaign.

In just seven weeks the Uganda and south-east Sudan border crossings had been closed, and key towns in the north-east placed under the control of Hoare's own 'District Commissioners'.

At 3 Group Headquarters, responsible for operations in the north-east, Chief-of-Staff Lieutenant Colonel Jacques Noel finalized plans for Operation *Violettes Imperiales*. This called for the seizure of Buta and Bondo, to the west of Paulis, involving two Commandos and the ANC. 5 Commando was tasked with taking Bondo, and 6 Commando with capturing Buta.

The run-up to *Violettes Imperiales* was marked by several incidents. After a failed counterattack at Aba, the enemy had fled across the border to seek refuge in the Sudan, prompting a successful follow-up operation by Peters, who was again in the forefront of the fighting when the rebels assaulted Niangara. At about this time Peters was promoted to Commandant by General Mobutu in recognition of an earlier action during the advance on Aba. Soon after, he was granted a week's leave and was accompanied from Niangara as far as Paulis by an eight-man escort from 57 Commando. The men were permitted to stay overnight in Paulis, but in allowing this their OC was contravening 3 Group orders, which stated that Paulis was off-limits to 5 Commando personnel. That evening his men were involved in an argument with some Katangese, during which their Congolese Adjutant was shot dead. Although not involved himself, Peters was held responsible by Hoare and immediately put on suspension pending an official enquiry.

Operation *Violettes Imperiales* commenced on 29 May 1965. Hoare's column of 110 men, an ANC bridging unit, and two Ferret Scout Cars left Niangara at dawn for the dash to Bondo. In spite of several brushes with the rebels, the 630-kilometre journey was completed in three days. Two Norwegian missionaries were rescued along the way and two more Europeans found alive at Bondo. One Belgian man had escaped death in November when he was tied up by the Simbas, put in a sack and flung into a river: somehow he managed to free himself and survived by hiding in an attic for six months until the arrival of Hoare's column. Further east, 6 Commando, spearheaded by a composite unit known as *Premier Choc*, under the command of Frenchman Bob Denard, had taken Poko and was proceeding towards Buta.

Hoare received a signal from Jacques Noel, ordering him to head immediately to Buta. Along the way lay Likati, home to a number of Greek and Portuguese traders and their families. As Hoare's column approached, the Simbas massacred the white population before fleeing into the surrounding bush. Only one woman survived. The mercenaries were enraged. According to Hoare, 15 rebels, captured at Bondo, were killed "while trying to escape", after which:

> We resumed the march considerably subdued and thoughtful. An unspoken order ran down the column – kill everything that moves. There is no stimulus like revenge and the column swept forward, searing the countryside with the bright flame of retribution. We halted at dusk at the cross roads, 74 km west of Buta.[8]

5 Commando entered Buta at 1000 hours on 3 June, an hour before 6 Commando, by which time just five white hostages remained alive.

★   ★   ★

Moise Tshombe and General Mobutu were delighted with the military successes in Orientale Province. However, the rebels were still being supplied from Burundi and across Lake Tanganyika from Tanzania. Hoare, who was nearing the end of his second contract, was offered a third to overcome rebel resistance in the Fizi-Baraka region, the domain of a fiercely warlike tribe called the Bahembi, stretching from Uvira, at the top of Lake Tanganyika, south along the coast for 240 km to Kabimba, and inland for 260 km to Kasongo. The mercenaries would be confronting a determined enemy who was well-equipped, well-trained and properly led. Significantly, during a recent rebel raid on Bendera, between Fizi and Albertville, one of the rebel dead was found to be a Cuban adviser.

After some persuasion, Hoare agreed to extend his service. Others who renewed their contracts included Majors Alastair Wicks and Peter Johnstone who was promised his own battalion and entrusted with safeguarding the north-eastern sector. Another battalion, to be based at Albertville, would be raised for service in the Fizi-Baraka area. In addition to the usual Commandos, there was to be a unit of 30 men to crew an 80-foot gunboat, the *Ermans*, and 6 PT boats to help police the border with Tanzania. Air power consisted of a dozen T-28s (reduced to 11 after a flying accident wrote off one aircraft), four B-26 bombers and a Bell helicopter.

Two incidents marred the training and combat preparation of the unit. Not for the first time, Hoare was faced with a mutiny by his men over delayed payment. Thoroughly fed up with the issue, Hoare met with Mobutu in Léopoldville and informed him that he would resign his command unless a more efficient pay system was implemented. The outstanding amount was paid within a week.

When he returned to Albertville, Hoare learned that in his absence four mercenaries in two Ferret armoured cars had been ambushed while escorting a Belgian *Adjutant Chef* and his three assistants to Bendera. Only one of the mercenaries had survived.

★　★　★

Because the terrain in the Fizi-Baraka pocket was predominantly hilly and wooded, Hoare decided on an amphibious operation, landing a motorized force behind enemy lines to seize Fizi, Baraka and Lulimba simultaneously. There were 300 mercenaries available for the mission, timed for 27 September. Force John-John was resurrected, once again under the command of Peters (apparently forgiven for the incident in Paulis), while Englishman Captain Hugh van Oppens was assigned Force Oscar. Two battalions of ANC were also available at Bendera and Lulimba. Peters and six others were to reconnoitre the landing site before the arrival of the main force. A suitable beach was selected, eight km north of Baraka, which was to be secured at dawn by Force Oscar, supported by Force John-John: Wicks was to lead a diversionary frontal attack on enemy positions along the Lulimba escarpment. After Baraka had been taken, Force John-John was to proceed to Fizi, and finally, Lulimba would be taken in a pincer movement from the front and rear.

The operation began in the early hours during a particularly fierce storm, so that Peters' beach reconnaissance party had to paddle their assault craft through very rough waters before finally reaching land. Recognition lights were hurriedly erected, but proved too dim to be of any use. Desperately, the team attempted to establish communications, only to discover that their radio was too weak. To make matters worse, Peters had arrived at the wrong beach!

Meanwhile, the PT boat towing the assault craft to its drop-off point 1,500 metres offshore had broken down and was drifting helplessly, its radar and wireless out of order. Already, the operation was two hours behind schedule: soon it would be getting light. Hoare decided to risk ordering in the first wave. PT boats sped towards the shore and offloaded the troops just as dawn was breaking. They immediately came under mortar and machine-gun fire, but the second wave came in and landed regardless. Patrols pushed forward to a road 50 metres from the water's edge and quickly established a beachhead. By 0515 hours, all were ashore. The perimeter was extended and soon after, the first six jeeps were landed.

The unfavourable weather continued to hamper the operation, with low cloud precluding any air support. The rebels at Baraka conducted a fierce defence. While Force Oscar pushed towards the centre, Force John-John bypassed the town, but was driven back: four mercenaries were killed and several wounded, including Peters. Enemy losses were an estimated 120 killed and an unknown number wounded. Amongst the dead was their commander Wasochi Abedi.

By dawn on day two the weather had cleared, enabling six T-28s to join battle. The aircraft, piloted by anti-Castro Cubans, were employed with deadly effect against an enemy led, ironically, by fellow countrymen.[9] The battle for Baraka continued for five days before the mercenaries noticed a change in enemy tactics.

Previously, the rebels had mounted fairly disciplined attacks at dawn and dusk, but now resorted to the more familiar mass attack punctuated by screams of "*Mai* Mulele!" Convinced that this could only mean that the Cubans had departed, Hoare began to concentrate his efforts on taking Fizi.

Earlier, Wicks had been withdrawn from Lulimba along with 300 ANC, and now joined Hoare for the advance south. After overcoming enemy resistance at the Mutumbala Bridge, 16 km from Baraka, the column continued towards Fizi, which was seized without incident on 10 October. Lubondja, the last major town before Lulimba, was reached soon after. But the victory was overshadowed by the news that President Kasavubu had sacked his prime minister and replaced him with Evariste Kimba.[10] With the rebellion almost over, Tshombe's usefulness was at an end. An election was scheduled for February, and Kasavubu clearly had no wish to retain in power someone whose popularity threatened his own position. Without Tshombe, the future of 5 Commando was uncertain. In spite of the unwelcome announcement, Hoare decided to press on and capture Lulimba. Peters, who had rejoined the column in spite of his injury, was again wounded and airlifted to Albertville the following morning. He was accompanied by Hoare who was keen to discuss matters personally with the Chief-of-Staff of Operations South – *Ops Sud*, Lieutenant Colonel Roger Hardenne. Consequently, 5 Commando was ordered to take Kasimia at the southern end of Lake Tanganyika's Ubware Peninsula, before heading south to Kavumbwe, leaving Yungu, east of Bendera, to the ANC.

★　★　★

On 24 November 1965, Lieutenant General Mobutu ousted Kasavubu in a bloodless coup, tacitly supported by the CIA. Mobutu declared himself President, and Lieutenant Colonel Leonard Mulamba became the new Prime Minister. By this time Hoare had fulfilled the conditions of his contract. After handing over command to John Peters, he boarded a flight for Léopoldville on the first stage of his journey home. Alastair Wicks went with him. Jerry Puren, who resigned from the ANC in January 1965, had been recruited by the Interior Ministry to collate information likely to affect Tshombe's position in the Congo; a dangerous, often frustrating, and ultimately futile task. Soon after Mobutu's rise to power he too departed, joining Moise Tshombe in exile in Belgium.

5 and 6 Commandos, the latter now led by Bob Denard, continued to serve Mobutu, and several mercenary officers, including Jean Schramme, commanded other, predominantly Katangese, units. On 23 July 1966, Katangese troops in Stanleyville revolted in support of the exiled Tshombe. Although Denard and his men are thought to have been in the town, they apparently did little to quell the rebellion: other units provided varying degrees of support, while some, including 5 Commando, remained loyal to the government. After several weeks of confusion, the Katangese and a number of dissident mercenaries were routed, allegedly by Denard who now appeared to be back on Mobutu's side.[11]

Early in 1967, Peters was superseded as Commanding Officer 5 Commando by another of Hoare's original officers, George Schröder (see chapter 6), a South African who commanded the unit until its disbandment three months later. By this time, Mobutu's ruthless purge of his political opponents was causing increasing concern in the international community. Another coup d'état was planned, this time by Jerry Puren.

Maurice Quintin, an acquaintance of Puren's, was asked to approach Jack Schramme to discover if 10 Commando might lead a revolt against Mobutu. Schramme, whose troops were considered by Mobutu as a potential threat, knew that it was only a matter of time before his unit was disbanded, so he agreed to the proposal. Quintin undertook two more trips to negotiate with Schramme, but on his last visit he was shot and killed, in circumstances which are still obscure.[12]

Unaware of Quintin's death, Puren flew into Punia with two of Tshombe's aides for discussions with Schramme, who agreed to a coup but insisted Bob Denard be included. Although Puren had doubts about Denard, he was forced to acquiesce when Schramme threatened to withdraw from the operation. A revised plan was finalized and D-day scheduled for 1 July. Puren returned to South Africa.

At the end of June, Puren arrived back in Punia with a dozen reliable mercenaries and a cargo of arms and ammunition packed aboard a DC4 piloted by Rhodesian businessman and adventurer, Jack Malloch (see chapter 2). Later that evening, Puren and Schramme discussed the forthcoming operation. It was now slightly behind schedule but, as events would soon show, this was to be the least of their concerns. On the morning of 1 July, Puren tuned in to Radio Brazzaville to hear that Tshombe had been kidnapped in an aircraft en route to join his supporters in Punia.[13] Without Tshombe, Puren decided there could be no coup, but Schramme disagreed, arguing that they were committed to carrying out their task; they would install a caretaker government, which could demand the release of Tshombe as nominated ruler of a sovereign country. The coup could still succeed.

At dawn on Sunday, 5 July 1967, Schramme's troops moved to seize control of Stanleyville where they were to link up with 6 Commando but, for reasons known only to Denard, he failed to gather his men; neither, it seems, did he warn them of the impending coup. The matter was partially resolved when Denard's surprised mercenaries reluctantly agreed to join forces with 10 Commando. However, 30 or so others based at Léopoldville had no such choice: all but one, employed as Mobutu's personal bodyguard, were arrested and killed.

The second objective, Bukavu, fell according to plan. But at Kindu the third strike force came up against heavy opposition and was pinned down on the opposite side of the Lualaba River. Furthermore, Mobutu's 3rd Parachute Regiment was on its way to Stanleyville. On the second day of the coup, the situation deteriorated further with the refusal of some of the Katangese to join the coup, and the withdrawal of friendly forces from Bukavu following a breakdown in communications.

At Kindu, the 200 mercenaries and Katangese were eventually overrun by an estimated 1,200 ANC. Some were captured and tortured to death. A few of Puren's Rhodesian and South African mercenaries, together with a number of Katangese, fought a fierce rearguard action before managing to escape into the jungle: four days and 200 km later, the exhausted survivors finally reached the safety of Punia. On 6 July, Mobutu's paratroopers arrived at

Stanleyville and began the first of a series of probing attacks. Two Portuguese mercenaries who were wounded during the initial assault were put aboard an Aztec Piper and flown by Puren to Henrique de Carvalho, in Angola. According to Puren's own account, he then proceeded to Luanda to discuss events with officials, anxious to know what was happening beyond their border. Subsequently, and to his "bitter frustration", he was prevented from returning to the Congo after his aircraft was found to be unserviceable and he was forced instead to sample the local beer and prawns in the company of old friends![14]

On 10 July, a number of wounded mercenaries, including Denard, were airlifted to Rhodesia. Schramme continued to direct the rebellion, but it was evident that his forces had lost the initiative. Although seizure of Katanga Province was the key to the success of the uprising, Schramme chose instead to converge on Bukavu, accompanied by some 200 civilians who hoped to escape the fighting by crossing into neutral Rwanda.

Mobutu intended to deal with Schramme at Bukavu, and to this end had prepared a formidable defensive perimeter around the town: the main approach road was made especially secure. But when Schramme's troops arrived, they attacked from three directions. Panic-stricken, the ANC abandoned their positions and fled for the sanctuary of Rwanda. By 10 August, Bukavu was firmly under Schramme's control, enabling the refugees – and scores of 6 Commando mercenaries – to cross the border.

Puren, his aircraft once again airworthy, chose this time to return. One of Tshombe's aides, Naweji, went with him and a Belgian, Bracco, piloted the machine. It was to be the aircraft's final flight. Unable to find a suitable landing site at Bukavu, Bracco was obliged to make a forced-landing on nearby Lake Kivu, but he and his passengers survived unhurt. Puren now joined Schramme who was busily improving Bukavu's defences in preparation for the expected ANC counterattack. By mid-September, Bukavu was surrounded by thousands of Mobutu's troops, making a breakout virtually impossible but, nevertheless, preparations were made for an ambitious plan to take Katanga, involving a diversionary attack by Denard from Angola.

On 29 October, the ANC launched a major assault on Bukavu.

Three days later, Denard began his offensive, only to be pushed back across the border by the ANC. The situation was just as critical in Bukavu. During the night of 4-5 November, the garrison began to withdraw across the Shangugu Bridge to Rwanda. It was all over. The last to leave were Schramme and Puren.

After a brief internment at Cyangugu, the hundreds of Katangese *Gendarmes* and camp followers – their wives and children – were herded aboard waiting trucks and returned to the Congo. In spite of Mobutu's promise of an amnesty, many, if not all, were killed. The 120 or so mercenaries remained in captivity for six months before being released on 23 April 1968.

Mobutu continued to rule his country with customary ruthlessness: political opponents, real or imaginary, were swiftly dealt with. In 1971, the President Africanized his name to become Mobutu Sése Séko, and the Congo became Zaïre.

After his kidnapping, Moise Tshombe was taken to Algeria and imprisoned, where he died, or was killed, two years later.

CHAPTER 2
RHODESIA, 1966-79

The mercenaries' war in the Congo was just one of several fought in Africa during the 1960s, and each conflict attracted its share of adventurers and opportunists. After the Imam was overthrown in the Yemen in September 1962, mercenaries assisted the Royalist guerrillas in their campaign against the Republican government; they operated in the Sudan; and also in the three-year Biafran war that started on 30 May 1967 when Colonel Ojukwu announced the secession of his homeland from the Federation of Nigeria. Those who made their names during this period were the German Rolf Steiner, 'Taffy' Williams and Count Carl Gustav von Rosen, an ageing Swedish nobleman who emerged as something of a national hero after a brief spell as a pilot.

Meanwhile, in Rhodesia, a comparatively minor skirmish was developing into a vicious war between black and white Africans, each defending their right to live as they chose in what they saw as their own land.

The origins of the Rhodesian War are rooted in the colonization of the region by white settlers in the late 19th century, and the dissent of black African leaders who rallied their people in the fight against white supremacy. In the early 1960s, two rival nationalist groups emerged in Rhodesia: the Zimbabwe African People's Union (ZAPU) under Joshua Nkomo, and the Zimbabwe African National Union (ZANU), headed initially by the Reverend Ndabaningi Sithole and later by Robert Mugabe. Both parties campaigned for majority rule, but were hindered in their efforts by political differences and tribal rivalries, which persisted throughout their armed struggle.

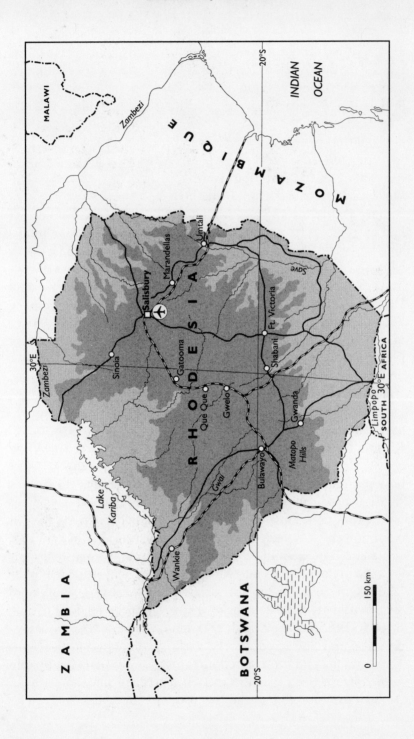

ZAPU was outlawed in September 1962 and temporarily replaced by the People's Caretaker Council (PCC), which was banned in August 1964 along with ZANU as a result of continuing internecine violence. Prominent nationalists, including Nkomo, Sithole and Mugabe, spent a decade in detention, while ZAPU and ZANU were directed by various lieutenants after relocating to new headquarters in neighbouring Zambia.

In July 1964, a unit of ZANU's military wing, the Zimbabwe African National Liberation Army (ZANLA), had ambushed and killed a white civilian, Petrus Oberholtzer, in the first act of war in Rhodesia since the 1890s. Although an isolated case, the murder had a profound effect on the country's close-knit white community. The following year, on 11 November 1965, Rhodesian Prime Minister Ian Smith severed ties with Britain, whose policies did not necessarily favour white interests, and proclaimed Unilateral Declaration of Independence (UDI). Five months later, on 28 April 1966, security forces killed seven ZANLA in a battle that would mark, for ZANU, the beginning of *Chimurenga* – their war of liberation. Less than three weeks later, survivors of the ZANLA unit murdered two civilians at their farm near Hartley.

The conflict continued at a relatively low-level until 21 December 1972, when ZANLA attacked Altena Farm in north-east Rhodesia. Meanwhile, the Front for the Liberation of Mozambique (FRELIMO), battling against Portuguese rule, had consolidated its gains in Tete Province, from where ZANLA was now allowed to operate in force. Clearly, for the security forces, the solution was to hit the enemy in their base camps and staging areas before they could infiltrate Rhodesia. Cross-border undercover operations by C Squadron, Special Air Service (SAS) had, in fact, commenced in the mid-1960s: security forces were also already engaged in hot pursuits into Mozambique.[1] Events soon led to the Rhodesian government authorizing an increasing number of 'externals' – as cross-border operations were termed. Less than three weeks after the attack at Altena, ZANLA murdered two civilians and abducted another, who was force-marched into Mozambique and imprisoned in Tanzania. This was the pretext needed for the first officially sanctioned parachute insertion of SAS troops into Mozambique: the operation commenced on 19 January

1973, and continued, with the approval of Mozambique's Portuguese administration, for nearly a month.[2]

In April 1974, a left-wing coup d'état in Portugal heralded the end of colonial rule in Mozambique. Within months, FRELIMO had formed a transitional government before officially taking control of the Portuguese colony in June 1975. These developments were as beneficial to ZANLA as they were disastrous to the Rhodesians, who now had to contend with an additional 1,100 kilometres of hostile border.

By 1977, the war had escalated and spread throughout Rhodesia. ZANLA, continuing to operate out of Mozambique, remained dominant in the eastern and central areas of Rhodesia amongst the Mashona, from whom ZANU drew much of its support. The use of bases in Zambia and Botswana and the allegiance of the Ndebele tribes in western Rhodesia, enabled ZAPU's Zimbabwe People's Revolutionary Army (ZIPRA) to remain active in the north and west.

The guerrillas were no longer the disorganized rabble they had been in the 1960s. They were now well-equipped with modern weapons and although many lacked basic military skills, a hard core of guerrillas had received training in Communist bloc and other sympathetic countries. ZANLA was primarily supported by China, ZIPRA by the Soviet Union. Weapons included the ubiquitous Kalashnikov and SKS-type rifles, light machine guns (the most common being the RPD and RPK), RPG-2 and RPG-7 launchers, and Soviet Fl and Chinese stick grenades. However, a far more impressive arsenal was to be found in the bush camps outside Rhodesia: during external operations the security forces faced mortars and 12.7 mm and 14.5 mm heavy machine guns, and towards the end of the war, heavier calibre weapons such as 122 mm multiple rocket launchers were also employed to combat Rhodesian raids.

In the wake of UDI, Rhodesia was subjected to economic and diplomatic sanctions but, nevertheless, managed to develop and maintain its fighting capability. With what was probably the most professional army in Africa, Rhodesia had a major advantage over its enemy in possessing air power. The Rhodesian Air Force included Hawker Hunter and de Havilland Vampire fighter-bombers and English Electric Canberra bombers, the Cessna Reims FTB 337G 'Lynx' and Douglas DC3 Dakota, while the Aerospatiale Alouette III served as the main helicopter until it was supplemented by the Agusta Bell 205.

On the ground, the British South Africa Police (BSAP) was responsible for law and order generally and also fielded formations such as the Police Anti-Terrorist Units (PATU) and Police Support Unit (PSU) or 'Black Boots', both of which were deployed against guerrillas within Rhodesia. The Army included the usual infantry, artillery and armoured elements. The war also spawned other, unorthodox, formations such as the Department of Psychological Warfare, or Psyac (propagandists); the Security Force Auxiliaries (SFAS: private armies whose loyalty lay primarily with moderate black nationalist leaders); Grey's Scouts (mounted infantry), and the Selous Scouts. The latter specialized in intelligence-gathering by tracking and infiltrating guerrilla units and by manning covert observation posts. While each had its own role in the war, much of the actual fighting was undertaken by just three units. The Rhodesian African Rifles (RAR), led by white officers until the integration of African officers late in the war, operated throughout the country, earning a fine reputation in the process. The First Battalion The Rhodesian Light Infantry (RLI), which eventually developed into an airborne-commando force, was deployed internally and on cross-border operations. The RLI sometimes operated in conjunction with C Squadron, later retitled 1 Special Air Service Regiment (Rhodesia), which was involved primarily in externals. The RLI and SAS were the only units not to be racially integrated, and each attracted experienced veterans from all over the world.

Rhodesia actively recruited foreign personnel. In the mid-1970s, some members of HM Forces were even sent letters offering them posts in the Rhodesian Army! Men attracted by the offer were required to make their way to Rhodesia's capital, Salisbury, where, at Army Headquarters, they were attested before signing on for the three years' minimum requirement. Some immediately volunteered for the SAS or other specialist units, but the majority joined the RLI with the option to transfer elsewhere later on. Virtually all applicants had to undergo selection and/or training.

In spite of the success of its recruiting campaign, or perhaps because of it, the Rhodesian government preferred to refute allegations that it was encouraging mercenaries to enlist. Even the recruiting brochure, *This is The Army*, stated, "With our emphasis on motivated manpower, mercenaries are not, and never have been, employed by the Rhodesian Army."[3] It was, perhaps, easier to deny the existence of mercenaries serving alongside regular soldiers and airmen for the same rates of pay and under identical terms and conditions. Certainly, many foreigners regarded themselves simply as professional soldiers, but there were also those who enjoyed being labelled 'mercs' and fostered the image by wearing on the shoulder of their combat uniforms a miniature of their country's flag! This may have been unthinkable during the formative years of Rhodesia's counter-insurgency units but, by the mid to late 1970s, dress regulations for those in the bush had relaxed to such an extent that virtually any suitable combination of clothing and equipment was permitted.

The RLI 'troopie' typified the Rhodesian soldier. In the latter stages of the war he usually operated as part of a four-man team called a 'stick' or 'stop group':

These were led by a stick leader/radioman who was responsible for an A63 set, codes, maps, mini binos, compass and a pencil flare. He and two troopers would be armed with 7.62 mm FN rifles, for which they carried a minimum of four magazines apiece. The fourth trooper carried a 7.62 mm FN MAG, and at least 200-250 rounds of link [7.62 mm ammunition in a linked belt]. Extra ammunition for the gun was distributed amongst the stick. We carried our own choice of grenades. These were invariably a mix of HE hand and rifle grenades, WP [White Phosphorous] and coloured smoke – the latter for calling in choppers for resupply or casevac.

Some troopers liked to carry a handgun. Those who were para-trained were entitled to draw the 9 mm Star pistol. A few owned captured weapons. Others, those who could afford them, sported privately purchased pistols or revolvers. A handgun was really only useful as a last resort. It looked good though!

37

Each stick was equipped with a well-stocked medic pack. Some of us also wore around our necks a syringe of sosegon or morphine, and most carried an extra saline drip. It was standard procedure to have your blood type marked on both webbing and shirt.

In the bush, clothing was quite basic. I had a one-piece camouflage 'jump suit'. In the event of a call-out I could quickly pull it on over the boots, shorts and tee shirt that I usually wore on base. Some guys preferred to wear just shorts and a shirt. Footwear could be boots – issue or civilian desert boots or 'takkies' – gym shoes.

Our web equipment varied considerably. Generally, it could be divided into three main categories. Chest webbing, captured from the enemy, was often adapted to fit FN magazines. The idea was so popular that before long local firms, notably Fereday's, began to manufacture custom-made sets at an affordable price. We could also purchase jacket webbing. Styles differed according to individual requirements. My own came with handy back pouches, obviating the need for a small pack. I also had extra padding stitched into the shoulders and waist, a small extravagance that resulted in equipment that fitted perfectly and could be worn, quite comfortably, for an indefinite period. The third type consisted of a combination of any number of pouches stitched permanently in place on a belt and yoke. The far superior items of East German, Soviet and Chinese manufacture were preferred to Rhodesian webbing, which was only really used when there was no other option.

In the bush, exposed skin had to be blackened with cam [camouflage] cream, and personal weapons – rifles and MAGs – were always painted in shades of green and brown. For the type of operation we would find ourselves in, it just was not practical to employ the more elaborate principles of 'cam and con' taught by other Western forces.[4]

Tactics were both simple and effective. As the war intensified, the Rhodesians perfected a system known as 'Fireforce' whereby troops could be rapidly deployed by parachute and helicopter. Such

tasks were usually the responsibility of the RLI and RAR. One of
the advantages of Fireforce was its flexibility: it could be based at a
permanent airfield, such as Grand Reef in eastern Rhodesia, or at
a temporary location in a threatened area. Fireforce reacted
quickly to terrorist incidents and sightings. The most reliable
reports were generally provided by OPs manned by Selous Scouts.
Those on Fireforce worked a rotating shift, with several sticks on
stand-by for immediate deployment by Alouette III 'G-Cars'. In
addition, up to 20 para-trained men were usually available as 'stop
groups'. A typical Fireforce comprised a DC3 Dakota 'Para-Dak'
(at least one of which was said to have operated over Arnhem in
1944), three G-Cars and an Alouette III 'K-Car'. The troop-
carrying G-Cars, each capable of carrying four fully-armed
soldiers, had single or twin Brownings mounted on the port side,
operated by an Air Force gunner/technician: when troops were
carried, the MAG gunner sat facing outboard, opposite the
technician to provide additional firepower if necessary. The K-Car,
or Killer Car, was the command gunship, armed with a 20 mm
cannon or quadruple-mounted machine guns. Besides allowing the
Commando OC to direct events from high above a 'scene', the K-
Car was also on hand to assist any stick in difficulty, with further
back-up provided by at least one Lynx. This little prop-driven
machine was armed with Brownings and SNEB rockets, and could
also deliver frantan (napalm) bombs with deadly accuracy.
Additional air support was sometimes available from Hunters,
Vampires or Canberras.

During Fireforce operations, advance to contact was extremely
nerve-racking for anyone unaccustomed to local procedures. After
deploying by helicopter, each stick would begin to sweep through
an area. The stick leader listened in on his radio and advised his
troops when the K-Car warned that they were nearing the enemy.
Sometimes the K-Car could not see where the guerrillas were, in
which case the element of surprise lay with the enemy. Either way,
the troops had to press on until contact was initiated, usually at
very close quarters. Often, guerrillas would break and run,
hopefully towards the waiting stop groups. Although that was the
theory, both the sweep line and stop groups could become
embroiled in their own little battles, with the operation developing

into a series of individual contacts – a nightmare for the commander trying to direct events from above. However, superior training and firepower usually prevailed and the few guerrillas who survived a firefight would try to surrender. But not always. Dave Armstrong was a Briton serving in 2 Commando (RLI). On 19 July 1975, he and the rest of 7 Troop were on stand-by at Mount Darwin, a forward airfield, which served as a Fireforce base.

During the morning, a Territorial Army patrol had been ambushed by a group of six terrorists and in the ensuing contact the TAs managed to kill two terrorists, the remainder of whom broke and ran. As there was no immediate prospect of regaining contact with the terrorists, 7 Troop was not called upon to respond immediately. The result was that Corporal Jannie de Beer of 10 Troop was deployed with his stick to assist the TA patrol follow up the tracks of the terrorists, since Corporal de Beer was an experienced tracker...

Several hours later, 7 Troop was called out as the combined TA patrol/10 Troop stick was ambushed in a narrow, twisting, overgrown river bed, or 'donga'. The donga was about 10 feet deep and not much wider with heavily overgrown banks which were very precipitous... There were two sharp bends about 20-25 yards apart. In the outside bank of the second bend, there was a wash-out fronted by heavy tree roots. It was in this extremely strong natural position that the terrorists had taken position. They had two major advantages and these were that it was very difficult for anyone to see into this wash-out without exposing himself in full view to enemy fire. In fact, it was more than difficult, it was impossible. The second major advantage was the fact that the floor of this wash-out was about two feet above the level of the riverbed.

The TA patrol/10 Troop stick had come around the first bend and thus exposed themselves to the terrorists who opened fire. The sergeant of the TA patrol and a member of Corporal de Beer's stick, Hennie Potgieter, were both killed. Ken Lucas, the gunner in Corporal de Beer's stick, was wounded in the legs.

It was into this situation that 7 Troop arrived. Major Meyer deployed Lieutenant du Plooy's stick and another to sweep through the area as at this stage no one was sure whether the terrorists were still there or not. The bodies of the two men in the riverbed were seen by the sweep-line and Lieutenant du Plooy ordered John [medic Corporal John Coey, from the United States] to see whether or not he could help them. As John climbed down into the riverbed he was shot by the terrorists who were still in their hiding place – right under Lieutenant du Plooy's feet!

During the rest of the afternoon, several attempts were made to get at the terrorists in their position, and this is where they used the strength of it to their advantage. As I said before, anyone attempting to assault the position was clearly exposed without in turn being able to see into the target area. We suffered two more casualties, one of whom was Lieutenant du Plooy. Also, any grenades thrown at the terrorists simply bounced off the tree roots fronting the position and exploded harmlessly below on the sand of the riverbed.

My stick was deployed 'downstream' about 30 yards from the main contact area as a blocking group, and towards dark more troops were flown in to provide a tighter cordon. Shortly after dark, the four terrorists broke out and in doing so managed to kill Corporal de Beer and wound another of his stick. Again, no one was sure whether the terrorists had continued with their breakout or had returned to their position.

The Special Air Service were asked for assistance as they were equipped with night sights, which we in the RLI didn't have.[5]

Six SAS, led by American Lieutenant Bob MacKenzie, (see chapters 4 and 12) arrived by helicopter and joined the RLI in trying to draw enemy fire by throwing grenades and shooting into likely hiding places. Unable to verify the guerrillas' position, and not even knowing whether it was still occupied, MacKenzie decided to investigate personally. An RLI corporal and a member of the SAS team accompanied the officer as he led the way along the boulder-strewn riverbed. Eventually, they reached the three casualties. As feared, all were dead. The hollow used by the guerrillas was nearby – and empty. A machine gun and ammunition from one of the dead was also missing. A follow-up operation the next day led to the recovery of the weapon which had been abandoned by the fleeing ZANLA. In Armstrong's opinion:

> One unusual circumstance and two mistakes occurred which contributed to this fiasco. It was a fiasco as well as a great tragedy... The unusual circumstance was that the terrorists were well-led and prepared to fight it out. (The RLI was definitely not prepared for this.) The first mistake was that too many people were in the riverbed initially and there was no flanking protection for the tracker. I can only assume that this was to enable the trackers to catch up with the terrorists and not be slowed down by having to wait for troops moving through thick bush on either riverbank.
>
> The second mistake was that of Lieutenant du Plooy in sending John into the riverbed without having completed the sweep of the area...
>
> The terrorist leader was identified by the Police Special Branch and we later heard that he had been killed by another unit. This would have been in 1976.
>
> Lieutenant du Plooy was killed in 1979, when the helicopter he was in was shot down near Mapai in Mozambique.[6]

Derek Andrews, an Australian (see chapter 4), served in Vietnam before arriving in Rhodesia in 1976, and after a brief period of training with the SAS, he transferred to the Grey's Scouts, remaining with the unit for about nine months before volunteering for the Selous Scouts.

> Approximately 300 multi-racial men with the same desire as myself climbed aboard trucks at the Selous Scouts camp at Inkomo and headed north to the training camp at Lake Kariba called 'Wafa Wafa' (Shona for 'I am dead, I am dead'). From the very start we were launched into heavy physical

training which began before sunrise and finished late at night with the singing of terrorist songs around the camp fire. We were not fed for seven days, but were given all sorts of information about bush survival. Unfortunately, even bush food was scarce at that time of year. None of the fruit which would be in evidence later in the year could be found and so the hunger was only surpassed by the physical exhaustion.[7]

The training syllabus included frequent lectures and lessons, covering not just bush survival, but tracking, map-reading and basic medical training. Candidates also learned about the enemy and familiarized themselves with enemy weapons. Battle drills were conducted using live ammunition, and in between the theory and practice there was more physical training.

On the sixth day without food we were taken by truck and dropped off approximately 30 kilometres away for a map reading exercise. I thought I noticed a wry smile or two as the instructors off-loaded us next to a banana plantation and then left. The bananas were forbidden, but in complete unity we disobeyed and approached the owner to see if we could have some bananas. He agreed but probably didn't expect us to consume his whole consignment which was due to be shipped out the next day. By the time we had finished it was getting late and our instructors were out looking for us. I don't think it took them long to work out where we were. This was a serious breach of discipline and we were ordered again and again to reveal the ringleaders, but we all stuck together and were eventually all dismissed from the course. What a crushing blow this was to us, as each man had sweated blood for seven days and each man was counting the days one by one until the end of the course. As we packed ready to leave, the chief instructor approached us with a proposition. We could leave or take the punishment they would hand out. Thirty of the 80 men involved had had enough and chose to leave, but the remainder jumped at the chance to stay.

The next day, in the clinging heat, we were told to run all day carrying mpani logs, which we began to do with enthusiasm, but with each passing hour, our muscles were racked with pain. Midday came, and the instructors gave us a chance to drop out, but we were determined and the decision was a very definite no. To our amazement they told us we could stop the physical torture and resume the course. That afternoon, we were told we would be eating that night. All afternoon, we could think of nothing else. We could hardly wait to sink our teeth into something substantial. Finally, the order came to line up and ... the instructors walked onto the parade ground and threw a dead baboon and a bag of mealie meal at our feet... We had to skin, chop up and boil the baboon with a large amount of curry powder. I must admit that when the time came to eat the unsavoury looking feast, it was heavenly!

The 25 day course came to an end at last, and one of the instructors walked up to me and welcomed me to the Selous Scouts.

Bush work with the Selous Scouts was exciting but highly dangerous. We moved around mainly at night in groups of five, consisting of two black soldiers and three whites, blacked-up and wearing Soviet or East German uniforms. The objective was to locate groups of terrorists in the area. There would be a group of approximately 30 black Selous Scouts masquerading as terrorists who would gain the confidence of the villagers and eventually find out where the real terrorists were hiding. We were constantly observing movement in the villages from nearby hills and would keep in contact with our group. When the terrorists were located, we called in Fireforce.

Our bush survival training was invaluable as supplies could not be brought into areas where we were working. Lizards, snakes, grasshoppers, grubs and beehive honey made regular meals. The honey the Africans brought from a hive one night was delicious. We had run out of supplies and so ate our fill. In the morning, eager for more, I took a handful ready to scoff it down once again, only to see, in the daylight, that it contained wriggling purple grubs. Although we had eaten cooked grubs many times, the thought of eating this live meal turned my stomach… Another time, we gathered guinea fowl eggs and brought them back to eat, but had forgotten whether rotten eggs sank or floated. We proceeded to eat them, only to find that many contained fully-formed young chicks. In an exercise of mind over matter, we remembered that this was a delicacy for the Chinese and continued to eat.

There was often competition for ownership of hills which were needed for us to be able to observe a village. They often formed part of the territory of groups of baboons and if we didn't win them over, they would make a great deal of noise and give away our position. The ritual would begin with us leaving some crushed corn on the hill and then retreating a short distance. The baboons, having seen this, would send their leader to eat it. If he took it, we would proceed to leave more and so were accepted without further suspicion. Many were the bush secrets my African friends showed me.[8]

The Selous Scouts and the SAS conducted numerous 'externals', often operating in small groups. The mid to late 1970s saw both units and the RLI carrying out large-scale cross-border raids. In November 1976, the two most important ZANLA bases were selected for attack: Chimoio was 90 kilometres inside Mozambique, and Tembue twice the distance. Although both were vital for ZANLA deployments into Rhodesia, Combined Operations (Com Ops) was reluctant to authorize any ground attacks because of massive logistical problems, and it was another year before the operation, code-name 'Dingo', was finally launched.

An estimated 9,000 ZANLA were at Chimoio, and 4,000 at Tembue. The assault force numbered 97 SAS and 48 RLI paratroopers, and 40 RLI heli-borne troops, with air support comprising six Dakotas, eight Hunters, six Vampires, three Canberras, 12 Lynxs and 42 helicopters.[9] Because of the distances involved, three administration areas were established inside Mozambique, 10 to 15 minutes' flying time from the targets. The first objective, Chimoio, consisted of 13 separate camps, five of which were to be targeted: essentially, the plan called for a boxing-in of the area, with two sides covered by the paratroopers, another by the heli-borne troops, and the fourth side by Alouette K-Cars.

Fifteen minutes before H-Hour, on 23 November 1977, a DC8 jet owned by Jack Malloch (see chapter 1) overflew Chimoio, panicking the guerrillas there and causing them to take cover. But when several minutes passed and nothing else happened, the guerrillas began to relax and assembled for their daily muster parade exactly as the Rhodesians had planned. It was hoped that the enemy would not be so quick to scatter the next time they heard an aircraft – which was when the first Air Force jet began its approach! Two minutes later, the Rhodesians began their insertion, followed by the helicopter gunships. Meanwhile, troops were landed at the proposed forward administration base to secure the area and await an air-drop of aviation fuel.

After deploying, the assault units immediately came into contact with terrified guerrillas as they attempted to break through the stop groups. Apart from a temporary delay, when the command helicopter was hit and forced to retire, the operation proceeded according to plan with the troops closing in on the main camp, killing or capturing the enemy in the process.

Amongst the SAS at Chimoio was Captain Bob MacKenzie:

Another 100 metres brought A Troop to the edge of the forest and a long zig-zag trench line. As our machine gunners sent burst after burst onto the lip of the trench, the riflemen threw grenades and then charged. Leaping in along a wide front, they found only a few enemy, mostly cowering at the bottom. Chimoio's perimeter was now breached, with several hundred metres of it occupied by the Rhodesian Army.

Calling in my RPD gunners, I ordered a brief break to reorganise and reload. Forming our own defensive position, I reported to Robinson [SAS Major Brian Robinson, commanding ground forces] and received permission to send out patrols to deal with pockets of guerrillas who were still fighting, and to capture secondary objectives that had been assigned during the planning of Op Dingo.

Leading a 15-man patrol back into the forest toward our next objective, the ZANLA intelligence centre, my point element signalled there were enemy ahead. The patrol deployed on line and advanced cautiously toward a large clearing. In the middle of the clearing stood a 30-foot tower with a DShK 12.7 mm anti-aircraft machine gun, its crew frantically blasting away at every plane in sight.

Preoccupied with aerial targets, neither the four gunners nor their security party on the ground saw the SAS patrol creeping to the edge of the clearing. Silhouetted against the hazy sky themselves, the crew were perfect targets. On command, my troopers opened fire. Bodies tumbled off the tower onto the group guarding the base of the tower, who were also shot before they could return fire. Still on line, my patrol swept across the clearing into the woods on the other side where we found another AA position. Unoccupied, this one had a Chinese twin-barrelled 37 mm cannon, still in cosmoline. Happily for the air force, it had not been put into action: a few pounds of plastic explosives soon ensured that it never would be.

Sweeping through another 150 metres of woods, during which 15 to 20 more terrorists were flushed and killed, my patrol reached ZANLA's intelligence centre. It comprised 18 grass huts which served as offices, classrooms and storerooms and, although surrounded by more trenches, had been abandoned. The compound was checked for defenders as the patrol moved through, then secured and searched in detail. My men brought piles of notebooks, diaries, files, and bushels of other ZANLA documents from the huts for a quick sorting by another of my officers and I before being backloaded to Rhodesia. There, they would get more intensive study by military and police intelligence experts.

While the officers were engaged in the drudgery of paper sorting, an excited shout from Corporal Bates Mare alerted the rest of the troops that he had found a darkroom and hut full of cameras – dozens of them. Aware as always of booby-trap possibilities, Mare and another NCO moved cautiously into the hut, and then came out with enough gear to equip a busload of Japanese tourists. Thousands of dollars' worth of new Leica, Pentax and Nikon 35mms, and a couple of rare video cameras – intended for ZANLA intelligence agents were now in the possession of a bunch of happy troopers.[10]

Later in the day, MacKenzie's troop reached a motor pool with about 20 vehicles, repair facilities, petrol and diesel tanks.

> Some 20 minutes later, charges had been placed on everything of value – except one pick-up truck – and connected into a long det-cord ringmain. Advising all aircraft of the impending bang, I sent everyone but a machine gunner away on the pick-up, then lit the fuse. The gunner and I walked a few hundred metres away, took cover where we could prevent any interference with the charges, and awaited the blast. Five minutes later the whole lot went up in a gratifying fireball and mushroom cloud.[11]

The pick-up was commandeered as MacKenzie's personal vehicle, until the last of the attack force was uplifted following a night of intermittent contacts. A day later, the SAS and a fresh group of RLI paratroopers were inserted into Tembue. Peter McAleese, (see chapters 3, 4 and 9) another member of A Troop, recalled:

> We moved from action to action, once flushing out nearly 50 ZANLA from a ravine in a tremendous rattle of automatic firing. On all sides, unseen actions took place, punctuated by the bigger 20 mm cannon of the K-Cars which we could call in with our ground to air A76 radios. We heard on the radios that the others in the SAS and the RLI were having as much success as us. The ZANLA command were totally disorientated and their fighters desperate to run away or hide. That night, we lay up in ambush just as we had at Chimoio, and several of the guys near me fired at terrorists trying to come through us in the night. We got little sleep but though we were 200 kilometres inside Mozambique, we felt very confident. We had ... inflicted terrible losses on the enemy. I never realised how many till the tally was made the following day... They stopped counting at 1,200 dead but the total at Chimoio and Tembue was well over 2,000.[12]

Both bases had been decimated; tons of weapons and equipment were captured or destroyed and a vast quantity of documents recovered. During these attacks, the Rhodesians lost one SAS trooper at Chimoio, a Vampire pilot died after crash-landing his battle-damaged aircraft, and several other soldiers were wounded.

Rhodesian casualty figures remained fairly low throughout the war, reflecting the professionalism of the security forces, which also accounted for a disproportionate number of enemy killed, wounded or captured. However, Rhodesian manpower was limited, and as the war intensified units suffered from a rising attrition rate.

Paul Courtenay was born in Kenya and raised in New Zealand. A graduate of Sandhurst, he had served in Northern Ireland, Cyprus and British Guinea before arriving in Rhodesia where he became 4 Troop officer in 1 Commando (RLI). Australian John Foran remembered him as "a man of courage, respected by his men".[13] On the morning of 24 December 1977, Lieutenant Courtenay and Foran were amongst those called out from Grand Reef.

I was in Para. One K-Car, three G-Cars, one Dakota, 28 troopies in seven sticks. We had an unknown number of terrorists on this mountain. It was raining quite heavily and continued to rain all day. The three stop groups were deployed. We were dropped behind the mountain. Climbing the rear side, we began to sweep down the terrorists' side, 16 troopers in extended line. This mountain was honeycombed with natural caves which we had to clear on the way down. Approaching the base camp, we had our first contact. Two terrorists broke cover and tried to bolt for it. We got one of these. We swept on through the base camp area, securing it and clearing a massive cave alongside the base camp. Lieutenant Paul Courtenay and myself then proceeded along this ledge, approximately 30 metres wide, to check it out. Midway along the ledge we came under fire from automatic weapons. We retreated to cover and marked the cave with a white phos' grenade for the Lynx aircraft. We moved back to allow him to drop a frantan bomb but he hit the wrong target, so we climbed up and over the ridge to come at them from the other side. The rain continued to belt down. On the way down the other side, I found myself directly above the cave entrance.

From my position I could see the lower portion of one terrorist's legs standing at the cave entrance. Informing Paul of this, I prepared to toss in two grenades, a WP and a HE. The white phos' was a mistake as in the heavy rain it hung there like a smoke screen. One terrorist escaped in this, despite the bullets and grenades we put in there. They still refused to come out [after] a failed frontal assault [which] saw Lieutenant Courtenay killed. The fight dragged on. I fired at least a dozen tear gas bombs into the cave along with HE grenades. We were about to use a bunker bomb when they called out they wanted to surrender. I moved to my old position above the cave. The terrorists were instructed to come out with their hands up. The first one emerged with his hands behind his back, trying to locate the voices. I shot him from point blank range. He did have a grenade in his hands. The next one came out with his hands up. Upon questioning him he admitted one more terrorist remained but was very badly wounded. He was sent back in to bring him out. When this had been done, I entered the cave to check it out. It was deserted. Three AK47s and one SKS lay on the floor. The wounded terrorist died. Night fell, and Christmas eve was spent on a muddy, wet mountainside with one dead troop commander, three dead terrorists, one prisoner. It was a very sad, very cold, wet and hungry Christmas eve. We were uplifted at first light.[14]

What was the attraction for the foreigners who served in Rhodesia? Many, if not most, believed that they were fighting for a just cause against an often ruthless, Communist-inspired enemy. But Rhodesia also presented an opportunity to participate in a real shooting war, something which many professional soldiers had been denied in the service of their own countries.

In December 1978, Tony Y, formerly of the Australian Army Reserve, described in a letter home his first major contact while serving in Support Commando (RLI):

Around three pm the siren went. The flying time was about 20 minutes and when we were dropped all we found were a lot of old and middle-aged Africans coming home from a beer drink. Regardless, we made a hasty road-block (so to speak) and started rounding up all the Africans in sight (regardless of sex or age). We had been doing this for about 15 minutes and had about 40 of them when all hell broke loose about one kilometre away. We could hear a lot of automatic and small arms fire and see the gun-ships firing into a village which was already starting to burn. All this action was happening where our Stop group 3 was (four men in each 'stop', there were three 'stops'). We heard over the radio that Stop 3 was having a contact so we left the Africans we had rounded up and were uplifted by chopper to Stop 3's area. There we joined with Stop 3 and started clearing a village. This meant clearing out each hut by working in pairs. Myself and another chap called Nigel W [an Englishman, see chapter 4] had cleared two small huts and were in the process of clearing the third which was large by African standards. It had two rooms, I was in the main room on one side of the doorway to the bedroom and Nigel was on the other side. It was Nigel's turn to go first and he had just pulled the curtain of the doorway aside when he suddenly jumped back and started firing into the bedroom. He had done this because as soon as he had looked inside, he had spotted an AK assault rifle sticking out from under the bed. Fortunately, that was all we found there. Because of this, we set fire to all the buildings in the village.

The next hut was my turn to go first – there was nobody inside but I also found an AK plus two sets of Communist webbing and three grenades. The reasons we burned the village were (1) punishment for harbouring terrorists and weapons and (2) because a common practice is for weapons and ammunition to be hidden in the thatched roofs. The latter proved to be correct for we had no sooner fired the last hut when ammunition in the roofs of the other huts started to explode.

We continued going through three – four other kraals, clearing as we went, finding more equipment and therefore burning all the kraals we went through. Once again my Stop (No 1) was up-lifted and taken by chopper to a kraal where a terrorist was seen running into a hut. We were dropped about 150 metres from the kraal and started towards the hut where the terrorist (gook) was supposed to be. It was my turn to clear the hut so I ran to the back (no windows) and set fire to the thatch, then positioned myself so as to be able to shoot anyone running out the door. The thatch was burning well by now and still no one came out. My stop leader indicated me to kick the door in (we were trying to capture him, not kill him). Anyway, I kicked the door in and jumped to the side of the doorway – no firing from inside. By this time it was starting to get a bit warm with the roof on fire, and with smoke inside the hut nothing could be seen inside so I put three rounds inside hoping to scare him out. Still no-one came out, but this time movement was spotted. To cut the story short, unfortunately (especially for the gook) I had hit him with one of my shots – we managed to get him out of the hut before the roof collapsed but he died shortly afterwards.

We cleared the rest of that kraal and were heading for the next when Nigel spotted a gook about 20 feet ahead of us in the bush. We both opened fire at the same time – another gook bit the dust – we were still trying for a captive so we went over to see how bad he was. Again, unfortunately for this fellow, though still alive, [he] was not healthy enough according to my boss so I was told to dispatch him. Although it may sound morbid we all had a bit of a laugh at the way he kicked his leg – just like in the movies where someone raises his leg and gives a shake as he kicks the bucket.

To try and cut this tale short again, we swept through another couple of kraals (burning as we went). The other stops got a few more gooks, but we did not shoot anything else except for a civvy who suddenly sprung up from some bushes in front of me. Before I realised she was a civvy I had put a round into her backside (her own fault for doing what she did). Anyway, I think I must not have hurt her too badly because she did not stop and we didn't see her again – not a bad instinctive shot from the hip I thought.

In that contact we culled seven gooks and captured three. One of the captives was the chief executioner of that area –

this bloke is the fellow who decides which targets are to be hit and he personally stabbed to death twelve Africans he suspected of being 'sellouts' (government supporters) in the past month.

Not a bad effort for my first 'big' contact – will have to put a couple of notches on my rifle.[15]

In 1979, fighting intensified as the war entered its final phase. In a seven-week bush trip in April-May, Support Commando, 1 RLI accounted for 165 insurgents, 28 of them during a cross-border strike, in return for four killed and several wounded and injured.[16]

On Tuesday 17 April 1979, elements of Support Commando were called out to Inyazura, in eastern Rhodesia. The following was recorded by the author immediately after the event.

At approximately 1100 hours Eagles One to Four jumped into a cultivated/kraal area where we were airlifted by choppers to a nearby kraal and told to flush out a gook who was hiding in a thick clump of bushes left of the kraal. We (Lieutenant Walters, Corporal Salzmann, Mike Moore and myself) fired several rounds into the bush and I walked up and threw an HE grenade into it whereupon, following a further bout of firing, myself and Carl Salzmann were detailed to run along a track in a flanking movement on the right of the bush, which we did, taking up temporary positions while Lieutenant Walters and Mike were ordered by the K-Car (Major Henson) to run across a cleared mealie field directly into the bush. They began to do so and seven or eight feet from the edge of the thicket ran straight into a burst of automatic fire from one, possibly two, weapons. Both men fell flat while bullets hit the ground all around them. Immediately following this incident, I saw a figure running back through the bush past me, 25 feet away, and I opened up but do not know whether or not I hit him. I then doubled back to some rocks as I was then lying in open ground, while firing into the bush behind me. I met up with Carl who told me that Mike had been hit and was still lying in the mealie field. After Lieutenant Walters had joined us, we learned that Mike was, in fact, dead, hit in the head and chest. We then called in a couple more sticks to help clear the bush and these duly arrived (one chopper recovering Mike's body on uplift). Following several frantan strikes by two Lynx aircraft and machine gunning from a G-Car plus much firing and grenade throwing by us, the bush was eventually cleared. No gook was found.

There then followed hours of hut clearing. I cannot say how many were shot up or burnt out. Several locals were 'questioned' as to the whereabouts of the gooks but to no avail – one seemed to have a fit during interrogation, another was beaten unconscious. During the clearing of one kraal, following several warnings to the inhabitants to come out, Corporal Binion [Australian Pete Binion] flung an HE grenade into a hut. On kicking the door in it transpired that it held a nanny and a piccanin. [The nanny] came out wailing and screaming and covered in blood. We just left her and carried on. During much of this time, fran' strikes and firing was going on in the distance. The sky was filled with smoke from burning kraals.

Finally, our stick – now reinforced by Koos Basson – was detailed to sweep across a fairly bushy area in search of a wounded gook. Before long, I found a blood-stained shirt and webbing in a dried-up riverbed. While I debated whether it could be booby-trapped, Koos and Carl began to clear a bush by firing into it. They immediately received return fire and Koos ran past me, one hand clasped to his neck and shouting that he had been hit. As he took cover up on the river bank, I knelt down and placed several rounds in the direction of where I presumed the gook was – this being only a few feet from where I knelt. For a few seconds I thought I had hit him, but when the dust and smoke had cleared, I saw that I had only 'killed' several large stones. I then patched up Koos – who had luckily only been grazed by the round – and we again called up reinforcements. Koos was casevaced and we continued our sweep, sometimes crawling flat on our bellies, our nerves by now quite taut. It was 'Binny' who finally flung a grenade at the gook who was subsequently shot up by several men and killed. We were uplifted at dusk.[17]

Mike Moore was killed on the first day of voting in a ballot that resulted in the election of Bishop Abel Muzorewa as the first black Premier of Zimbabwe-Rhodesia. This made little difference to those fighting the war, which dragged on for several more months. But while the security forces continued to defeat the enemy in the bush, their future was being decided by politicians at Lancaster House in London. On 21 December 1979, a cease-fire was announced, heralding the rise to power of Robert Mugabe and the birth of the state of Zimbabwe. The following year, some of Rhodesia's finest units were disbanded, including the Special Air Service, Selous Scouts and Rhodesian Light Infantry.

CHAPTER 3
ANGOLAN FIASCO: 'COLONEL CALLAN'S' MERCENARIES, 1975-76

In the mid-1950s, Portugal's African colonies witnessed the rise of black nationalist movements dedicated to the overthrow of the Portuguese. In Angola, three separate groups emerged: Agostinho Neto's Popular Movement for the Liberation of Angola (MPLA), followed in 1960 by Holden Roberto's National Front for the Liberation of Angola (FNLA) and, in 1965, Jonas Savimbi's National Union for the Total Independence of Angola (UNITA). In March 1961, the FNLA initiated a guerrilla war that continued for 13 years until Portugal's Marcello Caetano was ousted in an unexpected coup d'état. Soon after, Angola became internally self-governing.

The three liberation movements, although united in an uneasy alliance against a common enemy, were influenced by their own tribal followings and political doctrines. By June 1975, the Soviet-backed MPLA was engaged in heavy fighting with UNITA and the FNLA, the latter armed and equipped primarily by China, and both supported by the United States. The FNLA also had a useful ally in Zaïre, whose President, Mobutu Sése Séko, was Holden Roberto's brother-in-law. The prize for the victors, and their foreign backers, was a land rich in natural resources, including gold, diamonds and oil. Equally important were Angola's Atlantic seaports and links with landlocked neighbours, Zaïre and Zambia.

In October 1975, South African forces crossed into southern Angola in support of the FNLA and UNITA.[1] The following month, Angola was granted independence. When the MPLA announced the formation of a government headed by President Agostinho Neto, the FNLA and UNITA responded by forming a

56

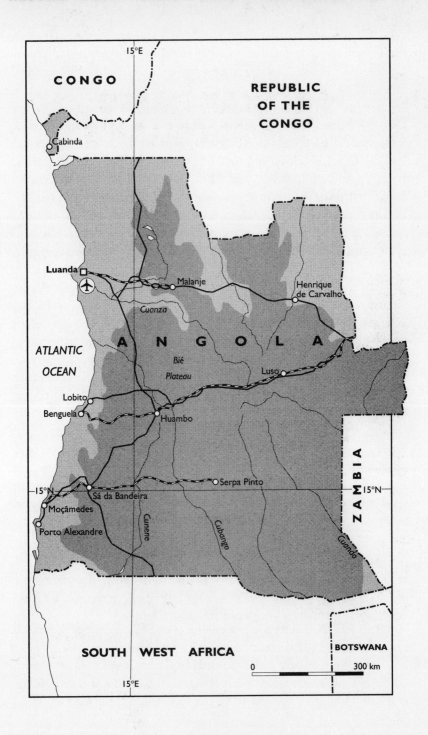

rival administration under Holden Roberto. Meanwhile, in England, various individuals had been monitoring events, and now saw in Angola an opportunity to realize their personal aims and ambitions and the chance to earn a small fortune in the process. Nick Hall, Mick Wainhouse, and Greek-Cypriots Charley Christodoulou and Costas Georgiou had served together in The Parachute Regiment: dissatisfied with civilian life, they were looking for alternative employment where their military expertise could again be put to use. Hall thought they might be appreciated in war-torn Angola and approached Donald Belford, the unofficial FNLA representative in Britain, to outline his proposal. Belford promised to pass on the details to Holden Roberto and, as Hall did not have a telephone, agreed to maintain contact via Georgiou.[2]

When Belford informed him that Roberto had accepted the offer and that the FNLA would fund the trip to Angola of one of the four, Georgiou immediately volunteered. The remainder were to follow at a later date. First though, the FNLA required a demonstration of support: the result was considerable fire damage to the Soho office of the Mozambique and Guinea Information Centre, which represented the MPLA in London. Soon after, on 28 November 1975, Costas Georgiou, now calling himself 'Tony Callan', left Heathrow airport accompanied by Colin Taylor, security officer for the FNLA in Britain. Donald Belford travelled separately. All three arrived in the Zaïre capital, Kinshasa, a few days later and after a short break were flown to the northern Angolan town of Negage. 'Doctor' Belford, a medical orderly who had progressed to field surgeon for the FNLA, was soon busy attending the sick and wounded at Negage, Carmona and Ambriz. 'Callan' worked as his assistant and later as an ambulance driver. During this period he was introduced to some of the white Portuguese fighting with the Angolan National Liberation Army (ELNA). Another organization, the Portuguese Liberation Army (ELP) formed by white settlers dedicated to returning Angola to white rule, also supported ELNA in its efforts to defeat the MPLA's People's Armed Forces for the Liberation of Angola (FAPLA).

On 18 December, Belford and Taylor left Angola to spend Christmas in England. Callan remained in Carmona, which fell without a fight to a combined Cuban/FAPLA force at the end of the month. After escaping to Negage, Callan organized a fighting patrol to prevent the town from being similarly taken. It is claimed that he and two Portuguese volunteers accounted for four T-34 tanks, four truck-mounted multiple rocket launchers, and over 60 men killed. A series of hit and run attacks followed, in which another 20 Cubans died.

Soon after, Callan returned to Kinshasa where, on 5 January 1976, he was joined by Hall, Wainhouse, Christodoulou and Taylor: Holden Roberto himself accompanied the four ex paratroopers to Angola. At São Salvador, the FNLA President announced that Callan was now his Field Commander, responsible for all military operations in the northern sector. Roberto returned to Kinshasa, with Hall as his personal bodyguard. During the trip, the FNLA leader discussed the possibility of hiring more British soldiers, and later that evening handed Hall $25,000 with instructions to find another 25 men within the next seven days. He also promised that Hall, Callan, Wainhouse and Christodoulou would be amply rewarded for their efforts – subject of course to an FNLA victory.

Nick Hall returned to London and approached reporter, Tony Geraghty, who had recently written an article for *The Sunday Times* about the problems encountered by insurance agent, Philip Woodley, when dealing with mercenaries. Geraghty put Hall in touch with Woodley, who suggested he contact John Banks (see chapter 8), another former paratrooper and the leading figure behind Security Advisory Services (SAS), a mercenary recruiting agency based in Camberley. Consequently, Banks and three associates Dave Tomkins (see chapter 9), a convicted burglar and safe blower; Leslie Aspin, an ex RAF NCO; and Frank Perren, a former Royal Marine, were entrusted with the recruitment and travel arrangements of the 25 mercenaries. The four knew several potential candidates who in turn knew of others: in this way, 23 men were quickly found. Banks and Tomkins also decided to join the team, which was placed under the command of Peter McAleese, (see chapters 2, 4 and 9) a tough Scotsman who had served in the Parachute Regiment and SAS.

Because of Tony Geraghty's involvement, the recruiters were concerned about the risk of a security leak. Aspin therefore arranged to meet the reporter, who agreed not to disclose any information if he was allowed to accompany the mercenaries as an accredited journalist. Hall, Banks and the other organizers decided that they would permit Geraghty to accompany them to Africa where he could be disposed of more easily. However, on 18 January, security ceased to be a problem when *The People* ran a feature about Hall and his association with the FNLA. The article bore the by-line of 'Trevor Aspinall', also connected with *I, Kovacs*, a supposedly autobiographical account of Les Aspin! Additional problems arose when Banks had to find replacements for several would-be mercenaries who decided to opt out. Others were found to be without valid passports, but in the event were able to travel on hastily produced SAS travel documents!

Before their departure, the mercenaries assembled at a hotel for briefings by Banks, Aspin and 'Major' Hall. As the meeting drew to a close Banks, who had earlier left the room, suddenly reappeared to make a dramatic announcement: he claimed that he had been double-crossed and now intended to work for the MPLA. Previously, Banks had made clear to his colleagues his intention to take over Hall's role once they were in Africa. Aspin was suspected of having informed Hall, who decided not to include Banks amongst the 25 men chosen for Angola. Banks had threatened to withdraw from the assignment altogether, prompting Hall to reconsider. Now, it seemed, Hall had again banned Banks, allegedly on the instructions of the CIA – the principal financiers of the FNLA. A compromise was hastily negotiated, whereby Banks would remain in England as the main recruiter. He seemed satisfied with what was a potentially lucrative (and safe) position. However, his alarming tantrum led to the withdrawal of two more men from the operation.

Hall and his depleted force were driven to Heathrow airport, where they were confronted by reporters and press photographers alerted by the exposé in that morning's *The People*. The publicity almost certainly saved Geraghty, who was informed by Hall that the invitation to accompany them to Angola had been withdrawn. By this time, the 22 volunteers had each been advanced $500, whereupon another two men took the opportunity to abandon the group. The remainder boarded Sabena Flight 614 for the first leg of their journey to Angola. During a stop-over in Brussels, yet another would-be mercenary decided to leave. So it was that 20 men arrived in Kinshasa to be met by Holden Roberto, who was clearly delighted with Hall's recruiting efforts. Accompanying the President was another recruit, Canadian Douglas Newby. The newcomers were treated to dinner before being driven to the Presidential villa where they were kitted out with boots, camouflage uniforms, web equipment and weapons – a mixed batch of 7.62 mm FN rifles and World War II vintage American .30 calibre M1/M2 carbines. They were then taken by bus across the border to Angola, travelling through the night and reaching São Salvador the next morning.

Arriving at the two-storey colonial residence that served as FNLA headquarters, the mercenaries joined some FNLA and Portuguese troops and formed up for presentation. As they stood at attention, Callan emerged from the HQ building and stared in silence at his men. Peter McAleese, now promoted by Hall to captain, reported to Callan who instructed him to dismiss the new arrivals and take them inside for some breakfast. There seemed to be no real order inside the building, with weapons and equipment scattered about. The men gathered in the dining area (which had a table but no chairs), Callan reappeared to welcome them, coffee was served by a jovial, portly Angolan, and everyone began to relax. But the mood was shattered moments later by the arrival of 'Captain' Wainhouse, who proceeded to berate the men for their civilian haircuts before marching out again. Shortly afterwards, the mercenaries were shown upstairs to their quarters, where there were beds but no mattresses, sheets or blankets. Callan had his own room, which served as his personal armoury, while Wainhouse shared with Christodoulou. Two Portuguese pilots were billeted in another room.

On their first day in Angola the mercenaries busied themselves with weapon training. They were given military-style haircuts and vaccinated against smallpox. Several were required to oversee a delivery of ammunition and other supplies. Former artillery man, Chris Dempster, took the opportunity to look over the vehicles, which were to be his responsibility. There were 13 Land Rovers, a Panhard M3/VTT armoured personnel carrier, a Dodge personnel carrier, a Panhard AML-90 armoured car, a Ferret scout car, a three-ton Mercedes truck and a heavy recovery vehicle. However, only two vehicles were in running order and there were no spares or tools. Most of the weaponry and equipment, much of it 'acquired' from the FNLA's allies, the Zaïrean Army, was in a similar state of disrepair.

That evening, Callan briefed his men, who learned that they were to be divided into four-man 'killer' teams for hunt and destroy missions against Cuban patrols. Although the mercenary commander appeared competent enough, an uglier side of his character became apparent when Dave Tomkins saw Callan with Wainhouse, roughly interrogating an FNLA soldier. As the mercenaries discussed the event, Jamie McAndless (formerly of the SAS) and Mike Johnson (who had served in the Royal Marines and French Foreign Legion) had a violent argument which ended with McAndless threatening Johnson with his FN rifle. Order was eventually restored, but some of Callan's volunteers must have been wondering about the reliability of certain individuals in their group.

The following day, Callan decided to reduce the number of African troops, whose fighting ability was often lacking. Immediately after morning parade the black soldiers were ordered to surrender their weapons and strip off their uniforms. Callan then called for volunteers willing to serve under his command. Fifty or so stepped forward and were told to get dressed while the remainder were driven to the main FNLA garrison at Quiende where, later that day, the disgruntled blacks mutinied. As soon as he heard, Callan led his mercenaries to the camp where the ringleaders were swiftly and ruthlessly dealt with. That evening, Dempster was witness to another cold-blooded killing when Wainhouse and ex-paratrooper 'Sammy' Copeland shot a suspected MPLA spy. Christodoulou, soon to be nick-named 'Shotgun Charley' because of a sawn-off shotgun he acquired, confided in Dempster that he too had taken part in a number of killings.

★　★　★

At dawn on 23 January, McAleese was dispatched to defend the coastal town of Santo Antonio do Zaïre, taking with him ex-paratrooper, Derek 'Brummie' Barker, Mike Johnson, Doug Saunders, Stuart McPherson, Mick Rennie and John Tilsey.[3] The other mercenaries, both British and Portuguese, together with the loyal Angolan troops, prepared for a move to Maquela, under threat due to a recent MPLA victory at Damba, further south. Under Dempster's supervision, enough vehicles were repaired to allow the men to depart in the early hours of the 24th. 'Fuzz' Hussey, a Briton, stayed behind to run the radio communications.

A terrible journey through rain and mud took its toll on the convoy vehicles. One slid off the road and was lost, and others had to be abandoned because they were unable to cope with the atrocious conditions. When the last of the mercenaries eventually reached their destination, Callan ordered them to proceed another 25 kilometres to Quibocolo. Meanwhile, Tomkins had been instructed to destroy a bridge at nearby Rio Zardi to hinder a possible outflanking movement by the enemy. Tomkins' expertise as a safe-blower was put to good use and soon the bridge was impassable, leaving just one route in from Cuban-held Damba into Maquela – and one route out if the mercenaries were forced to withdraw.

The demolition party rejoined Callan at a base camp outside Maquela. Another group of five Britons were deployed in an ambush position 15 kilometres from Damba. That morning they conducted a successful ambush on a Cuban/FAPLA armoured column, killing 21 soldiers and forcing the others to retreat. After withdrawing, the mercenaries rejoined their comrades to spend the next few days practising their own form of 'hearts and minds' among the local populace, dispensing cash payments to some, and casually shooting others. Callan's often mindless violence and unpredictability seemed to worsen with each day. When several FNLA dignitaries, including a cousin of Holden Roberto, arrived in their Land Rover at his base camp, Callan allegedly shot dead the President's relative and his aide before commandeering their vehicle! Sometimes, Callan's motives were frighteningly obvious. After taking a personal dislike to Dempster, Callan ordered his mechanic to undertake a virtually suicidal mission to Maquela to disarm a troublesome group of 200 former convicts known as Zorrens, but when Dempster achieved the task, Callan unexpectedly promoted him to 'Substantive Commandant' of Maquela!

On Thursday 29 January, Callan learned that another batch of mercenaries had arrived in Kinshasa. Meanwhile, Tomkins was preparing booby traps using anti-personnel mines and (when these ran out) Soviet POMZ-2 grenades, which were concealed in elephant grass alongside a section of road selected as an ambush site. In order to set up the grenades, a stake had to be driven firmly into the ground and a trip-wire attached to it. The wire was played out to the end of its 10-metre run where another stake was inserted, upon which a grenade and detonator were mounted. The spring-driven striker was primed, the striker-retaining pin inserted, and the end of the trip-wire clipped to it. Pressure on the wire pulled the pin and caused the striker to hit the detonating cap. Tomkins recalled:

I was coming to the end of the wire run and was holding the final POMZ, and was bending down, putting in the stake when one at the back of me, or one to the right, along the wire, went off. All I can assume is that the elephant grass … popped up … where I'd trod it down … sprang up and hit the wire, pulled it and it's gone off… I just heard a bang and … it shot me through the air – not the blast, but I think the force of the shrapnel. It whacked me in the legs and up the backside and dropped me into a drainage gully, and of course the wire that I was holding, which was attached to the last stake, pulled away … and wrapped all around my legs…

I knew that I'd been hit… So, with one hand I managed to get free to feel if I still had a pair of balls, and with the other I felt round the back and felt a bloody great hole, and the first thing I'm thinking about is, what colour is arterial blood…? I'm trying to figure out whether I've been done in the femoral, or whatever … because there's no pain at this time, and then I heard Charley (Christodoulou) shouting.[4]

Apart from those already suffering from tropical ailments, Tomkins was the first of the mercenaries' many casualties.

★   ★   ★

Jamie McAndless was another character whose behaviour was becoming a cause for concern. Immediately after Tomkins' accident he took Briton Bryan Lewis, Ako Joseph Nai (otherwise known as Joe Akoo – a Ghanaian who acted as an interpreter), and two FNLA soldiers on a 'snatch' raid to Damba. Initially, all went well: the patrol killed two Cubans and took two FAPLA captives. But during the return journey, a machine gunner fired at their Land Rover killing McAndless, the prisoners and both FNLA soldiers. Joe Akoo fled, leaving Lewis, who somehow succeeded in evading the enemy, shooting three of them in the process.[5]

On 30 January, Callan and 'Canada' Newby accompanied Tomkins to São Salvador en route to Kinshasa for medical treatment. That day John Banks also reached São Salvador with some of the 96 new arrivals, including John 'Spider' Kelly, a former soldier in The Parachute Regiment. He related how Callan had assembled the men and selected several with combat experience, when:

All of a sudden, Banks walked through the door, and Callan came and looked at him and said, "Who are you?"

He said, "I'm Major Banks."

Callan said, "You're fuck-all." He said, "You are nothing until you earn it, like these guys here. You earned fuck-all. Who's Kelly?"

"That's me."

"Do they call you Spider?"

I said, "Yes sir," straight away…

He said, "Right, as from now, you are Sergeant Kelly. These are part of your squad."

I said, "Fine sir."

He said, "That's how you earn your fucking rank Banks. Not by walking in here and telling me who you are."

Straight away, everybody clicked on then… Better watch what we say to this man.[6]

Banks did not stay long, returning to Kinshasa an hour later in

Holden Roberto's Range Rover and catching a flight home, abandoning his friend, Cecil 'Satch' Fortuin, who had arrived as one of Banks' two personal bodyguards. The next morning, Tomkins and a wounded FNLA soldier were evacuated to Mama Yemo Hospital in Kinshasa, soon to be joined by one of the newly arrived mercenaries, Hugh Morrison, a former French Foreign Legionnaire, who had been injured in a vehicle accident.

★ ★ ★

The long-awaited reinforcements began to arrive at Maquela, en route to Callan's base camp, on the afternoon of Friday 30 January. However, many of the newcomers had little or no military experience and were even less motivated than some of the original mercenaries. They were hardly inspired with confidence by the rapid exit of Banks, who they thought would be remaining in Angola as their commanding officer, and during their first parade the following day some of the men voiced their misgivings. Callan was enraged, but allowed those who did not wish to join him to stand aside. He then questioned the remainder, dismissing as unsuitable several other recruits, until 23 men had opted out or been rejected. They were relegated to fatigue duties at Maquela until other non-combative posts could be arranged in São Salvador. Callan took the remainder to the base camp, leaving newly promoted Lieutenant Dempster in charge of the fatigue party.

At about midday, the FNLA's Portuguese-piloted Cessna 174 reconnaissance aircraft landed, and Dempster was informed that the Cubans, supported by tanks, were dug in on the Damba road. Arriving back at headquarters, he was handed an urgent radio message from President Roberto advising Callan that Tômboco had fallen to an assault by Cuban tanks, which meant that Santo Antonio do Zaïre was now open to attack. Dempster left immediately for the base camp and reported to his commander. Callan decided to check for himself, taking with him a 106 mm recoilless anti-tank gun and some of the new men as his 'killer' group. Sammy Copeland was promoted to temporary base commander with Dempster as second-in-command. Before he left, Callan ordered his RSM to mount an assault on the Cubans outside

Damba. Copeland planned to drive in convoy to Quibocolo, then advance on foot under cover of darkness. Dempster was to be point man of one column, with 'Spider' Kelly leading the other. After a brief training session on the 66 mm LAW (light anti-tank weapon) Copeland set off with an advance party for Quibocolo, leaving Dempster to organize transport for his 25 men. Only three Land Rovers were left, so a number of men squeezed aboard two of these and departed for Quibocolo. Remembering that Callan's Toyota was being repaired, Dempster and another mercenary, Barry Freeman, took the third vehicle and left to check on the progress of the mechanics who were working on Callan's jeep at Maquela, where they were told that it would not be ready for another two or three hours. Dempster decided to return later. Before leaving, both men visited the 23 non-combatants who were given the opportunity to redeem themselves by volunteering for the night's operation. Dempster told them he would be back that evening and advised any who were interested to be ready to move. Among those at Maquela was former paratrooper, Kevin Whirity:

> We were left with a man called 'Butch', Brian Butcher, and Ken Aitken in command. The RSM, Copeland, left them in command. Aitken was Company Sergeant Major and 'Butch' was Company Quartermaster. 'Butch' got it into his mind that we'd all got to be kept in one place – a sort of guardroom.
>
> The guys that were there decided that at night we were going to make a break for it because it was clear what Callan was thinking of. Some of us thought even then that he was capable of shooting us. Butcher and Aitken herded us into a building which turned out to be the armoury, which suited us fine. After we were left alone, I said to the boys: "Grab yourselves a weapon and keep it close to you. If anything happens, pick it up and start firing through doors and windows." The armoury was a wooden building on a low brick wall which would have given some cover. During the day we wandered around, eyeing up the vehicles. A long-haired lad came along and said he could get a compass if we could raise some money. I gave him some money, others gave him cigarettes, and he came back with the compass.

Later we were in the HQ trying to get some food when Chris Dempster came in. He said he was up at the forward ambush position near Damba and the Cubans were coming that way. He said he would try and get back around nightfall but if anything came down the road after nightfall we would know it was the Cubans. He said this to Butcher and Aitken. As near as I can remember, he said that he was at the forward position with nothing but a group of men: "I can't hold them", he said, meaning the Cubans. "They'll wipe us out and they'll come up here. They'll roll right across Maquela. There's nowhere you can go. You can stay here and wait for the Cubans to come or you can come forward with us and try to stop them." Nobody wanted to go so he said: "Okay." Then he turned to Butcher and Aitken and said: "If by dark I don't come up that road, there'll be nothing coming but Cuban tanks, troops – they've even got their own bloody aircraft." And off he went.[7]

Back at the base camp Dempster and Freeman settled down to a couple of hours' sleep, only to be woken by two mercenaries who had been sent from Quibocolo with a message from Copeland, ordering Dempster and the others to join him as soon as possible. All four climbed into one vehicle and hurried towards Maquela. When they arrived, the place was in darkness. Someone produced a torch, which Freeman used to signal their arrival. There was no response. The next moment a missile slammed into the front of the Land Rover, stopping it dead. According to Whirity:

At about four pm, we noticed Aitken and Butcher looking a bit worried. They knew something was going on. You couldn't *not* know. Portuguese and black troops were coming in and at every key point they stationed a Portuguese or a black. There were some chaps on the far side of the compound watching. Watching us. We were under armed guard. It got dark. We had some grub served up – still in the armoury ready for a break. Butcher came in and ordered us all out into slit trenches. You could see the road winding for miles to some hills. Butcher and Aitken got into a Land Rover – Payden and I rode 'shotgun' for them as we toured the town perimeter.

68

I said: "Hey, look at that light." I saw a vehicle coming over the hill with only one light. Then another and another and another – until there were about nine. To me, there was only one thing it could be. Tanks travelling at night use only one light. Somebody wondered if they were Dempster's patrol, but somebody who'd seen a bit of service said wheeled vehicles don't use only one light. "Them's tanks", he said. A wind started up and over it everyone imagined they could hear the clatter of tank tracks. That was enough for Aitken and Butcher. "Get moving", they said. Before we could move there was a roar of a motor and a vehicle flashed past. It had two lights. So I thought: "Them's tanks and that's a Cuban scout car." Me and Dave were having a giggle at the thought that one moment we were under arrest and the next we've got weapons and were going to fight. The vehicle which went past us went up a slight gradient towards Maquela. We heard a bang and Aitken said: "Move out."[8]

★ ★ ★

At Cuimba, Terry Wilson, a former Rhodesian SAS trooper, had been placed in command of a detachment of FNLA guarding the border road. In the early hours of the morning his unit stopped two trucks heading for Zaïre. Aboard them were the 23 non-combatants from Maquela, who brought the alarming news that the town had been overrun by a Cuban armoured column. They claimed to have knocked out two tanks and killed 20 or so of the enemy before having to withdraw. It was assumed that any of Callan's men caught between Maquela and Quibocolo had either been killed or captured.

Whirity described events at the roadblock after Wilson ordered the men to get off the trucks and line up on the roadway:

We thought: "This is it." We had our weapons and were going to have a go at them. Then Ken Aitken came along. It all stems from Aitken, and if ever I see him I'll fucking choke him … Dave Payden will and all. Aitken came along, being the fucking big hero, and said: "Everybody behind the huts and into the bush." We all thought the Cubans were coming so everyone dived into the bush.

A few minutes later Aitken came along again, screaming and shouting: "If everyone isn't out of that bush in three seconds I'm going to start shooting. One, two, three" – and he fires a couple of shots. I thought this was bloody serious, there's something going on. He's set us up. So we came out of the bush and lined up again. Aitken said: "Throw your weapons on the floor. There's rifles pointing at you, machine guns pointing at you, heavy weapons pointing at you." There were all the vehicle lights shining on us. We thought: "This is it." Dave Payden and I were holding hands, squeezing, because we were frightened to bloody death. One boy dropped. The tension was too much for him. He just dropped. The tension was there. You knew what was going to happen.[9]

★   ★   ★

Not until daylight did the full facts began to emerge. Dempster's arrival at Maquela had been mistaken for a Cuban attack by the 23 mercenaries, who had changed into combat gear and armed themselves, ready to retreat to São Salvador. After opening fire on what they thought were enemy tanks, the panic-stricken men had commandeered three trucks and driven towards the border, only to be re-routed by Terry Wilson to Callan's location on the São Salvador road. Apparently, Tômboco had not been taken by the enemy, but under the misapprehension that Maquela had, Callan now ordered the men to prepare defensive positions on nearby high ground.[10]

When he learned what had really happened Callan was furious. Six of the non-combatants were ordered into his Land Rover and the remainder aboard two trucks, and driven to a waiting APC. The Land Rover reached it first, whereupon Callan told the half dozen anxious individuals to drop their weapons and strip to their underwear. They were then ordered aboard the APC and all the vehicles continued towards Maquela. By the time the convoy arrived, it was discovered that several of the 23 were missing, including Aitken and Butcher. The rest were lined up against the wall, disarmed and told to undress. Callan ordered the men who had been ambushed to fall in. Dempster, Freeman and another mercenary, Tony Boddy, came forward . The fourth had earlier gone to Quibocolo so two mercenaries, Paul Aves and Andy McKenzie, were detailed to take his place. Callan turned on those who had caused so much trouble, and demanded to know who had fired the rocket at Dempster's Land Rover. Philip Davies, a 22 year old from Birmingham, stepped forward.[11]

Callan allegedly produced his pistol and announced, "This is the only law here," and shot Davies three times.

Whirity was bending down, next to Davies, undoing his boot laces when Callan shot the boy in the leg and I felt blood and bits of leg splatter into my face. The boy fell against me and said: "Help me, Kevin", but I pushed him away. He fell back against the wall and Callan shot him in the body and then in the head, and finished him off.

Callan went back to Copeland and said: "You haven't tried the machine gun yet?" I saw Copeland looking at me. Callan said: "You, Para, are you prepared to soldier?" I said, "Yes, Sir." He said: "Out." I said: "What about him?", pointing at Dave Payden. "He's a good soldier." Callan called him out. Others said they wanted to soldier and Callan pulled them out of the line also, about half a dozen, including Dave and me. The rest of them, he told to continue stripping off, and when they were down to their underpants, he told them to get into the truck. He said to Copeland: "You know what to do." The truck moved off with a jeep with the machine gun in it behind, trained on the truck.[12]

In an open valley dotted with thorn bushes and tufts of long grass, but lacking any real cover, the men were ordered off the truck and gathered in front of Dempster, Freeman, Boddy, Aves, McKenzie and Copeland who, it is claimed, were covered by armed Portuguese. The condemned were ordered off the roadside whereupon RSM Copeland opened fire, followed by the rest of the execution squad. When it was over, at least 11 men were dead.[13]

★   ★   ★

After the executions, Callan announced his intention to lead the attack originally entrusted to Copeland. He and his men managed to knock out three tanks and kill 163 of the enemy. In turn, the mercenaries lost three killed and 19 wounded.[14] The following day, Callan organized another raid, accounting for an estimated 200 enemy and several tanks and vehicles destroyed or damaged. Colin Evans, who participated in the operation, later indicated that Callan directed two attacks, in the afternoon and evening of day two of the patrol. During the second attack, he thought they hit a tank (other accounts mention an ammunition truck), which blew up inflicting numerous casualties on both sides.[15]

The events of the next 48 hours are unclear. Callan was wounded in the leg and unable to walk. Another man, nicknamed 'Ginger', is believed to have also sustained a leg wound. Callan, and possibly 'Ginger', were carried from the scene by their comrades, who paused after two or three hundred metres to take stock of their situation and before deciding to go firm until daybreak. 'Ginger' apparently died that night.[16] In the morning, the survivors moved on and soon came to a hut belonging to a hunter, João Antonio and his wife, Sende Isobel[17]. By this time there were probably 12 men, including Callan, out of the two dozen British and Portuguese who had started out the day before. Copeland and another mercenary (possibly Scotsman John Malone) were sent to get help, followed some time later by Christodoulou and a Portuguese (probably Sergeanaro). All four reached Maquela.

After several days, two more left to seek assistance. One, thought to be Tony Boddy, was shot dead by a FAPLA unit and his companion, Andy McKenzie, was captured. The six remaining men moved on and soon after ran into an enemy patrol. According to Kevin Marchant:

We saw them and hid. But Callan, who had an M76 began to fire. We only had two automatic rifles and two pistols, one of which was Callan's. The FAPLA soldiers returned Callan's fire and Callan gave the order to retreat. He called the medic, McIntyre, to have a look at him, and then we started to run.

The FAPLA soldiers came after us, continuing to fire. We thought that Callan and the medic had been killed, because according to what Callan had said the FAPLA didn't take prisoners, and he was always saying to his men he didn't want any prisoners and that they didn't take prisoners – that they always killed them...

I didn't see Callan or McIntyre again. This is when we began our flight which lasted about 20 days. That night we rested and at day we walked northwards, guided by the position of the sun, because we had neither map nor compass.

During those 20 days we had to cross rivers and one of them had such a strong current that we lost the two automatic rifles that went to the bottom of the river. We were left with one pistol and one grenade which we later handed to the peasants that caught us. The group consisted of myself, Lawlor, Evans and Wiseman. We were caught in a village not far from Maquela. Me, Lawlor and Wiseman had gone to try and get some food. Evans had stayed because his feet were hurting. We three were taken prisoners and before the FAPLA arrived next day the people of the village caught Evans. The FAPLA took us to Maquela where they gave us food and medical treatment.[18]

Malcolm McIntyre remained with his commander until ordered to leave. Callan was captured soon after. McIntyre avoided a similar fate for two more days. 'Satch' Fortuin, who had been left behind after injuring an ankle early in the patrol, was also taken prisoner.

At about the time that Callan had departed on his ill-fated operation, Bryan Lewis finally turned up at the base camp. Shortly afterwards, he managed to steal an aircraft ride to Kinshasa with Barry Freeman and another mercenary, Pat MacPherson. Subsequently, Chris Dempster drove to São Salvador to arrange a diesel re-supply and met 'Fuzz' Hussey, following which the pair took a vehicle and headed for the border.

On Thursday 5 February, Peter McAleese, who had been appointed Callan's successor as FNLA Field Commander, began an investigation into the mercenaries' executions. Amongst those questioned was Freeman, who was acquitted after maintaining that he had been coerced into taking part. Christodoulou and Copeland were arrested in Maquela and summarily tried, the former being acquitted and the latter condemned to death. Before sentence could be carried out, however, Copeland broke away and fled towards the nearby bush. Several mercenaries promptly opened fire, wounding the fugitive who was then shot dead by Mick Wainhouse.

After arriving in Kinshasa, Dempster was also questioned about the Maquela executions but, like Freeman, managed to escape punishment after explaining the circumstances of his own reluctant involvement. A few days later both men flew back to England with 46 other disillusioned mercenaries.

McAleese returned to Maquela on Saturday 7 February with Bryan Lewis and Dave Tomkins who had recently been discharged from Mama Yemo Hospital. McAleese soon concluded that Maquela had become untenable and ordered the men to withdraw to São Salvador, subsequently dispatching half a dozen mercenaries and 140 black troops to assist with the defence of Tômboco. Meanwhile, FAPLA troops supported by Cuban armour had entered Santo Antonio do Zaïre, catching the defenders by surprise. Along with a (female) American journalist, Robin Wright, the mercenaries joined dozens of Angolans in a panic-stricken dash to the River Congo, where a motor-powered fishing boat had been moored for just such an eventuality. During the withdrawal Mike Johnson was shot and killed. Stuart McPherson, John Tilsey, Doug Saunders and Robin Wright were amongst those who boarded the boat, while 'Brummie' Barker vainly tried to organize an orderly evacuation. When the vessel cast off and headed into the estuary, he remained on the jetty to provide covering fire with his FN before diving into the river in a desperate attempt to reach safety. A burst of rifle fire into the water just ahead of Barker persuaded him to give up the attempt. Resignedly, the mercenary swam back to shore and captivity.

★　★　★

Even as the situation worsened, mercenary reinforcements continued to arrive. Some were recruited in the United States by

American Dave Bufkin in a similar manner to that employed in England by John Banks. Along with former Los Angles policeman Tom Oates, Bufkin had earlier visited Holden Roberto in Kinshasa to discuss the feasibility of providing American mercenaries. Bufkin had then gone home to organize travel arrangements for the first, and only, contingent. He returned to Kinshasa on 7 February with six men, one of whom opted out as soon as he learned about conditions in Angola.

★ ★ ★

On 8 February, Tomkins and Lewis volunteered to return to Zaïre to collect two Chinese tanks, a guided missile launcher and two multiple rocker launchers, which President Mobutu was donating to the FNLA. The following day, the convoy set out for the 400-kilometre drive to São Salvador accompanied by Holden Roberto, but 58 kilometres from their destination the convoy was held up by a collapsed bridge. Christodoulou and a black FNLA officer, Commandante 'Sonny' Lima, were overseeing its repair. While they were waiting, Roberto was recalled to Kinshasa and driven back by Lewis. Tomkins and Christodoulou accompanied Lima in his car to São Salvador, only to find that McAleese and the majority of the men had already left for Kinshasa. Among those remaining in São Salvador was Paul Aves, who had reappeared after being posted as missing; Mick Wainhouse, recently arrived from Maquela, and 'Canada' Newby.

At about this time, Mick Rennie and the other four mercenaries returned from Tômboco to report that the town had fallen to the Cubans. On 9 February, McAleese arrived in a Fokker Friendship with a fresh batch of 23, predominantly British mercenaries. They soon sustained their first casualty when Vic Gawthrop died, apparently after a heart attack during a foot patrol[19]. The following day, those at São Salvador were joined by the half dozen Americans. Dave Tomkins, two Portuguese and Fred Jones, a Briton who had been injured while testing one of the new tanks, returned with the Fokker to Kinshasa where, in the early hours of Thursday 12 February, Tomkins boarded a Swissair flight to Zurich, making a connection to Heathrow later that day.

★　★　★

The mercenaries, now consisting of about 45 British, Portuguese and Americans, were organized into three groups commanded by 'Canada' Newby, Charley Christodoulou and Mick Wainhouse, and deployed on reconnaissance patrols and the training of nearby FNLA units.

On Saturday 14 February, two mobile patrols, led by Christodoulou and an American, 'Gus' Grillo, headed towards Cuimba to report on the Cuban/FAPLA advance, but on the way, one of the vehicles broke down and everyone squeezed aboard the remaining Land Rover. They were ambushed a few kilometres from Cuimba. Christodoulou, killed instantly, tumbled from the still-moving vehicle, dragging American Daniel Gearhart onto the road with him. The survivors abandoned the Land Rover and ran for cover, but all six mercenaries and several FNLA soldiers in the group were quickly killed or captured.

It was now clear that the mercenaries would never be able to stop the enemy advance, although they could still delay it. With this in mind, Newby deployed a number of men on the evening of the 14th. The following morning, the Canadian took six mercenaries and drove in a single closed Land Rover towards Cuimba to try and locate Christodoulou's patrol. As they approached the town – now in enemy hands – the mercenaries encountered a truckload of FAPLA: those inside the Land Rover never had a chance. Newby, a Portuguese, an American and three British mercenaries were killed. Former US Marine Gary Acker was wounded and taken prisoner.

Soon afterwards, the remaining mercenaries abandoned São Salvador, crossing the border into Zaïre on 17 February, leaving only the Portuguese, who were not authorized to enter Zaïre, remaining in Angola.

★　★　★

In June 1976, the three American and ten British mercenaries held captive by the MPLA were subjected to a heavily publicized trial culminating in the deaths by firing squad of Tony Callan aka

Costas Georgiou, 'Brummie' Barker, Andy McKenzie and Danny Gearhart. The Americans ('Gus' Grillo and Gary Acker) and Britons (Kevin Marchant, Mike Wiseman, John Lawlor, Colin Evans, 'Satch' Fortuin, Malcolm McIntyre and John Nammock) received prison sentences ranging from 16 to 30 years. Joe Akoo, who had been captured following the death of Jamie McAndless, was acquitted after turning State's Witness. The two Americans were released in December 1982, and the seven Britons in March 1984.

Few of those who volunteered for Angola made any real money, although the FNLA certainly spent a fortune recruiting mercenaries. It has been speculated that much of this was diverted elsewhere by John Banks and his associates: if so, those responsible are saying nothing.

CHAPTER 4
FROM RHODESIA TO SOUTH AFRICA: SADF, 1975-82

Recce Commandos, 1980-83

Colonel Jan Breytenbach retired from the South African Defence Force (SADF) in 1987, after a long and distinguished military career. From 1950 to 1955 he served in the South African Army before joining the Royal Navy as a navigator in the Fleet Air Arm, taking part in the Suez Landings in 1956. In 1961, he re-enlisted in the South African Army and became a paratrooper. An exceptionally innovative officer, Breytenbach was credited with raising three specialist units and establishing the Army's Guerrilla School.

On 1 October 1972, Breytenbach formed 1 Reconnaissance, or 'Recce', Commando. By the late 1970s, the Recces had been expanded to four Commandos, including a Citizen Force (CF) unit (manned by those required to attend an annual call-up after completing their two years' national service), another comprising predominantly black troops, and a group specializing in amphibious operations. After the end of the Rhodesian War, some former members of the Selous Scouts and Rhodesian SAS were recruited to form two more Commandos. The South Africans' respect for Rhodesia's Special Forces was such that they were exempt from undergoing the usual selection and training – an arduous programme primarily intended to prepare soldiers for covert operations in enemy territory.

Jean C served as an officer in the French Air Force before joining the Rhodesian Light Infantry as a Trooper in January 1978. In March 1980, he volunteered for SAS selection. It was an open

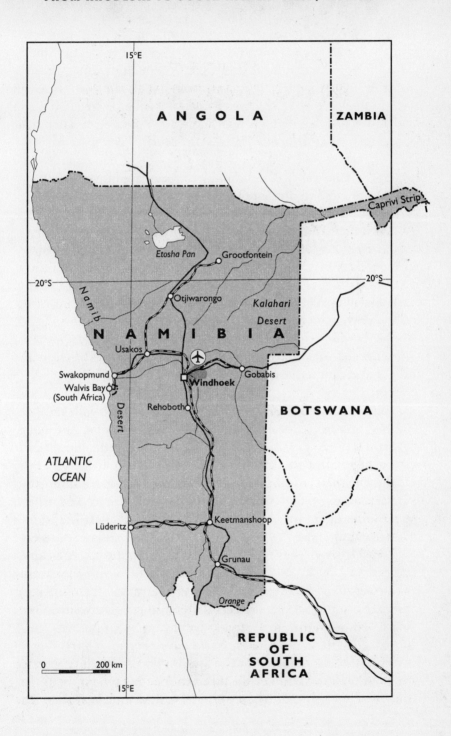

secret that South Africa was recruiting in Rhodesia and that passing SAS or Selous Scouts selection meant automatic qualification for South Africa's Recce Commandos. Tough months of training and mental preparation enabled Jean to get through selection with relative ease. As Robert Mugabe assumed power in what was now Zimbabwe, Jean and many others terminated their contracts with the former Rhodesian Security Forces.

> At the same time – this would have been about May 1980 – we were told to present ourselves at the South African Trade Mission, which effectively was the South African embassy, in Salisbury's Union Avenue. We were met by a man of military bearing, but dressed in civilian clothes, and signed our contracts for the SADF, while still serving in what was now the Zimbabwean Army. Our contract had been back-dated to the date of independence in Zimbabwe, and we were given a month to make our way to South Africa.[1]

In June, Jean boarded a coach for Beit Bridge on the Zimbabwe/South Africa border.

> When I got to Beit Bridge, I decided that I would walk across the Limpopo [River]. When I got to the other side, I turned around, took a last look at Rhodesia, and decided that was the end of it; I would never come back. I then walked up to the Customs and Immigration building, as I had done in Rhodesia two and a half years earlier... I was told to wait around. There was another chap on the bus, a Belgian, who was also joining the SADF. After about half an hour, a jeep arrived driven by an NCO. We were told to jump in the back.[2]

They were driven to Messina, where a huge, tented camp had been prepared – though quite unnecessarily – for an expected exodus of white Rhodesians in the wake of Mugabe's takeover. Jean remained at the camp for about two days, then took a train south to Pretoria and reported to the Special Forces recruiting office there. After attending a medical and completing other formalities, he was directed to Durban to join his new unit: 6 Recce. The

Commando, led by Lieutenant Colonel Garth Barrett, former commanding officer of the SAS, comprised 60 or so ex-Rhodesian SAS: about half of these had recently passed selection, others were former Territorials. Other officers who had served in the unit during the 1970s included Majors Colin Willis, American, Bob MacKenzie (see chapters 2 and 12), and Captain Peter Cole, a Briton. For men accustomed to the ageing equipment and comparatively Spartan lifestyle of the Rhodesian Army, joining 6 Recce was a revelation.

> Each of us received full kit, and for ex-Rhodesian soldiers who, at times, had to buy their own kit in various shops in Salisbury, it was like Christmas: brand new West German helmets, top quality bergens and webbing, 5.56 mm Beretta rifles – brand new – plus an AK [Kalashnikov rifle] and bayonet – brand new – and a 9 mm Beretta pistol each. But, unfortunately, we were all issued with awful chocolate brown denims worn by the entire SADF. The head-dress was the maroon beret, similar to that of the Parachute Brigade, but with the infantry badge – the Springbok head.
>
> Our camp was on The Bluff, a peninsula about two miles long overlooking Durban, that had been declared a military area years before. The camp was brand new and looked more like a university campus, with modern buildings, clipped lawns and very good facilities. Each of us had his own room, half of them with a sea view.
>
> I think that what surprised us and even, at times, shocked us – and eventually would effect our soldiering – is that we had come out of a full-scale war, and within days were living in another country where the war was thousands of miles away; and worse, a few minutes drive from South Africa's number one holiday and seaside resort with its beaches, its surfers, its night-clubs, its restaurants ... it was like being on another planet.[3]

Another surprise was that for the first few months there was little for the men to do except training and re-training. For some, the transition was altogether too much.

Every night, after training, we would drive down and find ourselves in the midst of thousands of holidaymakers. After a while, this started creating some discipline problems: the men were getting bored. They were having to wind down, and at the same time were frustrated at not being deployed. They would get into fights in the bars in town, or just go crazy, like the night when we started firing tracer through the windows. The South African Navy was conducting an exercise offshore and had to break radio silence as they thought The Bluff was being attacked. The next day, the Military Police came up and searched the place. But, of course, we had hidden everything and they couldn't prove anything.[4]

In late 1980 they began rehearsals for a secret mission. The commandos were issued with Rhodesian camouflage uniforms to mislead them into believing that they were about to deploy into Zimbabwe. In fact, their destination was Mozambique and the objectives three houses in a residential area of the capital, Maputo.

We trained extensively for house clearing in a derelict power station in an area adjacent to Durban harbour. The layout of the rooms, in what used to be the office block of a power station, was found to be suitable to prepare for the attack... We trained in denims, helmets and gas masks using AK47 rifles with drum magazines.[5]

After about three months perfecting their drills, the men were issued with FRELIMO uniforms and driven to a base camp on the Swaziland border with Mozambique.

Vehicles were waiting for us – all Russian-made, painted in the colours of FRELIMO. We left the camp that night with the drivers wearing night-vision equipment. We crossed the border, drove across country, and then reached what used to be the main road between Maputo, or Lourenço Marques, and the South African border – the border with South Africa was never closed, and there was still trade between the two countries. Once on the road, we drove down towards Maputo. It was an exhilarating experience: the night was cool, and everybody was really excited. We got to a junction indicating Maputo and then, amazingly, a number of us with cameras took photographs of the road sign saying 'Maputo'. This was the middle of the night, and we were using flashes, but nobody cared! We drove further down the road, and all of a sudden we stopped and waited. And waited. After a while, we learned that the operation had been aborted, so we turned around and drove back, and crossed back into South Africa without having been noticed at all.[6]

During the night of 29/30 January 1981, the operation was repeated. As before, the men crossed the border in disguised vehicles. They then proceeded to the Matola suburb of Maputo before dividing into three teams and continuing towards their respective targets.

This operation was a mixed success because of what occurred at one of the houses. A group of men went up to one of the windows. Someone threw a grenade, which should have gone through the window. In fact, it bounced off the window and fell on the floor. It exploded, hitting Rob Hutchinson and detonating a phosphorous grenade he had on him. Also, the house proved very difficult to enter and clear. Anyway, everything became a bit disorderly and the order was given to pull out. The two vehicles carrying this group drove away from the house, the people in each truck thinking that the other was carrying the body of Hutchinson. In fact, Hutch had been left behind.

The aim of the operation had been to capture ANC [African National Congress] personnel, including some senior officers who were based there. As it happened, a number of them were absent. We did capture some and, I believe, one of them was a very senior person. A large amount of information was also retrieved from the houses.[7]

In addition to those captured, the unit killed 13 members of the ANC. A Portuguese civilian worker also died in the attack.[8] The Commandos suffered three fatalities: Robert Hutchinson, Jim Park and Ian Suttil.

At about this time, the Reconnaissance Commandos were redesignated Reconnaissance Regiments: 6 Recce was absorbed by 1 Recce Regiment as 12 Commando, 2 Recce continued as a Citizen Force unit, while 3 Recce (ex-Selous Scouts) was amalgamated with 5 Recce. 4 Recce was retained as an amphibious specialist regiment. Two months after the Maputo raid, those in 12 Recce were given the option of extending their service or returning to civilian life.

> All in all, people had been disappointed by the lack of action... The South African Army was much more like a peacetime army and lacked flexibility. Eventually – and I guess this was the case for most of the Rhodesians – we had become 'guns for hire'. We had little sympathy for the South Africans, little interest in local politics and we didn't really believe in the cause. We were there because we just wanted to keep on fighting, since we didn't know what else to do.[9]

When warning was given of a two-month deployment, this time in the Gorogonza area of Mozambique in support of the Mozambique National Resistance (MNR or RENAMO), many, including Jean C, refused to be tempted. Others who stayed for the operation resigned after returning to South Africa, and by mid-1981 the Recces had lost the majority of its ex-SAS volunteers.

The amount of action a Recce operator saw varied widely between individual units. Paul was a British volunteer who was wounded in 1979 while serving with Grey's Scouts in Rhodesia. His injuries prevented Paul from attempting selection for Special Forces, and it was not until November 1981 that he left Zimbabwe for Phalaborwa, home of 5 Recce, to join a number of hopefuls preparing for Recce selection. Several weeks of training was followed by a three-week pre-selection course conducted by South African Air Force PTIs at the Pretoria suburb of Voortrekkerhoogte from where the candidates, including volunteers from 32 Battalion, 101 (Ovambo) and 121 (Zulu) Battalions were flown to Katima Mulilo in the Caprivi Strip.

We were issued SADF brown coveralls, each of which had a number painted on them. We were given World War II type webbing with a small back-sack. This sack was used to carry two x 60 mm mortar canisters for carrying six mortars, which were filled with concrete. The first phase of selection involved walking 150 kilometres along the cut-line, which is the border between South West Africa and Botswana, along the Caprivi Strip. We had three days to do this, although we didn't know the time-limit at the start of the exercise. The cut-line is just a soft sand road, ankle-deep in sand, and we had to stay on this track the whole way. We couldn't deviate from it at all. We were given no rations, no food of any sort, but we carried six water bottles. The good thing about the Caprivi is that there is an abundance of water. Every 10 to 15 kilometres there are water catchment areas where you can refill.

Every 25 kilometres or so the instructors had check-points just to tick you off going through. During this part of selection we lost quite a few people, and the course was whittled down to about 25 men. After about three days, we were halted and given a 24-hour ration pack each. We were told to dig a fully conventional fire-trench with overhead cover. Then we were teamed up, wherever possible, with an African. Once in the trench we had to adopt a tactical routine – which meant not being able to leave the trench until night. If we had to crap or piss, we had to do it in the trench. This exercise went on for three days, at the end of which we were pulled out of the trenches and each debriefed and asked questions about our partner, i.e. where he came from, name, date of birth, things like that. They wanted to see whether we'd made conversation with the African we'd been sharing with.

Once we'd been debriefed, we were formed up into teams and given a stretcher exercise. Each four-man team had to carry an injured man without knowing exactly how long for, or how far, or of being aware of any timings involved. Again, a psychological exercise. This lasted for about six hours, and then we were halted and told selection was over. Fifteen of us had passed the course.

Every member then had to undertake a Minor Tactics course, which was the mainstay of the Recce Commando. If you didn't make it on this, then you didn't become an operator. Minor Tactics is basically a Junior NCO's course, but incorporating Special Forces tactics: calling in artillery, calling in air support, setting up DZs, LZs and basically operating in four- to six-man teams. You were assessed at every step and at the end you had to take practical and theory exams, and that's make or break. The course lasted about six weeks. On completion, you undertook further courses – demolitions, small boats, heavy weapons, field-medic, and if you hadn't already done so, you did basic para and on to free-fall.[10]

After completing his training Paul was assigned to 5 Recce's 52 Commando.

5 Recce was formed to carry out a pseudo-operation role... 5 Recce worked on the same lines as the Selous Scouts in Rhodesia, with the added task of training indigenous guerrilla forces like the MNR and UNITA, etc. 5 Recce was formed up into three groups: 51, 52 and 53 Commandos. 51 worked in small teams: two- or three-man units that would free-fall into Mozambique, Angola or Zambia. 52 was a larger Commando group, assault Commandos of thirty to forty men, used for ambushing, blowing bridges and attacking of enemy key points. The last Commando, 53, was a pseudo-operation unit that operated from a military base in Ondangwa. It consisted of ex SWAPO captured by the security forces who [changed sides and] were used as pseudo-terrorists to infiltrate, control and contain certain areas of South West Africa and to locate [genuine] SWAPO groups, ambushing and killing or capturing as many SWAPO personnel as possible. 53 Commando was very successful in

this role, although they took a number of casualties themselves. This is understandable as the unit was operational nearly every single day. Little is known about 53, as the police special unit, *Koevat* (Crowbar), took most of the honours in South West Africa, but 53 played a major part in this theatre of operations.[11]

In mid-1981, Paul and four other operators – all of whom had served in the Rhodesian Light Infantry – were told to report to the Security Officer at Phalaborwa.

He was an ex Rhodesian Special Branch policeman whose job was intelligence and security at the base. [He explained that] we and four black ex Scouts operators would travel to Pretoria for a briefing at Special Forces HQ. We were told to travel in civvies, but to bring our bergens plus personal weapons, and we would also be taking along with us two RPG-7 rocket launchers. We travelled in two Special Forces Land Rovers. On arrival at Speskop [Special Forces Headquarters] we were met by some SF and intelligence officers. The briefing went as follows: we would drive in the Land Rovers to Beit Bridge where we would be met by another intelligence officer who would take us to a pump house on the Limpopo River. The task was to cross the Limpopo – as it was May, the dry season, parts of the river were very low and you could wade across at waist level – once on the Zimbabwe side, we'd set up a temporary base and there we would wait. That was the brief so far. Once we got to the pump house we'd have a further brief explaining our task once we were on the Zimbabwe side.

The drive to Beit Bridge took about three and a half hours. The sun was setting by the time we got to the border post. We took a small dirt track and followed the Limpopo River until eventually we reached the pump house. The whole South African side of the river had been cleared of vegetation and a three-metre-high rocket-proof fence had been erected with razor wire along the top and bottom. This was intended to keep any Zimbabwean refugees from crossing the river, though it was known that people still managed to breach the fence in certain places.

At the pump house we met the intelligence officer for our third brief. Once across the Limpopo, we were to RV with a European superintendent from the Zimbabwe Republic police. We'd exchange greetings and then he would hand over some equipment which we were to bring back across the Limpopo to the pump house. The op sounded quite straightforward.

We made our way in our civvies, carrying our personal weapons and the RPG-7s, and waded across the Limpopo. We also took with us two empty 45 gallon drums, painted white. These were to be placed on the dirt track that ran parallel to the Limpopo on the Zimbabwe side. This was to indicate to the oncoming police officer in his Land Rover where our position would be for the meet. It took us about 20 minutes to cross the river. We scrambled up the steep bank and made our temporary base, positioned the two white drums and then waited. We had been briefed that the Zimbabwe Army made regular vehicle patrols up and down the road parallel to this stretch of the river. Although we'd been there for about 45 minutes, we hadn't seen or heard any vehicles approach. Then in the distance we heard a motor. This could have been a Zimbabwe patrol, but it sounded like a lone vehicle. We heard it slow down. It must have seen the first drum and then, almost in front of our position, it came to a halt. The white officer de-bussed. One of our guys went forward. The meet had been made. We were called forward. I recognized the police officer. His name was 'Dave'. He came from London and had served in 9 Para Engineers in the UK. He had also served in the Rhodesian Engineers, and had one of his legs blown off in mine-clearance work during the war in Rhodesia. Dave was now a member of the Zimbabwe Republic Police and had helped train members of President Robert Mugabe's bodyguard team.

We exchanged formalities. He asked me what the situation was like down South. I said, it's okay. He said, once he'd taken his Land Rover back in one piece to Salisbury he'd be on the next flight out tomorrow morning if all went well. We then started lifting out the equipment from the back of the Land Rover. It was stored in wooden crates, about 12 of them each with a rope handle at either end. They were very heavy, and it needed two men to carry each one. Once we had offloaded all the crates we said cheers to Dave, he jumped into the Land Rover and off he went, back to Salisbury... Our priority was to get these crates down to the riverside and across the Limpopo as soon as possible in case we got compromised by a Zimbabwe Army patrol.

This whole process took about three hours. When we were finished, the sun was just coming up. It must have been about five o'clock in the morning. Back at the pump house, the intelligence officer greeted us and congratulated us on the work we had done. He said that we had deprived Mugabe of some valuable equipment. The crates were loaded on a Unimog and that left for Pretoria. We loaded our own equipment back on the Land Rovers and headed back to Phalaborwa.[12]

Afterwards, Paul and Dave were re-united in South Africa.

We started chatting about the op. Dave asked me if I had ever found out what was inside the crates. I said, no, we were never told the contents... He explained that they were Makarov and Tokarev pistols that had been donated by the Bulgarian Government in recognition to Robert Mugabe for his independence struggle. The weapons had only been in Zimbabwe for a week and had been housed at the Morris Depot, the police training camp in Salisbury.[13]

Dave, it transpired, had been working for South Africa's NIS (National Intelligence Service) as a member of the Zimbabwe Police, and was involved in various undercover operations including the bombing of ZANU PF (Zimbabwe African Union Patriotic Front) headquarters in Manica Road, Harare, and with sabotaging the munitions depot at Inkomo Barracks.

After the mysterious Limpopo mission, 52 Commando moved to Ondangwa, from where it was deployed in Angola during the run-up to Operation Protea, the largest 'external' to date. This amounted to a full-scale invasion of southern Angola by the SADF, with the main objectives being PLAN/FAPLA base camps at Xangongo and Ngiva. The Recces' role was to conduct night ambushes deep inside hostile territory. A typical operation involved a patrol of about 15 men, travelling in two Puma helicopters.

> We would fly about 250 kilometres into Angola and carry out an ambush on a strategic road point. On one such operation, we landed about four kilometres from our ambush position and walked in under the cover of darkness. We found our ambush position and were just setting up our anti-tank mines when we heard the noise of an approaching vehicle – vehicles travelling at night in southern Angola never used their lights because South African jets controlled the Angolan skies. As we hadn't had time to prime the anti-tank mines, we moved back to take up a firing position. My colleague suddenly picked up an RPG-7 and moved forward into the road. By this time the truck was only about 20 metres away. Suddenly there was a large explosion and the sky lit up. The whole front of the cab was ablaze. The rocket had penetrated straight through the engine block and into the cab. The vehicle kept coming. We recognized it as a six-wheeled Russian Gaz truck. On the back was an anti-aircraft gun, firing into the air. We opened up with everything we had, and soon we hit the ammunition in the back. The vehicle was ablaze, but still travelling in a straight line. Eventually it went past our position, veered off the road and exploded. The sky was full of pyrotechnics. Our patrol quickly extracted. We'd been walking for about 30 minutes when we heard mortar fire. This was common practice by the Angolans, though their reaction time was a bit slow in this instant. These type of operations took place for the next four or five weeks.[14]

A subsequent operation in southern Angola was less successful:

the Commando was parachuted in, along with 1 and 2 Recce Regiments, to ambush an armoured column reported to be heading for Xangongo, but unfortunately a navigational error resulted in the Commandos arriving at the wrong Drop Zone. Four men were injured, radio equipment damaged in the drop, and the operation had to be aborted. The task was reassigned to 32 Battalion, which succeeded in destroying or capturing dozens of vehicles, and thereafter the Recces reverted to the small-unit operations for which they were originally trained. For a while, 52 also experimented with mobile patrols, but decided against adopting such tactics due to their vehicles poor performance in coping with soft-sand conditions.

While 52 and 53 Commandos were active in Angola, 51 had been busy in Mozambique, where individual operators and small teams were deployed to assist RENAMO guerrillas against the Marxist government. After Operation Protea, 52 returned to Phalaborwa to construct a training camp for the MNR guerrillas until the project was taken over by military intelligence, who closed the base and established another in the Kruger National Park. In the meantime, 52 continued to conduct re-supply operations for their colleagues in 51 Commando, and remained on standby to act as a rescue force and destroy any South African helicopters forced to put down in Mozambique.

Paul stayed in the Recces for two years before taking up a civilian job in South Africa. A number of foreigners remained, and some were still serving well into the late 1980s, but for the majority, there was little incentive to continue with a military career. Gordon Harland, formerly of the British and Rhodesian armies, who led a fairly uneventful existence as a medic in 4 Recce, maintained that the SADF recruited ex Rhodesians not for their expertise, but because "they wanted to disband the Rhodesian Army, so Mugabe didn't have a reliable fighting force",[15] a notion shared by many former Rhodesian soldiers in South Africa.

Os Terrivis – 32 Battalion, 1975-89

One of the tasks of the SADF during Operation Savannah in 1975 was to reorganize Angolan soldiers who had defected to the FNLA from the MPLA after their military commander, Daniel Chipenda, failed to wrest control from the Angolan President Agostinho Neto. After forming the Reconnaissance Commando, Breytenbach had remained with his unit for more than two years before being posted to Army Headquarters. Eight months later in August 1975, he was dispatched to southern Angola to raise a new unit from Chipenda's FNLA, assisted by a Special Forces team of South African officers and NCOs and several Portuguese SNCOs. The result was 'Battlegroup Bravo', which joined 'Battlegroup Alpha' (an indigenous force under Commandant Delville Linford) to form 'Zulu Force'. The two units were in action from the early stages of Operation Savannah. Later, 'Battlegroup Bravo' was reinforced by two more companies and detached to fight alongside 'Battlegroup Foxbat', a unit recruited primarily from ex UNITA troops.

Breytenbach intended to use Bravo Group as a specialist counter-insurgency formation, to track and destroy guerrilla units in their own base areas. On 27 March 1976 Bravo Group was officially recognized as part of the South African Defence Force, and by the time Savannah ended, early in 1977, had been redesignated 32 Battalion: Alpha group was retitled 31 Battalion. 32 was based at Omauni in South West Africa (Namibia), dispatching foot patrols into southern Angola where the People's Liberation Army of Namibia (PLAN), the military wing of the South West African People's Organization (SWAPO), had established a number of bases. The PLAN guerrillas were actively supported by FAPLA forces so both became targets for South African operations.

As the war continued and PLAN began to develop from a guerrilla force to a semi-conventional army, 32 battalion adapted its tactics, operating in battalion strength when the situation required. On 4 May 1978, Operation Reindeer heralded the first of many SADF cross-border raids when airborne troops struck at SWAPO at Cassinga while mechanized infantry assaulted Chetequera. Rifle companies from 32 Battalion then cleared SWAPO's forward operational bases east of the town. The operation was an unqualified success, resulting in some 1,000 PLAN killed and hundreds wounded or captured. Casualties included a number of FAPLA and Cuban troops.

In 1977, Breytenbach reluctantly left the Battalion to attend a Staff and Command duties course. His replacement, Commandant Gert Nel was in turn succeeded by Colonel Deon Ferreira in January 1979. During the four years of Ferrerira's command, the role of the Battalion was extended: his men were deployed as motorized infantry with heavy support weapons, company-sized search and destroy teams, airborne assault troops, and on fireforce-type missions. The unit's Recce Wing also carried out various tasks, including ambushes deep inside Angola. Because of its flexibility, the Battalion became the prime strike group of Task Force 101 (later redesignated the South West Africa Territorial Force).

By 1980, a number of former Rhodesian soldiers had joined 32 Battalion, which by this time had expanded to seven rifle companies, each of three or four platoons, an 81 mm mortar company and a reconnaissance element. Few people outside the Battalion were even aware of its existence. The black troops lived on base with their families, while white officers and NCOs were based in tented accommodation nearby. During their time together, blacks and whites alike lived in the same Spartan conditions. As the emphasis was on self-reliance, contact with other units was discouraged, but South African troops passing through were naturally intrigued by the presence of so many foreign soldiers, and rumours began to circulate about the *uitlanders* (outsiders) near the Angolan border. The shroud of secrecy was lifted in 1981 when Lance Corporal Trevor Edwards, a Briton who had deserted from the unit, went public and accused 32 Battalion of committing atrocities under the command of white mercenary officers and NCOs during anti-guerrilla operations in Angola. His story was denied by Colonel Deon Ferreira, who claimed, "Every patrol that went out was under the command of a South African officer. Foreign elements were not allowed out on their own; they never were."[1]

Breytenbach later wrote: "I can state categorically that any commanding officer would have quickly become aware if atrocities were being committed, because guilty secrets like that could never be hidden or covered up. More importantly, neither I nor my successors would have wanted to cover anything up and we would have quickly brought culprits to trial."[2]

The denial of such allegations is understandable, as was perhaps the xenophobia of some of those in command. But according to Nigel W, (see chapter 2) an English volunteer in 32 Battalion, the unit did operate in Angola under the command of former Rhodesian soldiers.[3] Tim (see chapter 11), another Englishman, who served as a junior NCO in the Battalion Reconnaissance Group in 1982, also confirmed that "foreigners did take patrols into Angola".[4] As for the alleged atrocities, Tim recalled, "When I was in 32, they were clamping down on killings. It had got out of hand. The blacks were just stringing up Angolans and watching them swing while they were drinking their tea." He also admitted that his group had killed a man during interrogation, but maintained, "It was an accident... We used a sort of primitive water torture – we just put a towel over their heads and then poured water on it – and he had a heart attack. He must have had a weak heart."[5]

The unwelcome publicity generated by Edwards may have contributed to the decision by the SADF not to renew the contracts of (white) foreign military personnel unless they applied for South African citizenship. Some who refused to accept the new terms remained hopeful that the SADF might rescind this policy, and refused to discuss their service careers with anyone outside their own close-knit circle lest it jeapordize their prospects of re-enlistment. Several years after leaving the SADF, Nigel was still wary about being interviewed: at times he could be extremely brusque, particularly when pressed to describe the modus operandi of 32 Battalion.

> What you did was walk around the bush ... and when you walked into the gooks, who might number one, or might number three hundred, you attacked them. You might win, or you might have to run away![6]

That, according to the former NCO, just about summed up a month and a half of operations in Angola. Nigel was eventually persuaded to provide sufficient information to enable a short, but accurate, account to be compiled.

During a typical deployment, a company would be inserted either by helicopter or by simply walking across the SWA/Angola border, and a temporary base (TB) established from which to mount reconnaissance or fighting patrols, depending on the nature of the operation. Each platoon worked a rotating shift, enabling half of the men to patrol for two or three days while the remainder rested.

Following spoor across the flat, featureless, landscape, patrols would regularly encounter enemy forces. Clashes frequently occurred in the evening, when both sides simultaneously converged on the same bore hole or at an old Portuguese dam to replenish water supplies. This invariably resulted in a 'punch-up' followed by days of patrolling as each side attempted to ambush the other. If the soldiers of 32 caught up with the enemy first, the platoon or company commander usually initiated the contact. The men followed the example set by their leader, who was always point man. On his command of "Advance!", they would charge headlong at the enemy, firing at anything that moved. The location of the TB was changed as the unit scoured its area of operations. Patrols lasted anything up to six weeks, with helicopters providing re-supply and evacuating casualties.

The men carried several days provisions in bergens weighing up to 100 lbs. Their uniforms were similar to those once worn by the Portuguese Army in Mozambique, and now widely used by enemy forces although all items of clothing had been stripped of manufacturer's labels and were therefore untraceable to any particular country.[7] Footwear consisted of canvas and leather 'Special Ops' boots. Troops were issued with a unique pattern of jacket webbing designed to carry AK47 magazines as everybody was armed with captured Soviet or Chinese weapons. White soldiers were required to blacken their hair and skin with camouflage cream so that, from a distance, the men were indistinguishable from a SWAPO or FAPLA patrol. In effect, should the Battalion be obliged to abandon anyone killed in action, there would be no evidence that the SADF was engaged in operations beyond South Africa's borders, and accordingly, the SADF did not release the names of Battalion members killed on active service: they simply ceased to exist. It was a convenient and effective procedure, and one that was very nearly applied to Corporal Nigel W.

Nigel and another Rhodesian corporal were in joint command of about 50 men involved in an uneventful patrol, until the NCOs acquiesced to their bored men's pleas and attacked a FAPLA unit. Following a short fire fight, both groups broke contact. The resolute enemy then tracked the patrol, and managed to approach undetected as the exhausted troops lay resting in the open. As in much of Angola, the terrain was devoid of any real cover and so the patrol had deployed in an outward-facing U-shaped configuration of three straight lines, the platoon commanders positioned at both angles.

Nigel's first indication that something was amiss came when he spotted movement in the bush 50 metres in front of them. He was still staring at the spot when a 40 mm rocket-propelled grenade exploded in their midst. A moment later they were subjected to what Nigel described as "the most intensive fire I have ever experienced". According to Nigel, "the air turned green" with incoming tracer. When both NCOs ran for the negligible cover of a solitary tree, they were beaten to it by a trooper, just before he was sent cartwheeling by an exploding RPG. The pair were powerless to do anything except lie absolutely flat, using their bulky packs as their only form of cover. The harrowing experience continued for about 20 minutes – a long time to be under fire – until "everything a foot above ground level had been sheared away, all bushes, all trees, everything!" Nigel looked back at his colleague to see him hit by several bullets. Tracer rounds landed, spinning and hissing , inches from his own face. The perforated canteens in his bergen leaked water, "from about 20 bullet holes ... like something from a kid's comic". Nigel was himself shot through the head and chest.

Eventually, the survivors stood as though obeying a silent command and, screaming wildly, charged the enemy. Six FAPLA were killed and the remainder driven off. Amazingly, the two platoons lost only one man killed, although 22 were wounded. Five hours later, the patrol was uplifted by helicopter.[8]

The troops' ability to remain calm and then launch a successful counterattack says much for the courage and high standard of discipline within the Battalion. Indeed, discipline was maintained in a manner that shocked even the hardened veterans of the Rhodesian War. Misdemeanours were dealt with in various ways. One of the milder forms of punishment, it is alleged, was to have the miscreant, wearing helmet and pack, manhandle a truck wheel along a road for 36 kilometres. Because the road was mostly sand, the wheel could not be rolled, but had to be turned over from one side to the other. The punishment could take up to two days to complete. More serious offences could result in a trooper being publicly flogged with a sjambok [whip made from rhinoceros or hippo hide], and it is claimed that the ultimate penalty was invoked on at least one occasion when a soldier was shot on the parade square of the Battalion camp after he dared to voice his grievances over pay. Afterwards, the CO asked the formed-up Battalion if there were any other complaints: unsurprisingly, there were none.[9]

Small wonder then, that when unleashed, 32 Battalion proved such an efficient fighting machine. Its ferocity in action inevitably earned the grudging respect of its enemies, as well as the apt sobriquet, *Os Terrivis* – The Terrifying Ones!

The Battalion was involved in many of the publicized externals carried out by the SADF in the 1980s, including Operations Sceptic (May-June 1980), Protea (August 1981), Super (March 1982), Mebos (July-August 1982) and Askari (December 1983 – January 1984). The unit also carried out clandestine missions and was active in assisting UNITA against FAPLA in 1985 and 1986. By this time, 32 battalion had been supplied with Valkyrie 127 mm multiple rocket launchers, 120 mm mortars, 106 mm recoilless and anti-aircraft guns, Milan anti-tank missiles, plus additional 81 mm mortars and Browning M2 .50 calibre machine guns; and all personnel had undergone extensive retraining in conventional warfare.

Many of SWAPO's fighters were now being used to reinforce FAPLA in its campaign against UNITA and this, combined with a steady attrition rate, was beginning the have a noticeable effect on PLAN's fighting capability in Southern Angola and SWA. However, FAPLA, already bolstered by an estimated 30,000 Cuban troops, was further strengthened by some 3,000 Russian and East German 'advisers' together with Soviet and East German military equipment.

Towards the end of 1986, Colonel 'Jock' Harris succeeded Colonel Eddie Viljoen, who had taken over as 32 Battalion Commander from Ferreira in December 1982. Harris stayed with the unit for a year before handing over to Colonel Mucho Delport. The war was now entering its final phase. In 1987 Operation Modular saw the SADF supporting UNITA against FAPLA/Cuban forces in a series of successful actions in which both sides made extensive use of their artillery, armour and air power. FAPLA's defeats resulted in Cuba dispatching even more troops to Angola, which prompted the SADF to launch Operation Hooper to pre-empt further offensive enemy action.

Political negotiations to end the war led to South Africa withdrawing its forces from Angola in August 1988. The implementation of United Nations Security Council Resolution 435 (providing for UN-supervized elections in SWA/Namibia) was scheduled to come into effect on 1 April 1989. This should have ended the fighting. Instead, on the night of 31 March/1 April, an incursion of SWAPO insurgents from Angola led to renewed hostilities and a suspension of UNSCR 435 before order could be re-established.

In November 1989, the long-awaited elections resulted in victory for SWAPO and 32 Battalion was withdrawn to a new base at Pomfret, on the edge of the Kalahari Desert in South Africa's northern Cape Province.

The Philistines: Pathfinder Company, 44 Parachute Brigade, 1980-82

Colonel Jan Breytenbach was back in action by May 1978, this time as commanding officer of 44 Parachute Brigade. In 1980, he developed a concept that would provide the Brigade with an independent force specializing in unconventional operations in the border areas of South West Africa. The new sub-unit was to be known as Pathfinder Company.

At the time, 44 Parachute Brigade was organized into three separate battalions. The 1st, based at Tempe, included a regular cadre and was responsible for airborne training and selection of

National Service (NS) volunteers. Brigade and 2nd Battalion Headquarters (located at Hammanskraal, Pretoria) and 3rd Battalion (at Johannesburg) were each manned by Citizen Force personnel.

Pathfinder Company consisted of foreign volunteers, almost all of whom had served in Rhodesia. They were quite different from other soldiers in the SADF, most of whom they regarded as being overly serious, ridiculously pious and unbelievably xenophobic. Colonel Breytenbach spent much time with his new command, and while his proven abilities should have earned him the respect he undoubtedly deserved, his presence was not always appreciated. Sean Wyatt, a Canadian who served as a JNCO, remembered him as 'The Joker', a nickname coined as a result of the Colonel's unorthodox tactics, but conceded:

> He had a good deal of organisational skill and he was a far seer, a forward thinker... He did have a lot of personal courage, but he was past it by the time he served with us... He should have been up there conducting higher level operations instead of running around with basically what amounted to an oversized platoon.[1]

Company Commander was Captain Piet Botes, who had previously served in 32 Battalion. He was another of the few South Africans associated with the group. Wyatt recalled that

> Captain Botes was definitely a Boer of the Old School. However, he was a skilled soldier and we all liked him a lot. He didn't know how to treat us foreigners until he'd seen us all perform on selection, and I think he developed quite an affection and respect for us.[2]

Company Sergeant Major was WO2 Peter McAleese (see chapters 2, 3 and 9) who Wyatt remembered as

> a unique individual, to put it politely... He didn't like me, I didn't like him. We didn't get along. However, I'll give him full credit in that he's probably one of the finest instructors

I've ever encountered ... and one of the few leaders that would inspire total confidence. I can state unequivocally that most of us would follow him to the gates of hell... He was a leader and he was definitely good under fire. He was a very deadly individual and ... the finest soldier I've ever come across.[3]

McAleese and Botes devised an intensive training programme for those joining the new company: subjects were frequently taught by the 'recruits' themselves, many of whom had specialized during their previous military service. After about five months, enough men had been gathered at Mabalique camp, on the border with Zimbabwe, for McAleese to run the first of several selection cadres. These took place in the Drakensburg Mountains, southeast of Pretoria. Wyatt's first attempt at selection failed when "I checked in at the top of the first hill, 400 metres from the start, having fallen ... over twice. Too young and unfit with absolutely no drive. A poor effort all round on my part."[4] After several weeks of training at Mabalique, 19-year-old Wyatt was ready to try again.

Selection worked out to be a five- or six-day route march... It changed with different courses but, essentially, for the first two days you carried (in addition to your rucksack and full fighting order with its rations and everything) an 80 lb box of ammunition on your back. I don't know how to explain how difficult it was. The altitude took a toll on you... During the first day of selection, I lost 10 lb and two pant sizes, and I was in good shape. It was just sheer, physical punishment.

You had to navigate your way through the Drakensburg Mountains. The first day, we set off with 17 people in our selection. The route was laid out, with the check points you were supposed to arrive at... I think it worked out that in five days you were expected to cover 170 kilometres... That may not appear too bad, but it was so brutal. First day, 17 of us started off. We went across an interim mountain range, climbed up over one little group of hills, down, across a river, up a hill, a sheer cliff and, finally, on to a road. By the time we crossed the river, there were six of us left. Myself and KD [American 'KD' Clarke] stuck together because we had done that first part before, so KD and I worked together... We got up the hill – basically, climbed the damn cliff to get up there – helped each other, and then KD's leg gave out, popped to hell... Captain Botes was following us and he proceeded to beat me with his stick and encourage me to carry on!

By mid-morning the next day, when we hit the road, there were four of us left – myself, KD, Dave Barr and Gordon Brindley... It was just brutal... We carried on, did all that was required of us, made the check point, carried on and dumped the boxes, then carried on without them. I was totally dead. My knee had given out, I had blisters everywhere. It was too horrible. Anyway, we made it down to the final portion... Then they made you go out with your fighting order and rucksacks, run six kilometres, and then sent you back. Basically, the six-kilometre run was a sickener. Throughout the run you had directing staff yelling in your ear, telling you to quit... Now, I had every intention of doing this whole thing and telling them to fuck off... I was pissed off, and I did not like being treated like this ... and we carried on ... got to the end of it and Captain Botes said, "Did you like that? Are you ready to carry on?" My body was going, No, No, No, but my mouth for some reason said, "Yes". At that point he said, "Fine, you've passed. Take your kit off. Have a shower."... And that was it. That was selection. The four of us passed. Of those who did not, some were asked to come back, and some were not.

After that we did more training at Mabalique and helped with training for the next group who went for selection, and then we proceeded to act as directing staff on selection of that group.

It was at this time that we got a little feed-back on what had been going on up in South West Africa with the first teams that had deployed.[5]

The initial selections produced enough Pathfinders to be divided into two sections under McAleese and WO2 Dennis Croukamp, formerly of the RLI and Selous Scouts. In January 1981, following a period at Mabalique spent perfecting attacks against guerrilla camps, the Pathfinders were attached to C Company of lst Parachute Battalion for Operation Vasbyt 5. This was to be an attack against SWAPO and FAPLA positions near the Angolan town of Cuamato, in conjunction with 31 and 32 Battalions.

Ken Gaudet was decorated for his service in Vietnam with 173rd Airborne Brigade, and fought with the RLI throughout the last year of the Rhodesian War before arriving in South Africa. One of the original intake of Pathfinder Company in September 1980, he described how the assault force arrived at Cuamato in Puma helicopters.

> The advance unit hit a hot LZ [Landing Zone] as they landed in the town of Cuamato, the site of our planned FOB [Forward Operating Base]. The resistance was light though, and after a brief fire fight the SWAPO terrorist unit in the town fled, leaving two KIAs [dead], one usable RPD light machine gun and a couple of AKs.
>
> My chopper was the second one in and we landed next to the local well. Our lieutenant immediately put our men out in a defensive position on the north side of town to cover the road entrance. My fellow Pathfinder was a Frenchman, Corporal Busmey, and Frenchie and I settled down under a big baobab tree to cover the road.[6]

When the airforce reported enemy troops heading north, C Company was ordered in pursuit. In addition to Lance Corporal J Busmey, Lance Corporal Gaudet's patrol included 12 South African paratroopers. Suddenly

> the forward scouts spotted two terrs [terrorists] to their front. They radioed the information to the lieutenant, and he split the patrol into two groups, and moved out with one of them to the scouts' location. The sergeant was left back in command of my group. The word was passed by radio that terrs had been spotted and the lieutenant and his section were in pursuit. About 10 minutes later, small-arms fire broke the

silence, followed by mortar fire. The lieutenant radioed back that they had followed the terrs all the way to their base camp, and now they were under heavy fire. We monitored his call back to the FOB commander requesting more troops.[7]

Reinforcements, including McAleese and the rest of the Pathfinders, soon arrived.

CSM McAleese asked for volunteers to assault the terrs' trench line and establish covering fire while the remainder of our force moved in. One of the Pathfinders, Corporal Gilmour, and two of the Paras spoke up.

McAleese and the three men charged across the open area between us and the first bunker while we laid down covering fire for them. Two terrorists jumped out of the bunker to take them on, but Gilmour killed both. He then tossed a white phosphorous grenade into the bunker.

The other terrs in the outer trench line fired back on the advancing Paras while falling back to their inner trench line. As soon as McAleese and his team reached the outer trench line, the *valk* I was attached to charged across from the tree line to join them.

The outer trenches soon were in chaos, filled with Paras who seemed not to know what to do next. The terrs were hitting us from the inner trench line with everything they had – AKs, RPDS, even 14.5 mm heavy machine guns and a 75 mm recoilless rifle.

The Para sergeant told his lieutenant he was going to move forward and capture the 75 mm recoilless rifle. He moved out to throw a grenade, but was hit in the head and fell in a lifeless heap. The young lieutenant saw his sergeant go down and went out to help him. When he turned around to give his Paras instructions, he was shot in the back. One of his troops went out, pulled him under cover, and started working to stop the bleeding.

Word came down for us to pull back out of the trench line into the trees and await further orders. Four Paras grabbed hold of the dead sergeant to move him back to the tree line, and CSM McAleese carried the wounded officer. During the pull-out, panic set in among some of the Paras and they began to run.

CSM McAleese, with the aid of the Pathfinder corporals, stopped their flight. "Hold your ground!" McAleese bellowed. "Paratroopers don't run from terrs!"[8]

As the men hurriedly reorganized in preparation for a more orderly withdrawal, they were subjected to a creeping mortar barrage, anti-aircraft HMG and small-arms fire, which resulted in another man killed and two more wounded. That night, the survivors dug in near Cuamato.

The following morning, the enemy base was mortared and attacked by South African helicopter gunships in preparation for another assault by the Paratroopers and 32 Battalion infantry. The operation continued for much of the day, then the tired troops were airlifted back to Ondangwa. In return for two South African fatalities and several wounded, at least 66 enemy were killed and five captured, along with a considerable quantity of arms and equipment.[9]

Graham Gillmore served in the Grenadier Guards and then as a signaller with the Rhodesian Light Infantry before joining Pathfinder Company as a senior NCO in charge of radio communications. He recalled that

By early 1981 two selection courses had produced Pathfinders to man a convoy of vehicles being prepared in the workshops of the Department of Scientific and Industrial Research. This consisted of three Toyota Landcruisers, two mounting .50 calibre Browning machine guns and one with a 20 mm cannon bartered from the Air Force. Three Land Rovers would carry twin 7.62 mm FN MAGs [general purpose machine guns] mounted on the back plus a single machine gun for the commander. Three Unimogs were to be used for the fuel, rations and ammunition needed for long-range patrolling. All vehicles had smoke dischargers and winches as well as foam-filled tyres (as a preventative measure against puncturing from thorns).[10]

The convoy arrived at Murrayhill only days before the Company set off for Sector 10, the operational area in South West Africa that borders Angola. It was to be a slow drive with frequent stops made in order to plan and practice techniques and drills.

The Pathfinders took two weeks moving up through the Kalahari Desert along the Botswana border, trying out ambush and anti-ambush drills, laagering and patrol formations. It was decided that two vehicle sections worked best with the commander in a Landcruiser and the 2IC in a Land Rover. This provided a satisfying blend of firepower. All vehicles had VHF radios for internal use and section commanders carried HF sets for communication to base camp.

One unfortunate incident which marred the journey was a bitter fight between CSM McAleese and W02 Green, an Englishman who had been involved in converting the vehicles. The two men had a long-standing grievance and after it erupted into violence McAleese was returned to Murrayhill to concentrate on training the next batch of Pathfinders. His position was filled by W02 Croukamp, a Rhodesian with a cool, confident approach to combat.[11]

Soon after arriving at their new camp, the Pathfinders were deployed on their first mobile operation.

This was to be a dawn attack on a known SWAPO base. Following a preliminary air strike, the base was to be assaulted by 32 Battalion, with the Pathfinders providing close support with their machine guns.

The Company received its orders and prepared kit. Dress was optional. South African brown uniform mingled with Rhodesian camouflage and anything else available, usually of Communist origin. Webbing choice was also left to the individual. Personal weapons consisted of the 5.56 mm R4 [South African version of the Israeli Galil] which was not as popular with the men as the old Rhodesian-issue FN FAL. Most disliked its smaller calibre and 'tinny' feel. Some took along hand guns, both privately owned and the issue Star 9 mm. Each vehicle carried a quantity of M79 grenade launchers and an RPG-7 rocket launcher.

The day before the attack the Company crossed the cut-line (border with Angola). Aided by aerial photographs, the Pathfinders drove north, seeking a route through thin bush. When the bush thickened, hampering progress, a Unimog was called to the fore and these marvellous work-horses would crash, bend and batter a road through for the others to follow.

By last light, the Company had managed to link up with 32 Battalion. Before dawn, the terrorist camp began to buzz with activity. The enemy had discovered that something was up and started putting down speculative fire on likely approach routes with BM-21 multiple rocket launchers.

The air strike went in on schedule and was met by spirited anti-aircraft fire from several points around the camp. The ground forces commenced their advance into the camp area. A well-disciplined sweep line was formed by 32 Battalion, the vehicles of the Pathfinders spaced at intervals along it. As we progressed, fire was put into likely enemy cover. There was no return fire, however, and it soon became apparent that apart from the anti-aircraft gunners everyone else had fled.

While 32 Battalion was left to deal with two unexploded bombs, dropped by the Mirages on the initial strike, the Company moved out to clear the anti-aircraft positions. Supporting helicopters had reported seeing terrorists wheeling off heavy machine guns, but we located one position with three 14.5 machine guns still intact. When we arrived a SWAPO, wounded in one leg and unable to escape, chose to shoot himself in the head.

After checking them for booby traps, the guns were lifted out by Puma helicopter. Later, Colonel Breytenbach managed to retrieve one and it was mounted in a Unimog for our own use.[12]

On their return to South West Africa, the Pathfinders moved to

Ondangwa and established a camp alongside that of 1st Parachute Battalion. During the next few months, the Company was deployed on long-range vehicle and foot patrols and also acted as a cut-off group during cross border operations. Although many Pathfinders were wounded, only one died on active service. In July 1981, 16 men were involved in a foot patrol deep inside Angola. Australian, Sergeant Derek Andrews (see chapter 2) and a newly-qualified Pathfinder, Steve Hadlow, were flown out by helicopter to join the group. Shortly afterwards, two suspects were captured. Some of the men were in favour of killing the prisoners, but Sergeant Major Croukamp had another idea, as Andrews recalled:

> He suggested that we send the two to the terrorists with a challenge to come and fight us. We all thought he was joking and had a good laugh, until we saw that he was deadly serious and so we all agreed. After all, it had been a very boring trip with little action up until then. The note went something like:
>
> > "To the Political Commissar: Dear Comrade,
> > We consider you to be wimps who fight only women and children and unarmed old men. If you consider yourselves soldiers, we will be waiting for you at the big river (Canani)"
>
> The note was given to the two suspects who were told to take it to their comrades. They obviously realised that they had escaped death, and the look of fear suddenly vanished from their faces and they proceeded to break the land speed record as they departed north to the terrorist camp. Truthfully, I don't think any of us expected anything to come from our bravado but, being cautious, we dug in that night and patrolled the next day without anything out of the ordinary happening. We radioed base and gave a report and were told that we would be re-supplied the next day. My friend, Steve, became very quiet and asked if he could go out on that re-supply chopper. Often, a soldier would get a type of

107

premonition – a feeling of foreboding – and they would be allowed to go back to base. But Steve's request was denied and although he remained uneasy, he just accepted the decision. The next day, the re-supply chopper came and went and once again we filled our packs and gave the left-over supplies to the nearest village.

Having reached the big river in the afternoon, we dug in as usual in a good tactical position with all-round defence, but something didn't seem right. When my turn came to relieve the sentry, I took two grenades out of my pack and kept them beside me. There was a definite feeling of unrest. At sundown we all went to our foxholes and stayed ready just in case of attack. Nothing happened, although the eerie feeling remained. Once again, the sentries were posted and the rest of us bedded down for the night.

I must have been exhausted because I don't remember anything until 4 a.m. when I sat up to the sound of heavy firing. Our boys were firing on the perimeter, so my first thoughts were that they had seen something, but my mind soon cleared as that heavy concentration of green tracers came flashing through the camp. My experience of the Soviet green tracers in Vietnam and Rhodesia left me in no doubt that this was the enemy and the sheer density of fire meant that it was a large force. For a moment, it all reminded me of Bonfire night, and then the adrenaline started pumping and I scrambled from my sleeping bag into a well-placed ant-bear hole. As I struggled to put on my chest webbing, sand flicked at me from the rounds that hit the ground only centimetres away, and cracking sounds filled the space above my head as rounds passed perilously close.

I couldn't return fire from my central position because of the troops on the perimeter and ammunition re-supply. I called out to see if anyone was wounded or needed my help, hoping that no-one would respond, but back came the call that someone was hit. I would rather have stayed in the relative safety of my hole but instead leapt out, and dashed in the direction of the wounded man, running as close to the ground as I could. In the dimness of first light, I could see the silhouettes of the enemy advancing, but I had to put that out of my mind to attend to my mate. When I reached him all I could see was a black splash on his forehead. He was conscious and able to tell me that he had a headache. I dressed his wound and made him comfortable and then returned fire. The enemy was very close by this time, and we could even hear their orders being yelled to fix bayonets.

This was a confident force preparing for the final assault in which they would try to overrun us. We must have all sensed this, as we all switched from semi-auto to automatic and sent everything we had at them. We could see that we were scoring a lot of hits and this must have been just enough for them to falter because they soon started to retreat, dragging their dead and wounded with them, which is a sure sign of well-disciplined soldiers. Our confidence soared as we all yelled insults at them in our own languages and accents. The enemy must have wondered who we were with so many countries represented.

While the enemy retreated, our lieutenant took those men who were not involved in the firing and swung around in front of our position in a counter-attack. In the meantime, we reloaded and I called for a situation report. At this stage, we had one dead and one wounded. I had no time to dwell on the fact that it was my friend, Steve, who lay dead in his foxhole. Out in the open, the counter-attack continued, when a new sound sent shivers down our spines, and we knew that this was by no means the end of the attack. The enemy had started using mortars and at that moment I was thankful that I had chosen a treeless area for our camp. When mortars hit trees, the shrapnel is sprayed down into the foxholes and there is no way of sheltering from it. The first barrage landed among the eight men in the counterattack, which sent them running for their foxholes but, methodically, the enemy increased the range until the mortars were dropping among us. Seven of the eight soldiers in the counterattack were wounded. It was like all hell had broken loose. I felt very vulnerable lying on top of my wounded friend in his foxhole, as I was above ground level and had no protection from the terrifying explosions and incoming rounds...

There was an horrendous explosion that left me dazed. I felt something hot running onto my hand, and crazy thoughts of my skull being shattered or my head blown to pieces ran through my mind. I raised my hands slowly to my head and was greatly relieved as, inch by inch, my fingers explored undamaged flesh. As I felt my earlobe, I realized that the blood was coming from a small shrapnel wound.

I imagined that hours had passed since the mortars first began to drop when, all of a sudden, they stopped and there was deadly silence... We lay there in shock, just listening to the silence.[13]

The enemy did not resume their attack, and shortly afterwards the patrol was airlifted back to South West Africa. In addition to Steve Hadlow's death, there were at least eight wounded. The following month, Pathfinder Company was ordered to Omuthiya, and joined other units in rehearsals for Operation Protea. Pathfinder Company was to deploy in an anti-tank role, being equipped for the occasion with French 89 mm Strim rocket launchers. 'Gilly' Gillmore's following account was compiled from the former Sergeant's operations log.

On 21 August [1981] we received a warning order to be ready to move any time after 1700 hours. The following day, at 1100 hours, the Company was given its final briefing. The Task Force would attack target 'Yankee' – the town of Xangongo and the FAPLA armoured brigade there. Because of our role as tank hunters, the Company would remain uncommitted but ready to be deployed as required.

By 1745 hours the Task Force was on its way to the FUP [Form Up Point]. At noon on the 23rd it reached Okolongo, 30 kilometres from the cut-line, where a major refueling programme took place. The FUP was reached shortly afterwards. The move from the FUP to the target began at 0230 hours the next morning. On crossing the cut-line, a multiple launch rocket system, a Stalin Organ-type Unimog, detonated a mine, becoming the first casualty of Op 'Protea'.

110

At exactly 1200 hours the SAAF [South African Air Force] Mirages struck Xangongo. The ground forces, including the Pathfinders, were already on the outskirts. 32 Battalion provided the assault troops, who were supported by the artillery with their 155mm G-5 guns. By 1900 hours, the fighting was over and the town was firmly in South African hands.

The Pathfinders themselves were not engaged that day and spent the night near an old Portuguese fort overlooking a bridge. They were stood-to for most of the night due to some fighting in the centre of town, on the far side of which could be heard the distinctive sound of mortars firing.

All was quiet by midday on the 25th, so Colonel Breytenbach arranged for his men to become attached to Battle Group 30. Joining up with the Ratel infantry combat vehicles, the Pathfinders sped along the tarmac road towards a FAPLA camp, 80 kilometres north-west of Xangongo but, annoyingly, it was already deserted by the time the column arrived.

At last light the units dispersed for the night, a Ratel remaining on the road to halt any FAPLA coming down from Cahama in the north. The Pathfinders laagered 200 metres off the road, about a kilometre down from the Ratels.

Corporal Dave Barr was the gunner on Colonel Breytenbach's Landcruiser. Due to his wealth of knowledge, learned on US Marine helicopters in Vietnam, he was responsible for all our heavy machine guns. At 2200 hours, he was on guard when a convoy of petrol-driven trucks passed by, heading north. As all the friendly forces had diesel engines, Barr quickly woke the sleeping crew members. By now, the convoy had reached the Ratels blocking the road and a sharp engagement was heard to take place, lasting for five or ten minutes. It was followed by a silence broken only by the sound of the FAPLA convoy now driving back the way they had come. By chance, they stopped right next to the Pathfinders, who were now stood to at their vehicles.

At a command by Colonel Breytenbach, all the vehicles on the side nearest the road opened fire. Men from the far side assisted with M79s and the 60 mm mortar. An incredible amount of red and green tracer streaked across the sky, while a nearby artillery unit added to the surreal scene by firing illumination shells.

The FAPLA firing stopped and all was quiet again. The Pathfinders had no casualties or damage, but the enemy were not finished yet. Noises coming from the far side of the road indicated that they could be setting up mortars, so a patrol under Captain Veldhuizen was quickly formed and, armed with the 89 mm rocket launchers, silently inched their way towards the sounds. On the other side of the road they saw two Russian Gaz lorries and several FAPLA soldiers setting up mortars. The Pathfinders crossed the road unseen to form a firing line. On a signal from Captain Veldhuizen, they opened fire. It was dramatically effective. Both lorries exploded, hit by 89 mm rockets. After only a few minutes, Captain Veldhuizen's men ceased firing. There was neither sight nor sound of the enemy. However, because of the dangers of sweeping a contact area in the dark, the patrol returned to the laager.

With the action over for the night, sentries were posted while the rest caught up on some long overdue sleep despite the continual din caused by exploding ammunition in the burning vehicles.

By morning, the Company was up and ready to move. The night's contact area would now have to be swept prior to all else. To everyone's great satisfaction, the entire FAPLA convoy was found deserted on the road. It consisted of a fully-equipped radio jeep, two BTR armoured cars, two BM-21 multiple rocket launchers and four other Gaz trucks, each with a twin 23 mm anti-aircraft machine gun mounted on the back. These nine vehicles captured, plus the two mortar lorries destroyed, made a successful night's work. Although no enemy bodies were found, it was evident that their casualties had been removed, due to the quantity of blood spoor in the area.

After returning to Xangongo for a quick clean-up, the Company set off to work independently, heading north to the town of Chivemba where reports indicated a FAPLA force of unknown size. Deliberately making their presence known in the town area, the Company then lay in ambush along the road, hoping to catch any patrols reckless enough to come after us. This tactic showed no results so it was decided to visit suspected SWAPO and FAPLA camps. Before entering a camp area, we would call over helicopter gunships, but no enemy were encountered. The camps had been empty for a number of days.

By the 29th of August all possible enemy positions outside Chivemba had been checked and found to be deserted, so it was decided to enter the town itself. As a Land Rover had broken down, Colonel Breytenbach elected to leave the mechanics behind, protected by two other vehicles, while he approached the town with seven vehicles and 26 men. The column got no further than the kraals on the town outskirts when the Colonel's Landcruiser was destroyed by a landmine.[14]

One of the first on the scene was Sergeant Andrews.

Dave Barr had both legs shattered and received quite severe burns, and Graham Gillmore had his foot blown out of its socket. It was one of the many times my medic training really helped, and apart from attending the other wounded men, I grabbed the dislocated foot, which was still connected by some of the flesh, and stretched it back into position, securing it with bandages.[15]

Andrews' prompt action saved Gillmore's foot, but Barr's injuries were far more serious and would result in the American losing both legs. Breytenbach and his driver were both extremely lucky to escape with only minor injuries.

After the two badly wounded were evacuated, the Colonel was advised by the Air Force of an estimated 1,000 PLAN/FAPLA in Chivemba and prudently decided to withdraw. The Company continued to check likely enemy camps until Protea ended three days later.

After a period of leave and re-training which included a

parachute conversion course, the Pathfinders were parachuted into Angola during Operation Daisy in November 1981 as part of an assault force ordered to destroy a PLAN headquarters at Bambi and a base area at Cheraquera. In December, the Company was again deployed on mobile patrols. At about this time, Colonel Breytenbach was posted to a new command and replaced by Colonel Frank Bestbier. Shortly afterwards, Pathfinder Company was transferred to 32 Battalion's Reconnaissance Wing. According to Englishman Tim W:

> It was obvious from the start we weren't wanted. They made us live outside the [camp] perimeter and treated us like shit. Some of the kaffirs had bunkers to sleep in, proper rooms, and we were outside in tents.[16]

Furthermore, the Pathfinders were required to pass a selection course. This culminated in Operation Missing Link, a fruitless search for guerrillas in South West Africa. A search and destroy operation in Angola, codename Handsack, lasted six weeks, during which there was one minor contact. Upon returning to SWA the Pathfinders were informed that they were being posted back to 44 Parachute Brigade. The majority left the SADF upon completion of their one year contracts.

★ ★ ★

After leaving 44 Parachute Brigade, Colonel Breytenbach seems to have been involved in the formation of another specialist unit intended to carry out secret operations in Zimbabwe on behalf of Chief of Staff Intelligence (CSI). The unit included both white and black former Rhodesians, including a number of ex ZIPRA guerrillas. At least one operation took place, which resulted in the deaths of two Rhodesians, Staff Sergeant Dave Berry and Sergeant Bob Beech. Sergeant John Wessels, a Briton, was captured, tortured, and later executed. It was rumoured that the men were involved in an unauthorized mission, possibly to rescue political detainees. Another, curious, explanation, is that they had been trying to retrieve a cache of ivory. The truth has yet to emerge.

⋆   ⋆   ⋆

All (white) foreign military personnel in the SADF were eventually required to adopt South African citizenship. This enabled the government to deny further accusations that the SADF employed mercenaries. Ironically, there was remarkably little concern about the numerous black foreigners who continued to serve in the SADF for the duration of the border war.

CHAPTER 5
COUP AND COUNTER COUP: COMOROS, 1975-95

After the Congo, 'Colonel' Robert Denard (see chapters 1 and 6) continued to work for anyone who could afford his services. His notoriety would eventually surpass even that of 'Mad' Mike Hoare, whose reputation owes much to his autobiographical *Congo Mercenary*[1] and *The Seychelles Affair*. However, unlike Hoare, Denard did not seek publicity. Others have recorded his exploits, and not always accurately, but Denard has done little or nothing to put the record straight.

Denard's most recent activities resulted from his long-term involvement with the Comoros, a group of four islands (Grande Comore, Mayotte, Anjouan and Moheli) that lies between Mozambique and Madagascar, dominating the shipping route from the Indian Ocean into the Mozambique Channel. Mayotte, the southernmost island, was annexed by the French in the mid-nineteenth century, while the rest of the archipelago continued to be ruled by local Sultans, avoiding colonization until the 1880s. By the turn of the century, Sultan Said Ali of Grande Comore, the largest and most northerly island, had emerged as the dominant potentate.

In July 1961, Said Mohammed Cheik became the first President of the Comoros. He was succeeded nine years later by Prince Said Ibrahim, son and heir of Said Ali, but a vote of no confidence forced him to step down in favour of Prince Said Mohammed Djaffer in October 1972: Ahmed Abdallah Abderemane was elected as the new President two months later. France planned to grant autonomy to the Islands, but was pre-empted by Ahmed Abdallah's unilateral declaration of independence in July 1975.

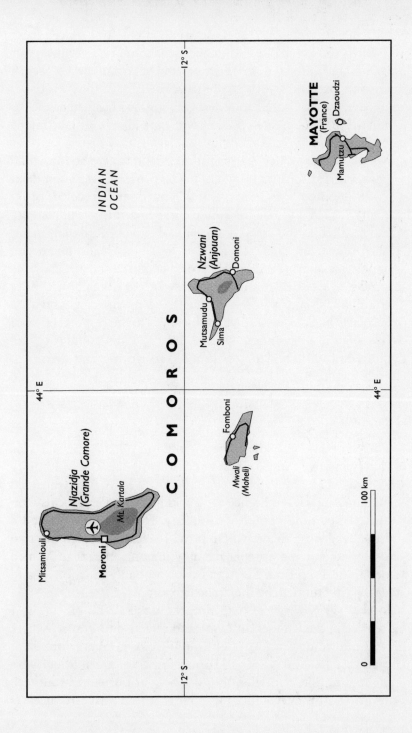

The French President, Valéry Giscard d'Estaing, was placed in an awkward position, but ruled out military action. The situation was further complicated when Mayotte opted to remain under French rule. Soon afterwards, Abdallah was ousted in a bloodless coup; Said Mohammed Djaffer took over as interim-President while Ali Soilih, the main figure behind the coup, controlled events from the background.

Abdallah, meanwhile, fled to Anjouan from where he continued to pose a threat to the ruling party. The problem was soon dealt with. In September 1975, Bob Denard and several other mercenaries led a locally recruited force in a raid on the island, which resulted in the arrest and eventual exile of Abdallah. After Denard's departure, Soilih emerged as the islands' leader and began to impose his own ideas and beliefs on a bemused constituency. He severed all ties with France, dispensed with the islands' more puritanical Islamic traditions, legalized marijuana, and in a particularly bizarre move gave the local youth the responsibility of overseeing the rest of the populace. By 1978, his popularity had dwindled, and increasing tension led to rioting and deaths in Grande Comore.

★   ★   ★

Denard had not been idle since his mission to Anjouan. He was probably involved in Cabinda and with Angola, and in January 1977 had led an abortive attack on Benin, West Africa, which led to his standing trial in France for the killing of several locals who had dual Beninois/French nationality. Now he was offered a contract to depose the very man he had helped to install not two years previously, and to replace him with none other than Ahmed Abdallah. His return to the islands was probably sanctioned, and at least partly funded, by the French government.

In May 1977, French ex paratrooper Hugues de Tappie cut short his service in the Rhodesian Army and returned to France, where he was placed on stand-by for an undisclosed operation. That Christmas, he and another former Rhodesian soldier were instructed to join a trawler, the *Antinéa*,[2] at Lorient in southern Brittany. There they met four men, one of whom was introduced as a medic, another as an administrator – the advance party of Denard's mercenary team. Also aboard were several crewmen, preparing the vessel for what they had been told was a geological survey. Only the advance party were aware of the true identity of their employer, 'Mr Thomas' – aka Bob Denard.

At the end of March 1978, the *Antinéa* sailed for the Canary Islands where the engineer, who had become increasingly suspicious, was paid off and replaced. Before leaving the Canaries about a week later, 40 men were secretly embarked. Hugues de Tappie recalled:

> The Spanish authorities, and even those on the boat – the electricians and so on – did not know they were aboard. So, early the next morning, when they showed themselves, the crew were very surprised. What the hell is going on? Well, don't worry, they are divers for the operation, all divers [indicating short haircuts], yeah, sure.[3]

The *Antinéa* headed south, rounding the Cape and continuing north, through the Mozambique Channel. Denard planned to launch his operation during the night of 12-13 May. With just three days to go, he briefed his men.

> Denard revealed where we were going and what we were going to do, and split us into three groups… The night before the coup, we turned off the lights on the boat and put up curtains, and anchored a few miles off Itsandra beach, where we were to land. The sea was rough but we had to continue because … it was a Saturday morning and the army was off [for the weekend], so it was a good opportunity for a landing.[4]

Leaving little to chance, Denard assigned one of the mercenaries to guard the *Antinéa* and her crew. To ensure that the landing would be a complete surprise, he decided against liaising with a contact who was to have provided information about the situation ashore. According to Hugues de Tappie:

Denard told me, "Forget it. We're going, anyhow, and at least we know that nobody will expect us. We can't be betrayed."… So, we anchored and disembarked in three Zodiacs … wearing black fatigues, hats and with blackened faces. There was a torch behind each Zodiac, and all were following Denard. I was with Denard, obviously, being his radio operator.

We were only armed with pump-action shotguns, a few hunting rifles and diving knives and had very basic walkie-talkies. Nothing else… We intended, as we did, to pick up weapons from the enemy.

We landed on the beach after an initial attempt in the wrong place, where we almost capsized. We were almost thrown onto the rocks but, eventually, with Denard steering, we managed to turn about and landed… Once on the beach, we secured the Zodiacs.[5]

The mercenaries hurriedly established a beachhead. Personnel were detailed to cut nearby telephone lines, to look after the Zodiacs and to guard the main coast road, while two teams were instructed to seize the military camps at Kandani and Voidjou. The former was just east of Itsandra beach, and the other several kilometres away between the capital, Moroni, and the island's international airport.

Denard led another group to the Presidential House and was the first to contact the local defence force. There was an exchange of fire as the mercenaries bypassed Kandani, leaving the base to be dealt with by the team following close behind. Kandani and Voidjou were quickly overrun. Denard then found his route blocked by a sleeping sentry.

The guy was resting in his guard-house and apparently had not heard the shooting because of the [dense] forest… We kept quiet while one of us crawled forward to [indicating throat being cut] and as our guy approached, the sentry woke up, but he could not fire his weapon for some reason. He was knifed, but it took quite a long time. It was very difficult because the guy was screaming, for two minutes maybe, then it was over.

Then, just before dawn a Renault 4 approached from the Presidency. We did not know then, but it was the Chief of Police. We did not know whether our shooting had been heard by those at the Presidency ... but Denard told us, "Shoot the car", so we all shot at it using Brennek ammunition – 12 gauge – it is very efficient.[6]

All three men in the Renault were killed. The mercenaries then proceeded to assault a nearby building, believed to have been used as an interrogation centre. They took the sentries prisoner and re-armed themselves with the soldiers' MAT-49 sub-machine guns and AK47s. While Bob Denard, Hugues de Tappie and another team member handcuffed the prisoners and searched the building, the rest of the group headed for the Presidency. Two mercenaries gained entry after firing at the door lock, and found Ali Soilih in bed with two women. After a brief interrogation, he was left under guard while the rest of the team entered Moroni, linked up with the other mercenaries, and soon had the next target – a radio station on the outskirts of the city – under their control. So far, they had achieved their objectives without incurring a single casualty. The enemy had lost less than 10 men killed.

It was now daylight and a vast crowd began to gather in Moroni as the population realized what was happening. The mercenaries were surrounded by cheering men and shrilly ululating women, but Denard had not yet completed his mission. One of the main objectives was a barracks in Moroni that housed the *Commando Moissi*, Ali Soilih's 'elite' unit of guards.

So far, we only had to deal with the army, but the soldiers were not fanatics like the *Commando Moissi*, and we did not know how they would react, this so-called Commando... They were kids... But they did not react, actually. We arrived at their barracks and they had all vanished. Then we went to the jail and liberated its political prisoners, one of whom would be the next Minister of Defence a few days later, and only then, in the jail, was one of us injured accidentally by a ricochet from Denard ... but it was not too serious. That was it. The coup was over.[7]

Denard's men maintained security, standing by in case of any retaliation from Soilih's remaining supporters. An interim 'politico-military directorate' was formed by Denard, Abdallah Mohammed and Abbas Djoussouf before the return of Ahmed Abdallah and another of the coup instigators, Mohammed Ahmed, on 22 May. A new government was installed with both men as co-Presidents. The post of Prime Minister went to Abdallah Mohammed, while Djoussouf became Defence Minister.

And what of Ali Soilih? Patrick Ollivier, another French ex paratrooper and a former captain in Rhodesia's Grey's Scouts, arrived in the Comoros in 1981 and served under Denard for 16 months. When questioned about the fate of Soilih, he maintained that

> When … President Ahmed Abdallah arrived, he decided that Ali Soilih had to be shot. Bob Denard … told me, and I think he didn't bullshit me for once, that he disagreed with having to shoot Ali Soilih.[8]

Denard undoubtedly appreciated the potential value of keeping Soilih alive. While he lived, the former President continued to pose a threat to Ahmed Abdallah, but if Soilih were to die, Denard would lose a valuable pawn and Abdallah could consolidate his position with no further need of mercenary support. Abdallah decided that Soilih would stand trial in front of a tribunal, which virtually guaranteed the death sentence. But by 29 May, Soilih was already dead. What happened is unclear. One story suggests Soilih was encouraged to flee and was 'shot while escaping'. Another version is that he was killed by a mercenary, apparently on the orders of Abdallah and other unidentified parties.[9] It is difficult to believe that Denard was not also somehow involved, but the question remains: why order the death of someone who faced execution anyway?

Denard remained in the directorate for another two months before resigning to concentrate on his responsibilities as Chief of the Army and Security. By this time, the army of the old regime had been replaced by a new force, trained and led by the mercenaries.

The coup prompted a predictably unfavourable reaction from

the Organization of African Unity (OAU), causing Denard to adopt an increasingly low profile, "even though he was really very much appreciated by the [local] population. They called him 'Colonel Papa', and that's how they felt about him."[10] Nevertheless, the presence of white mercenaries in general, and of Denard in particular, continued to attract unwanted attention. France applied pressure on Denard to withdraw. Initially, he refused, but agreed to reduce his force to15 to 20 military 'advisers', and remained until the end of September 1978, by which time he had taken a local woman, Amina, as his wife. In his absence, a new arrival, Commandant 'Charles'[11] took over as mercenary commander and military adviser to Abdallah who assumed sole power in December. Later, Denard was able to return unobtrusively. He converted to Islam, and settled in Daché, north of Moroni.

By late September 1979, South Africa had agreed to fund the Comorian Presidential Guard in turn for various concessions. These are said to have included a site on the islands for a secret listening station and a base from which to transit arms shipments destined for the Middle East, RENAMO in Mozambique and rebel forces in Afghanistan.[12]

Little is known about Denard's mercenary activities since the Comoros, though he was certainly responsible for a secret operation in Chad in 1982.

★　★　★

On 11 August 1960, Chad was granted independence from France, but in a region divided by religious, ethnic and tribal differences, it was inevitable that civil war would follow. By 1969, significant gains by rebel forces prompted President François Tombalbaye to seek military assistance from the French, whose troops remained in Chad until December 1971. In April 1975, Tombalbaye was ousted in a coup d'état staged by his Defence Minister, General Félix Malloum. The new regime evolved into a coalition that included one of the main faction leaders, Hissène Habré; but Libyan-backed rebels, led by Goukouni Oueddeï, continued to pose a threat and the French were again asked to intervene. Before they left in May

1980, in-fighting had led to the resignation of Habré and Malloum and the formation of the Transitional Government of National Unity (GUNT) with Oueddeï as President and Habré as Defence Minister. After renewed clashes between Oueddeï and Habré, the former again approached Libya's Muammar Gaddafi for assistance. Habré was forced to flee to Cameroon and then to western Sudan where he began to regroup his forces.

Denard was approached and asked if he could help Habré, and dispatched a small team to Chad to organize an offensive. Of the three mercenaries involved in the operation, one was killed in action in Chad, and another later died in a shooting accident in the Comoros. Hugues de Tappie is the only survivor.

> We just got our usual wages from the Comoros Islands. We were not paid by Hissène Habré but hoped that our efforts would later be rewarded. So, we joined the fight, which was pretty hard – taking weapons only from the enemy. It proved to be very successful.
>
> I mainly reorganized the signals – well, organized them in fact because there was nothing there. As we moved forward, we took equipment from the enemy, but no one knew how to use it, so I had to train them... The two other guys set up a mortar section and were mainly involved with training [the rebels] and repairing heavy machine guns. We were using 14.5 mm and 30 mm anti-aircraft weapons, Katyushkas [Soviet multiple rocket launchers] and so on... In mid-82 we took [the capital] N'djamena ... and two months later, I resigned.[13]

After the fall of N'djamena, Oueddeï escaped to Libya. Several more of Denard's mercenaries arrived to assist the forces of Hissène Habré, followed later by French troops. In addition to the threat presented by Goukouni in the north, Habré faced opposition from other factions in the south. In October, 1986, dissatisfaction amongst his own supporters led to Goukouni joining forces with Habré. Unwisely, he chose to make his announcement while visiting Tripoli, and was promptly apprehended on Gaddafi's orders!

During the next few months, Habré, with French and American

aid, conducted a successful campaign against Libyan forces in Chad. Habré remained in power until 1989 when he was deposed by his Chief of Staff, Idriss Deby.

★ ★ ★

The Comoros also underwent a change of government in the same year. On the night of 26/27 November, Ahmed Abdallah Abderemane was killed and Said Mohammed Djohar installed as interim-President. The circumstances of the death of Abdallah, who was shot several times, remain a mystery. Denard is the prime suspect, but denied being directly involved: "As Chief of his guard I was responsible for the President's death, but not to blame for it."[14]

South Africa responded by suspending assistance to the Presidential Guard, while the French assembled a Task Force in Mayotte – a clear warning to Denard that his time in the island paradise was over. On 14 December the first of the mercenaries began to leave the Comoros and the remainder, including Denard, departed the following day.

Bob Denard stayed in South Africa until 1 February 1993 when he returned to France to stand trial for his involvement in the Benin affair. In April, he received a five-year suspended sentence. Denard may yet to be tried in connection with the killing of Ahmed Abdallah, following a civil action opened in 1990 by the Abdallah family, accusing him of murder.

During the night of 27-8 September 1995, 33 mercenaries transferred to two inflatable dinghies from a vessel moored off the coast of Grande Comore. Once ashore, the men split into teams, rapidly secured their objectives and captured President Said Mohammed Djohar, who was accused of misrule and misappropriation of government funds. There was only token resistance from the Comorian forces, several hundred of whom opted to side with the mercenaries. Bob Denard had returned, having accomplished another coup.

On 4 October France staged a counter-coup with 600 troops who quickly seized control of key installations before accepting the surrender of Denard and his mercenary-led army. The ageing

'Colonel' left on the first stage of his journey to imprisonment in France, while the unpopular Djohar was flown to Réunion, ostensibly for a medical check-up, and replaced by an interim government under the moderate Caabi el-Yachroutu.

The Comoros continued to be troubled by internal disputes, resulting mainly from the inability of local leaders to agree about the continuing role of France in Comorian affairs. In August 1997 Anjouan and Moheli seceded from Grande Comore. The following month at least 30 people were reported to have been killed when then-President Mohammed Taki ordered troops to Anjouan in an unsuccessful attempt to restore central authority in the Island.

CHAPTER 6:
COMEDY OF ERRORS:
SEYCHELLES, 1981

Roger served in the Parachute Regiment, RLI and Rhodesian SAS before volunteering for the South African Defence Force. While waiting for his application to be processed, he was approached by another ex Rhodesian soldier, American Barry Gribbon, who informed him about a forthcoming 'scene'.

At first I didn't believe him, but said, yes, I was interested, and left it at that. About three days later, Barry had to phone the person he was dealing with. He contacted Mike Webb[1] who told him that the scene was on. So we jumped down to Durban to find out what it was all about. When we arrived, we spoke to Mike Webb who gave us a brief run-down, saying that it was to be a coup d'état, but he didn't say where. He said there was going to be a meeting soon – that Mike Hoare [see chapter 1] was organizing it – and that payment was to be US $10,000 for approximately two weeks' work.[2]

It was early November 1981. Three weeks later, a mercenary force landed at the main island of Mahé in the Seychelles to attempt a classic coup d'état.

***

The Seychelles, an archipelago of nearly 100 islands with a population of only 64,000, is situated in the Indian Ocean 4(40´ south of the equator, 300 kilometres north of Madagascar. Colonized by the French in the mid-18th century, the Seychelles

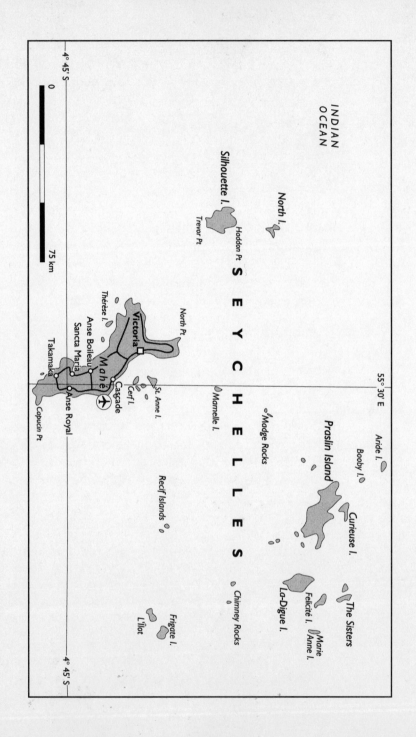

Above RLI troopers on a parachute course at New Sarum, Rhodesia, 1979. From the left: 'Beetle' Bailey (Canadian), Jean C (French Moroccan), John Banks (Rhodesian), Charlie Dickens (British), Koos Basson (Rhodesian), Anthony Rogers (the author), Mike Moore (Rhodesian), Barry Gribbon (American), Nigel W (British). Rhodesian Air Force Dakota in background. (Anthony Rogers)

Below Selous Scouts in Mozambique during Operation 'Virile', December 1977. (via Derek Andrews)

Above RLI awaiting uplift at the end of a cross-border strike, Mozambique, 29 April 1979.
Australian Tony Y (standing) with captured SKS rifles. (Anthony Rogers)

Below Derek Andrews, an Australian serving in the Selous Scouts, on board an Alouette
helicopter en route to an operational area in Rhodesia, 1977. (Derek Andrews)

Showing the flag: American Jeff A serving in 1 RLI, kitted up for a parachute jump. (Jean C)

British members of 32 battalion SADF seen in Angola during the early 1980s. (Private collection)

Right Wounded American volunteer, Fred Verduin and SWAPO KIA after the Pathfinders sent a message inviting SWAPO to join them in battle, Angola, mid-1981. (via Tim W)

Below Pathfinders take a break during Operation 'Protea', Xangongo, Angola, August 1981. American 'KD' Clarke (left) and a British volunteer. (Private collection)

Above Belgian volunteer, Mike Deceunick with 32 battalion SADF in Angola during Operation 'Handsack'. *(via Tim W)*

Below Spaniard 'Mario Vidal', ex-Spanish Legion, French Foreign Legion, RLI and Rhodesian SAS, seen in the early 1980s while serving with the Recce Commandos, SADF. The weapon is an RPG-7. *(Jean C)*

Above SADF Pathfinders and a 'Jackal' vehicle (Private collection)

Below Selection for Pathfinder Company, 44 Parachute Brigade SADF, Drakensberg mountains, South Africa, 1981. (Private collection)

British volunteer 'Gilly' Gillmore in the SADF Pathfinders, seen in Angola during Operation 'Protea', 1981. Note the graffiti. (Private collection)

SWAPO casualty found after night attack on a Pathfinder patrol, Angola 1981. (via Tim W)

Paul (middle) ex-RAF Regiment and Grey's Scouts, seen serving with 5 Recce during Operation 'Carnation' in mid-1981. (Private collection)

Above *The Antinea which carried Bob Denard's invasion force to the Comoros, seen in dry dock at Las Palmas, the Canary Islands, March 1978. (Hugues de Tappie)*

Below *Rio, one of three French mercenaries sent by Bob Denard to Chad to support Hissène Habré, seen in mid-1982 repairing a BM-16 MRL. In 1983 Rio was killed in a training accident in the Comoros. (Hugues de Tappie)*

Left Mike Pemberton (sitting) and John Richards, both ex French Foreign Legion, with former Royal Marine/TA Paratrooper 'Finny' (with shotgun), Surinam, 1989. (via Alan 'Bowen')

Below British mercenaries in Surinam, 1989. Bill, ex TA/ex French Foreign Legion, flanked by Paratroopers Alan 'Bowen' (left) and 'Finny' outside their quarters, the old YWCA hostel, Moengo. (via Alan 'Bowen')

Right Roy Kaulback (left) and Dave Tomkins during the first of three operations involving British mercenaries in Columbia, August 1988. (Dave Tomkins).

Below Rehearsal de-brief for mercenaries tasked with killing Pablo Escobar, Columbia 1989. (Dave Tomkins).

Above Former Royal Marine Keith Phillips (left), an instructor with 'Đuro's men', a 'Special Police Anti-Terrorist' group, Nin, Croatia, February 1992. *(Anthony Rogers)*

Below British mercenary Karl Whitburn seen serving with the Croatian forces, alongside a knocked out T-34/85 near Karlovac, December 1991. *(Anthony Rogers)*

Above Laszlo, a Hungarian former-paratrooper who served in the HOS before becoming second in command of 104 Brigade's Reconnaissance Commando Platoon (IDV), Bosnia 1995. (Tony Kendall)

Below Turkish mujahideen attached to the Croatian 104 Brigade HOS contingent, Bosnia 1992. (Tony Kendall)

Above Raymond, from the Netherlands, fought mainly with a Dutch volunteer unit around Gospic, before joining the HOS in 1992. He is seen here serving as a reserve officer commanding the IDV, 104 Brigade, Bosnia 1995. (Tony Kendall)

Mercenaries at Karlovac, Croatia, winter 1991. Back row from the left: Danny (Canadian-Croat), Mick (Australian-Croat). Front row from the left: Britons Ian, Paul and Roger. (Alan 'Bowen')

Brian Madden, a British mercenary serving with the HOS in Mala Bosna, Croatia, December 1991. (Anthony Rogers)

Above British mercenary Ben Bronsten, serving in the Croatian 110 (Karlovac) Brigade, Croatia, December 1991. (Anthony Rogers)

Above Front line OP manned by foreign volunteers of 104 Brigade's IDV, Bosnia, Summer 1995. (Tony Kendall)

Below Sukhoi Su-25 bomber flown by mercenary pilots from 'Executive Outcomes' against UNITA guerrillas in Angola, 1993-5. (Al J Venter)

Above The French Foreign Legion remains the world's most famous mercenary unit, still attracting volunteers from many countries. (Private Collection)

Above The British Army still retains a much reduced force of Gurkhas, some now based in the UK after the withdrawal from Hong Kong. (Anthony Rogers)

Below Legionnaires of the Spanish Legion's 2nd Tercio Duque de Alba seen in 1985. (via Tim W)

were later seized by the British, who remained until 1976 when the Wilson government imposed (largely unwelcome) independence. The Chief Minister at this time was the flamboyant James Mancham, whose pro-Western Seychelles Democratic Party had been elected six years previously. Britain's terms for independence decreed that a coalition government should take over the running of the Seychelles, and in 1976 Mancham was obliged to join with France-Albert René, leader of the opposition Seychelles People's United Party. It was a ludicrous alliance, formed out of necessity and doomed to failure.

A year later, while Mancham was in London attending the Commonwealth Leaders' Conference, René mounted a coup in the time-honoured fashion and declared himself President. He instituted a one-party State and recruited a small but oppressive army with the assistance of Tanzania's President Nyerere. Tanzanian military 'advisers', who formed the core of the force, also served as René's personal bodyguard. During the next two and a half years it is thought that various schemes for a counter coup were considered by Congo veterans Mike Hoare, George Schröder (see chapter 1) and, possibly, Bob Denard (see chapters 1 and 5).[3] Certainly, in May 1979, Hoare approached the South African government on behalf of pro-Mancham exiles, but failed to win Pretoria's backing for a coup.[4] The following November, René announced that a mercenary plot to overthrow him had been thwarted by his government.[5]

In 1981 the South African government was again approached and this time agreed to help: René's overtly Communist posturing had become a source of some concern. While permitting the USA to maintain a satellite tracking station on Mahé, the President also allowed the Soviets to construct a military base on Coetivy Island, 320 kilometres south-west of Mahé.

By November 1981, a plan had been formulated to reinstall 'Jimmy' Mancham. Mike Hoare was entrusted to carry out a coup with the tacit approval of the governments of South Africa and Kenya, also uneasy at René's increasingly pro-Soviet stance. Kenya's Minister for Constitutional Affairs, Charles Njonjo, was particularly concerned about the influence asserted over President René by Tanzania's socialist government. It was agreed that South

Africa would supply a mercenary force with arms and ammunition captured by the SADF in Angola – such weapons would not be easily traceable, and they used the same type of ammunition as the weapons of the Seychellois army, which was an important consideration if the mercenaries needed to re-supply themselves in a prolonged battle. Njonjo promised that Kenyan troops would be placed on readiness to move into the Seychelles immediately after the takeover, whereupon the mercenaries would be discreetly evacuated.[6]

Among the Seychellois leaders involved in Hoare's plans were Eddie Camille and Gerard Hoarau, whose liaison skills were to prove invaluable. Hoarau was to become 'Vice-President elect' before replacing a now reluctant Mancham as leader of the new government. Robert Frichot, the Attorney General under the Mancham administration, was another adept negotiator whose loyalty was to be rewarded with a suitable diplomatic position. Hoare conducted three reconnaissances to Mahé: in September 1978, he visited the island with fellow Congo veteran Jerry Puren (see chapter 1), returning alone in June 1980, and again in late 1981 with Tullio Moneta, another ex Congo mercenary. Moneta and another Congo veteran, Barney Carey, organized the initial recruiting for the coup. Martin Dolinchek, of the National Intelligence Service (NIS), considered by Hoare as a useful contact, was also taken on board. One unlikely team member was Hoare's brother-in-law, former jockey, Bob Sims, whose job was to set up a safe house in Mahé's capital, Victoria.

The SADF provided Hoare with the arms and ammunition needed for the operation, and recruiting began in earnest. In addition to Hoare's ex Congo mercenaries, 20 former members of the Rhodesian Security Forces volunteered, along with 20 or so SADF (Citizen's Force) Recce Commandos.

After a few days in Durban, Roger joined about a dozen men at the Coastland's Holiday Flats where they met Mike Hoare and his son Chris, who was in charge of administration. They were given a briefing about the political and military situation in the Seychelles, and told that their mission was to take control of the government there. They were assured that the operation had the full backing of the South Africans and was also supported by

Kenya. The men were to travel as tourists to Mahé, where they would be issued with weapons smuggled onto the island.

> Mike showed us an AK47... It didn't have a butt on it, but he didn't mention he was going to take the butts off all the weapons. At the time I thought the butt had been taken off just to make it easier to carry around town while we were in South Africa. But in fact all the weapons had the butts removed.[7]

During the operation, the mercenaries were to be split into three assault groups consisting of one ten-man team and two groups of about twenty. Group One was to seize the Seychelles radio station and army barracks at Union Vale, just north of the capital, Victoria. Group Two was to take the airport and main army barracks at Pointe La Rue, at the south end of the airstrip. Group Three would attack targets in Victoria: the telex office, army headquarters, barracks, State House and Presidential Palace. The success of the entire operation depended on achieving total surprise. Once Mahé was under their control, the mercenaries were to await the arrival of James Mancham and the Kenyan troops, whereupon they would revert to being 'tourists' and return to South Africa.

Mike Hoare asked the assembled men if they were interested: all of them were, and each received 1,000 rand advance payment. A few days later (by which time everybody had been divided into teams), all attended another, more detailed briefing. Six mercenaries were selected for an advance party under the command of Barney Carey to arrive a few days before the main body. Their task was to recce the targets and to provide protection, if necessary, for the main force on its arrival at Mahé airport.

During this second briefing the mercenaries were shown aerial photographs and scale drawings of Mahé, and were brought up to date on the organization and deployment of the Seychellois army. It was also announced that they would be travelling as a drinking club called 'The Ancient Order of Frothblowers'. A final, ingenious ploy, intended to weaken the resolve of even the most cynical airport authority officer, was the distribution of toys as supposed gifts for local underprivileged children.

The mercenaries were completely confident, most of them convinced that their task would be over within an hour or two of H-Hour. In the meantime, Hoare told them, they were to act like good tourists, to go easy on the alcohol, and generally behave themselves.

On Saturday 21 November, Hoare arrived at Durban's Louis Botha airport and met four of the advance party scheduled to depart that day. Barney Carey, Ken Dalgleish, Aubrey Brooks and Des Botes were each handed a carrier bag with a concealed weapon, and casually informed that there was nothing to worry about as the airport's X-ray machines had been shut down. The arms and ammunition had not been delivered to Mahé after all: the men would have to smuggle in their own rifles and two magazines apiece, packed in the bottom of their holdalls. Hoare assured them that the method had already been tried and tested.

Carey's group departed South Africa without incident, to arrive some four hours later at Mahé International airport. They passed through passport control and customs with ease, then made their way to the Beauvallon Bay and Coral Strand hotels in the north of the island. On Sunday 22nd, Roger and Charlie Dukes (an American who had also served in the Rhodesian SAS) arrived at Louis Botha airport where they were greeted by Hoare and presented with their weapons. They too experienced an anxious but uneventful trip, travelling via Réunion to Mahé. They were met by Carey, who saw them onto the bus to the Reef Hotel, just south of the barracks at Pointe La Rue.

Also in Mahé at this stage were Bob Sims, accompanied by his fiancée, Sue Ingle, and Martin Dolinchek. On the morning of Wednesday 25th, the remaining mercenaries were issued with weapons. This unexpected development was too much for one man, who wisely decided to opt out of the operation. The rest were driven across the border to Swaziland to board a chartered Fokker F-28 of Royal Swazi Airlines. The flight plan included a brief stop-over at Moroni, in the Comoros, which caused considerable speculation amongst Bob Denard's mercenaries who had occupied those islands three and a half years previously (see chapter 5). However, the Fokker took off again shortly afterwards, and landed at Mahé on schedule later that afternoon.

Outside the airport terminal the advance party waited apprehensively in hired cars. A tense quarter of an hour passed before Mike Hoare and the first of his men appeared at the main entrance and cheerfully greeted Carey. Everyone relaxed. So far, it was all proceeding as planned.

The last half dozen men were filtering through Customs when one of them inexplicably headed towards the red 'Something to Declare' channel.[8] Apparently, the mercenary was asked to accompany a Customs officer into a private room, where his bag was searched and the AK47 discovered. The Customs officer, or another official, then took charge of the weapon and rushed out of the office, presumably to alert his colleagues. He was promptly shot and wounded by one of the mercenaries. In the confusion, one of Hoare's men, Johan Fritz, was also hit, and died immediately.[9]

Outside, the advance party had been alerted to the fact that one man had been apprehended. When firing broke out, they knew they had to respond immediately if the operation was to have any chance of success. Hoare ordered four of them to drive to Pointe La Rue to prevent the army from deploying. Brooks, Dalgleish, Roger and Dukes sped to the barracks and stopped just outside the entrance barrier. It was quickly decided to take the guardroom without shooting and alerting the entire camp. According to Roger:

> We made an attempt to capture the guardroom intact. We didn't open fire straight away. We began to get out of the vehicle and told the guys on the gate to lay down their weapons and they wouldn't get hurt. Two of them got the message and ran away, but the third panicked and just cocked his weapon and opened fire. His initial burst wounded two of us... Aubrey Brooks was wounded whilst getting out of the car behind me, so I don't know how that particular bullet missed me. Aubrey was shot through the back of the leg and Charlie Dukes was wounded in the arm.
>
> We all took cover when the shooting started and returned fire but the guard ... moved into a position behind a wall in

the guardroom and was fairly difficult to remove… After the initial exchange of fire a 12.7 mm opened up on us and so our position wasn't too healthy. There were rounds hitting the car, parked immediately in front of us, so we pulled back out of the way.[10]

Despite the injuries sustained by Dukes and Brooks, all four succeeded in climbing a small hill opposite the barracks from where they observed most of the garrison, accompanied by a Soviet BRDM (amphibious scout car), escaping through the rear entrance.

Shortly afterwards, elements of the main party were seen approaching, and covering fire was put down to suppress the 12.7 mm machine gun about 300 metres away. However, as the butts had been removed from the mercenaries' weapons so that they would fit inside the men's holdalls, accurate fire at that range was impossible.[11] Nevertheless, the little group continued to provide covering fire as best they could while their comrades prepared for an assault on the barracks. It was obvious to all of them that unless some kind of action was taken, they would soon lose the initiative.

For those still in position above the barracks, the situation was all the more frustrating, knowing that the enemy had abandoned the camp, leaving it wide open to attack. Hoare could not have known this, however, and refused to consolidate the position.

Meanwhile, Brooks was rapidly going into shock. He was advised to go back down the hill and join the main group. When it became apparent that Hoare was not about to attack the barracks, Roger, Dukes and Dalgleish decided to follow Brooks, only to discover that he had not made it. He was presumed – correctly – to have passed out somewhere along the way, but the gathering darkness and dense vegetation prevented a satisfactory search.

Hoare now demonstrated his apparent reluctance to engage in night-fighting – a curious failing that seemed to originate from his Congo days – and decided to withdraw to the airport terminal, planning to return and capture the barracks in the morning. He joined the other mercenaries aboard their commandeered transport, abandoning not just the unfortunate Dukes, but also their one real chance of taking Pointe La Rue and the airport runway.

At the airport terminal, the men de-bussed and awaited further developments. They did not have to wait long. A BRDM, possibly that previously seen leaving Pointe La Rue, appeared on the scene, firing in all directions. The mercenaries took cover and vainly tried to knock out the armoured car with their AK47s. When the BRDM made a third pass, the men concentrated their fire on its tyres. Apparently unconcerned, the driver continued to the end of his chosen route, where he tried to turn the vehicle around. To everyone's delight, it promptly crashed into a monsoon ditch. Some of Hoare's men approached the vehicle and called on the occupants to surrender. Not surprisingly, the terrified crew preferred to stay where they were. The situation soon developed into a tragi-comedy as somebody fetched some petrol, which was poured over the armoured car. Those inside still refused to budge, so the petrol was set alight. According to Roger, "Three of the four-man crew came out, and the last one opted to remain inside, so he got shot for his troubles."[12]

The BRDM was eventually pulled out of the ditch with an aircraft-tow vehicle. Unfortunately for the new owners, their attempts to capture the crew had also burned out the electrics, without which the armoured car was useless, so the smoke-blackened hulk was positioned across the approach route and left as a road-block.

While this was taking place, mercenaries in the control tower were busily talking down an Air India Boeing 707. Flight 224 from Salisbury to Bombay, scheduled to make a refuelling stop at Mahé at 2230 hours, was apparently persuaded to land by Charles Goatley (ex Rhodesian air force) and Vernon Prinsloo (a former officer in the Rhodesian Light Infantry), who believed they were acting on Hoare's orders. Hoare later claimed that he had dispatched one of his men to the control tower, with an order that the aircraft was *not* to land, but that the messenger had deliberately altered the command.[13]

As the airliner touched down, a wing glanced off one of two vehicles abandoned on the runway by local troops. Having averted one disaster, the pilot, Captain Umesh Saxema, taxied his aircraft to a halt and found himself facing Mike Hoare and another potentially lethal situation. At about the time that the

'Colonel' was briefing the incredulous pilot, the airport terminal was shaken by two hits from a 75 mm recoilless rifle. Several 40 mm rockets followed, but these and all subsequent rounds overshot the target. The explosions convinced Hoare that he had to move fast to save the passengers on the Boeing. Following a telephone call to government officials in Victoria, a cease-fire was negotiated, allowing the aircraft to be refuelled and prepared for take-off.

This also presented an ideal opportunity to escape. Here was a half-empty airliner about to depart with sufficient fuel to reach South Africa. The alternative was for the mercenaries to remain in Mahé and attempt to wrest control from a now alert defence force equipped with heavy weapons and armoured vehicles. Hoare's men had only their AK47s, a few grenades and a dwindling stock of ammunition. Roger maintains that "Mike Hoare ... asked [Saxema] to fly us out. He agreed. I was told there was a payment of 5,000 rand [made] to the pilot to fly us out, although he later denied this, so I'm not sure who was telling the truth."[14] Whatever the deal, when Air India flight 224 took off it had most of the mercenaries on board, including the body of Johan Fritz.

Half a dozen of Hoare's men, and one woman, remained behind. Some, like Aubrey Brooks, had no choice in the matter. Others thought their chances of survival were better on the island. As far as Roger was concerned

> I had been there for two days before the main group arrived, and had all my belongings in a suitcase at the hotel. Also, I had seen the defences at the other end of the runway and I wasn't aware that some sort of deal had been made ... and that a cease-fire had been arranged... I seriously did not believe that the aircraft would get off the ground... So I stayed behind with Barney Carey with the intention of getting back to the hotel and acting like a civilian. Barney had pretty much the same idea.[15]

As did Dolinchek, while Jerry Puren decided to hide in the surrounding hills. Sims and Ingle, it seems, considered themselves above suspicion. Roger and Carey watched as the Boeing roared along the runway, lifted into the night sky and set course for Durban. At this point, Carey casually mentioned that Hoare had left some documents in his car, abandoned outside Pointe La Rue barracks. What documents? Roger wanted to know. Carey told him: a list of all those involved in the operation! Roger was appalled. As he said later, "Had I known about that I would have definitely got on the aircraft."[16]

The two men parted after agreeing to retrieve the incriminating papers, if at all possible. The airport at Mahé is built on land reclaimed from the sea; with high ground covered by tropical forest on one side, and the coast on the other. For Roger, the best option seemed to be to return to his hotel by heading south along the runway, keeping to the seaward side and away from the airport lights, but halfway along the runway he was fired on, rounds snapping past the back of his head. Roger had discarded his weapon and now lay flat, terrified that whoever had shot at him might decide to finish the job. He remained perfectly still for half an hour and listened to the confused firing still going on in the distance. The Seychellois army had not yet realized that the main force of mercenaries had departed with the Air India flight, and were continuing to shoot up the airport terminal.

Concluding that it was safe to continue, Roger slowly crawled 500 metres or so to the end of the runway. To bypass the barracks, he was obliged to take his chance in the shark-infested sea, but his luck held, and at dawn he finally reached the Reef Hotel. The wet and exhausted 'tourist' explained that he had been for an early morning swim and was let into his room, now occupied by a total stranger. With a curfew in force, those stranded had to be accommodated wherever space permitted. Roger knew that he would still have to explain his absence to the hotel manager but, in the meantime, took the opportunity to revive himself with breakfast. So far, it seemed, his ruse had worked.

★ ★ ★

Meanwhile, Air India flight 224 was en route to Durban where its arrival would place the South African government in an extremely awkward predicament. It landed at 0500 hours local time. The (fare-paying) passengers were allowed to disembark after two or three hours. Eventually, the 45 mercenaries emerged and were flown to Waterkloopf air base from where they were driven to Sonderwater Prison, outside Cullinan.

★   ★   ★

On Thursday morning, Seychellois troops rushed the airport at Mahé, only to find it occupied by 60 or so petrified civilians, cowering in the transit lounge. "We were all lying jam-packed together, unable to move", one was later quoted as saying. "I'll never forget the sound of the rockets and mortars. You could hear them coming from about a quarter of a mile away and with every thud you thought the next one would get you. It was terrifying."[17]

Barney Carey watched the final assault from a vantage point above the airport, having decided to hide in the bush until things had quietened down. He was captured later that day, when the army and police carried out a search of the area. Aubrey Brooks was apprehended soon after. While in police custody, the two men were subjected to a harrowing ordeal: both were systematically beaten and convinced that they were about to be shot.

★   ★   ★

After breakfast, Roger was taken to see the hotel manager.

> I told him that I had been driving past the airport when the commotion started and got kidnapped along with my friend Charlie Dukes, who was also in the vehicle. I said that our car was taken from us and we had to walk back from the airport. I told him that I'd lost Charlie … in the ensuing confusion, and he seemed to believe me, so that was the story I stuck to.[18]

Charlie Dukes, of course, was now back in Durban.

Roger was allocated another room where he stayed for the rest of the morning, having decided to bluff his way through any investigations until he could catch a flight out. Later that day he was questioned by the police, and repeated his kidnap story. The police appeared to believe him, but confiscated his passport. At lunchtime the following day, they returned and asked Roger to accompany them to the police station. No explanation was offered. At the station, Roger was invited to sit in an office while various individuals arrived to stare at him. These were the civilians who had been present at the airport on Wednesday night and, though he was unaware of it at the time, Roger was soon identified as one of the mercenaries. He was locked in a cell and, on Saturday morning, handed over to the army and taken to their headquarters in central Mahé. The cell was "like a cupboard, two feet by two feet, with enough room to stand. You couldn't sleep properly… You could sit down, but only with your knees up under your chin."[19]

Roger was kept tightly handcuffed during his three days of imprisonment. Once a day he would be dragged outside and roughly interrogated. After repeating his story, he was thrown back into the stinking hole and left to ponder his predicament. He was neither fed nor given anything to drink, and had to perform his bodily functions where he sat. Soon the heat and stench were unbearable. After three days the interrogators told him that Aubrey Brooks and Barney Carey were also prisoners. This prompted Roger to admit his own involvement.

Late that night, Roger was hauled from his cell, bundled into a vehicle and driven to Pointe La Rue barracks. He was badly beaten during the journey, sustaining a broken nose and rib and severe bruising. At the barracks, he was dragged to another cell where he received a further beating. After the soldiers departed and the dazed prisoner had recovered slightly, he became aware that he was not entirely alone. Carey and Brooks were in nearby cells and had both undergone a horrific ordeal at the hands of their captors. That night, all three had hoods placed over their heads and were told they would be shot the following morning. Somehow, the hours passed. The prisoners were convinced that they were about to die. Each man, lost in his own anguish, waited in dread for the guards to return, until

I heard them coming down the corridor, opening the doors one by one and I thought, this is it… They finally opened my cell door, and gave me a cup of coffee! It was the biggest anti-climax of my life.[20]

Roger now knew that the soldiers were bluffing.

> The immediate anxiety of being shot passed. But then, of course, there was still the worry of what was going to happen to us... There was a great deal of pressure on all of us at this stage. We didn't know what was going on. The sense of disorientation is very great when you are in a cell on your own, all of the time. There are all of these external fears: a fear of death ... of being beaten up again... Psychologically, it was quite a difficult period for us all.[21]

The mercenaries spent a week at Pointe La Rue. Although kept in almost pitch darkness, conditions were marginally better than at army HQ. After two or three days, Brooks and Roger were returned to the police station and shown to the press: Carey was still too badly hurt for public display. His colleagues, who clearly had also been mistreated, appeared in newspapers and on world-wide television. They seemed mildly bemused by all the attention, uncertain whether to smile for the cameras or not. They were subjected to a barrage of questions, to which each tried to reply as best he could. But by encouraging such publicity, the government had also revealed the plight of their captives, a fact that both men were quick to grasp.

During their temporary imprisonment in the police cells, Brooks and Roger encountered Dolinchek. Roger knew him only as "the guy from the South African government".[22] Apparently, Hoare's 'intelligence officer' was an unpopular figure with the majority of the men. He was considered as "a bit of a pain in the neck ... a know-all", who (conversely) "didn't know a great deal".[23]

Sims and Sue Ingle had been arrested on Saturday 28 November, possibly as a result of the papers left behind by Hoare. But Sims had also failed to destroy some documents in his possession, which in turn had implicated Dolinchek.[24]

After their press interview, the mercenaries, now including

Dolinchek, were ordered into the back of a truck and taken to Pointe La Rue. Within half an hour of being locked up, Dolinchek called for the guards, and requested to speak to someone in authority. He explained that he was not a mercenary, but a South African government agent!

Until that moment the authorities had been unaware of any government's involvement. Dolinchek would soon set the record straight. His collaboration led to an immediate easing of the pressure. All four men were transferred to the prison at Union Vale barracks and put in solitary confinement; but at least there were lights in the cells and beds to lie on. The food, consisting mainly of bread, fish and rice, washed down with mugs of tea, was a definite improvement. For a while, the prisoners were also permitted 15 minutes' exercise each day, until the guards grew bored with the disruption of their routine. Thereafter, the men were left in their cells. The only other real discomfort was that during the first two months of solitary, all were kept permanently handcuffed.

On or about 20 December, those at Union Vale were joined by Puren who had given himself up after two weeks in the surrounding hills. Roger, Carey, Brooks, Dolinchek, Puren and Sims appeared in court for the first time on 5 January, charged with illegal importation of firearms, and remanded in custody for a fortnight. Such a charge could, however, only really be applied in Puren's case. The others had arrived before the main group of mercenaries who were the only ones known to have definitely brought their weapons to Mahé.

During their imprisonment, the men became fairly well acquainted with their gaolers, who included supporters of both René and Mancham. Only two continued to be openly hostile: the senior officer, Major Marengo, and another guard known only as Henry, described by Roger as "quite a nasty piece of work".[25]

There was another brief court appearance in January when the prisoners were again remanded. On 4 February, the accused, now including Sue Ingle, appeared in court to face a new charge: treason, the only crime that carries the death penalty under Seychellois law. Remanded for another two weeks, the men were taken back to Union Vale, while Ingle was returned to her cell at the central police station in Victoria. Their trial was scheduled for April.

★　★　★

In South Africa, Hoare, Moneta, Duffy, Goatley and Dalgleish had been granted bail after being charged with 'man-stealing'. The 40 other mercenaries were released without charge. A month later, in January 1982, warrants were issued for the arrest of all the men, who were then charged under the 1972 Civil Aviation Offences Act. The previous charge against Hoare and the four other men was dropped. This sudden reversal by the South African authorities no doubt resulted from the international outrage that followed the earlier release of the mercenaries. It may also have been an attempt by the government to dispel accusations that it had been involved in the failed coup.

On 10 March 1982, the accused appeared before the Natal Supreme Court to face charges relating to the unlawful seizure of an aircraft; jeopardizing aircraft and airport safety; and unlawfully possessing arms and ammunition. The trial lasted a little over four months. Mike Hoare was sentenced to 10 years' imprisonment, and the remainder received custodial sentences ranging from five years to (for the majority) six months. Charges were dropped against two men in return for their turning State's Witness. Charlie Dukes, who was incapacitated at the time of events and therefore posed no threat, was acquitted.[26]

★　★　★

In April, the South African lawyer representing many of the accused, including those in the Seychelles, suddenly withdrew on the grounds that there was a conflict of interest between his clients, thereby forcing the Seychellois to again remand their case. In Britain, the father of Ken Dalgleish arranged for Nicholas Fairburn MP QC to represent the seven in Mahé. When the trial opened on 16 June 1982, Fairburn presented an eloquent and logical argument: a charge of treason was only applicable if the defendant was a Seychellois citizen or local resident – his clients were neither. The attorney General responded by insisting that under Seychelles law any person could be so charged.[27]

Fairburn did succeed in persuading the court to release Ingle, who had become involved only through her association with Sims. She was allowed to return to South Africa. Her release also led to the Attorney General dispensing with the charge of treason against her fiancé. Sims was to plead guilty only to the illegal importation of firearms.

On their lawyer's advice, Roger, Carey, Brooks and Puren then pleaded guilty to treason, intending to end the trial before it could really begin. A plea of guilty would result only in a speech by Fairburn in mitigation, and then sentencing. There would be no trial and therefore no more publicity. Indeed, executing the mercenaries could even prove detrimental to René's regime, and would certainly harm the already ailing tourist industry. It was probably the mercenaries' only chance, but was nonetheless a courageous and desperate gamble.

It failed, thanks to Martin Dolinchek. He alone chose to represent himself. When he "pleaded guilty, but not really guilty",[28] he provided the Chief Justice with the pretext he needed to adjourn the hearing, granting the State time to consider these latest events. The court was now able to produce the evidence it had amassed, including the documents abandoned by Hoare, and segments of tape-recorded messages by Mancham, Hoareau and Paul Chow Singh, another leading activist of the exiled Resistance Movement. The tapes had been set on fire in an unsuccessful attempt to destroy them and left at the airport during the mercenaries' withdrawal.

The trial lasted nearly a week, although a verdict was not reached until 5 July. In the meantime, Roger, Carey, Brooks, Puren and Sims remained in their miserable cells to contemplate their fate. After two weeks, Dolinchek was found guilty as charged. When the court reconvened to hear pleas in mitigation for the other accused, Fairburn attempted to gain sympathy for his clients by describing the ill-treatment suffered since their arrest. He again questioned the right to charge anybody with treason against a country other than their own, and even inferred that the mercenaries' mission was not wholly dissimilar to René's takeover in 1977! In spite of Fairburn's efforts, Roger, Carey, Brooks and Puren were all sentenced to death – Roger, in fact, received two death sentences; one for his participation in the attack at Pointe La

Rue, and another for his involvement at the airport. Sims and Dolinchek received custodial sentences of 10 and 20 years respectively.

Before leaving Mahé, Nicholas Fairburn lodged an appeal against the severity of the sentences: the date for the hearing was scheduled for 20 September. However, a few days later, the six mercenaries were taken to meet René himself. The president was clearly concerned about possible repercussions which might arise from the findings of an independent tribunal. René therefore proposed that, if the prisoners withdrew their appeal, he would endeavour to exchange them for ANC prisoners held in South Africa. The alternative, he explained, was an indefinite postponement of the appeal hearing, with the men facing many years in solitary confinement. It was also made clear that Fairburn was not to be allowed to return to the Seychelles to act on their behalf. Having no option but to trust René, the six agreed to his terms and withdrew their appeal.

Following their agonizing decision, an event occurred that undoubtedly contributed to a re-assessment of the prisoners' plight. In August, simmering discontent among the Seychellois army officers flared into open revolt with a mutiny of the Union Vale garrison.

The mutineers seized several key points – namely those targeted by the mercenaries the previous year. However, the Presidential Guard remained loyal to René, and the Pointe La Rue garrison was dissuaded from joining the uprising by the Tanzanian troops in Mahé. When the troops at Pointe La Rue refused to occupy the airport, the rebellion collapsed. Although the rebels announced on the local radio that they had control of Mahé, most of the mutineers were soon quite drunk and incapable of maintaining the offensive. Some approached the imprisoned mercenaries and, speaking through an interpreter (a prisoner named Jean Dingwall, the only Seychellois to be detained in connection with the mercenaries' coup attempt) asked them to join the rebellion. On Dingwall's advice, the prisoners declined the soldiers' invitation, though Roger believed that "Had they made the offer earlier we would have taken it... By the time they did make the offer, things weren't going very well at all and so we decided it was best to just sit on the fence and wait to see what was going on."[29]

Towards late afternoon, the Presidential Guard began to mortar Union Vale barracks. When the first bombs landed the garrison fled, leaving the prisoners on their own. For the mercenaries, who were on the top floor of the jail, it was a particularly harrowing time as they were forced to listen to the fluting warble of each incoming round before it detonated with a resounding bang. The barrage continued for most of the afternoon. That evening Puren shouted across to Roger, who was in a cell previously occupied by the South African. There was a small hole in the wooden ceiling through which rainwater occasionally leaked. If forced, suggested Puren, the ceiling might give way, Puren suggested, enabling Roger to break out.

The barrage ceased towards nightfall, only to start again the following morning. Fearing that sooner or later a bomb would come crashing through the roof, Roger decided to follow Puren's advice, using his upended bed to reach the ceiling, which collapsed as soon as he began to pull at the rotting woodwork. "I was able to get out of the cell, get into the office where the keys were kept ... and then I went around and released everybody else."[30] Roger and the others trooped downstairs where they were comparatively safe. Dingwall suggested that they should do nothing as the rebellion was as good as over. Two pro-René captives, jailed by the rebels, were also released. Together with Dolinchek, they left the barracks to contact the government forces. The rest waited until the barracks was occupied by the Presidential Guard.

As a result of their conduct during the uprising, the prisoners were now treated altogether differently. For the next two months they were permitted to live together in one room. While they welcomed each other's company, the men had also been affected by their months in solitary: tempers were short, and there were numerous arguments. The problem was alleviated somewhat in October after President René expressed concern over the welfare of the prisoners and announced that they were to be transferred to one of the outer islands in the Seychelles. For the next nine months the men lived on Platte, a sandy cay measuring just 800 by 500 metres. A small detachment of soldiers acted as their guard: an easy task, with the surrounding waters teeming with sharks!

> We had a little house where we all slept. We weren't allowed out at night but during the day could do as we pleased, and just walked around the island, eating pawpaws and coconuts … collected sea shells, went swimming and got a sun-tan.[31]

In July 1983, the six were visited by a reporter from Britain's *Sunday Mail*.

> She took photographs and interviewed us… She gave us the word… "You might be getting released soon." After she had gone, about two days later, a plane arrived for us. We jumped on it and went back to Mahé.[32]

Clearly, some kind of a deal had been negotiated. Roger suspected that their release, one week later, may have been in return for South Africa commuting to life imprisonment the death sentence on half a dozen ANC prisoners.

★   ★   ★

In South Africa, 34 of the mercenaries imprisoned the year before were released on 17 November 1982. Vernon Prinsloo was freed five months later, followed, in November 1983, by Ken Dalgleish, Charles Goatley and Mike Webb. Tullio Moneta, Pieter Dooreward and Peter Duffy were released in May 1984. The 'Colonel', Mike Hoare, was eventually freed in May 1985.

★   ★   ★

Gerard Hoarau, tipped to become President had the mercenaries succeeded, was assassinated in London by an unidentified gunman on 28 November 1985.

In 1990, Sir James Mancham (who, as an honorary KBE,

became entitled to be so-addressed after adopting British nationality six years earlier) founded the Crusade for the Restoration of Democracy in the Seychelles. He was invited back by Albert René in 1992 and in the first elections since the return of democracy polled 40 per cent of the votes to become the Opposition leader.

CHAPTER 7
MALTA, 1984-85

Many more mercenary operations are conceived than ever actually take place. Such an example was a plan to overthrow the Socialist government of Malta in the mid-1980s.

Malta, measuring just 28 by 13 kilometres, is the largest of three main islands 100 kilometres south of Sicily in the central Mediterranean. Its location and excellent natural harbours have led to numerous battles for control of this strategic post. In 1814 Malta became a British dependency, providing the Royal Navy with an ideal base. During World War II the islands withstood a two and a half year siege by Italy and Germany during which Malta was mercilessly bombed from the air. The fortitude of the Maltese was formally recognized on 15 April 1942, when King George II awarded them the George Cross, the highest honour that a grateful British Sovereign could bestow on a community. Malta was granted independence in 1964, but continued to provide Britain with a military base until 1979.

Since independence, Malta has been governed by either the pro-West Nationalist Party (PN) or the socialist Malta Labour Party (MLP). At the time of Britain's withdrawal, the Maltese were ruled by Dom Mintoff's MLP. The Maltese, virtually all of whom are Roman Catholics, are a devout people, yet Mintoff persisted in challenging the Church on a variety of issues, causing dissent even amongst his own supporters. He continued to outrage his opponents by encouraging cultural and diplomatic ties with Libya, and by seeking support from Russia, China and North Korea. Local elections were frequently accompanied by violent demonstrations by MLP supporters, and accusations from the PN of gerrymandering. The political climate of the early 1980s spawned at least one plot to oust Mintoff: in 1981, it was claimed that there were plans for 300 British mercenaries to mount a coup after which "Malta was to be governed by a council representing all the sectors of the Maltese nation".[1]

Several years after the furore of this non-event another, unconnected, operation was initiated, designed to destabilize the government, damage the economy, and set the scene for a takeover by the opposition. The details of this conspiracy are known only by a minority of individuals and, until now, have never been made public.

In the early 1980s, 'Tony', who had served with British forces in Malta, was approached by a Maltese friend, a businessman and well-known local political activist, who expressed an interest in aquiring military firearms. Nothing materialized from this conversation until about a year later, when the businessman contacted Tony again with the same request. Tony decided to confide in 'Mike', a former soldier who had served with the British Territorial Army, Rhodesian Security Forces and the SADF.

Mike still maintained links with mercenaries and others likely to be useful. He claimed that he was able to obtain virtually any kind of infantry weapon – for a price. So, I got back to my man in Malta and told him that the merchandise he required was available, and asked him to confirm that he was still interested. He claimed to be, but seemed uncertain and hesitant which threatened to put me on the spot because I had already got things moving and didn't want to let down Mike and his contacts. But the Maltese connection – we'll call him 'Joseph' – said he would not commit himself until he knew exactly what was available and for how much. I explained that I was unable to price anything until I knew what was required. It was all quite ridiculous, and also evident that he didn't have much of a clue when it came to weapons, but was acting on behalf of somebody else. Anyway, I stressed that he could have whatever he wanted, but he still insisted on a list so I had no option except to sort one out.

I got back to Mike who, of course, agreed that he was

unable to provide a realistic quote without at least having
some idea of the end user's requirements. Nevertheless, we got
to work and Mike managed to present a very rough estimate
for basic infantry weapons such as FN SLRs and MAGs,
various handguns, ammunition and also explosives. These
details were then delivered to Joseph.[2]

In November 1984, Tony received an unsigned,
typewritten note. It read:

Hello, I am the person who will be coming over to do the
dealings, (you know me very well) but for now no names.
    I am in possession of your last letter, and at this stage all I
can say is that *we definitely* want some stuff, as to the
quantity, I will let you know very soon.
    Will be over there approximately by the end of this month
with another person, so you can wait for me to come and
knock your door and when you see who I am you'll know
what we came for.
    Regards and thanks.

Soon after, Tony received a telephone call from the letter writer,
actually an old acquaintance, 'Mario'. He assured Tony that 'they'
wished to purchase arms and ammunition up to a value of £10,000
sterling.[3]

I told Mario that this was really an insignificant amount and
so it was decided that we had best meet to discuss matters. I
called Mike and put him in the picture and while he expressed
disappointment at the amount involved, he seemed relieved
that something finally seemed to be happening.

In December, Tony met Mario and his partner, 'Vincent' at the
ticket office of London's Euston Station.

We ventured into the city, chatted for a while over a coffee
near the West End, and then I left them to meet Mike. As
arranged, I joined him that evening inside Shakes Pub,

opposite Victoria Station. We caught the tube to Green Park and continued to an hotel where I introduced him to Mario and Vincent.

For the next half hour or so we discussed what was available. Mike had a contact who could supply a new Heckler and Koch G3, some FN rifles, pistols, a few 66mm LAWs and grenades. If additional items were required, Mike said, it would necessitate some overseas travel. He claimed to have a source in Italy for Ingram machine pistols, which was the type of small, concealable weapon Vincent seemed keen to acquire. I remember that he also wanted a tranquillizing gun, which surprised us, but then it was explained that they did not intend to inflict casualties on innocent people in whatever it was they had planned. Eventually, they explained just what this was.

They intended to destroy a radio mast near Għargħur, in north Malta. They also wanted to blow up some gun boats – patrol boats – moored at Marsamxett Harbour. We discussed various ways of carrying out these tasks. Then, all of a sudden, the conversation switched. "Listen," said Vincent, "supposing we decided to hire outside help instead of buying this stuff for ourselves? Supposing we wanted to hire some men to do these jobs for us? Is this possible?"

The four discussed this 'new' idea at length. The two Englishmen agreed that the radio mast could probably be brought down with a minimum of fuss, but dealing with the patrol boats would require more time and careful planning.

We also talked about assassinating the Prime Minister, Mintoff, which would presumably have dispensed with the need to carry out acts of sabotage as the whole idea seemed to be to persuade the ruling party to step down or, at least, agree to a free and fair election. Mike thought the task could be achieved for £1 million, which didn't seem to faze Mario or Vincent, but certainly surprised me.

With hindsight, I realize that I should have pulled out at that moment. I think I knew then that everything was liable to get out of hand and jeapordize whatever we had so far. I mean, knocking out some lightly protected installations was one thing, but this talk of killing Mintoff and the sum of money involved was slightly ridiculous. I'm not saying it couldn't have been done, but I doubted whether the Maltese would actually put up the kind of money Mike was asking. For the moment, at least, it was decided that we concentrate on raising a team to take care of the mast and boats and Mike agreed to go to Malta in order to present a feasibility report. He was provided with a return airline ticket and expenses for a brief visit. I was unable to accompany him at such short notice. If the targets could be taken out, the operation would take place within the next two months. Our contact, from now on, was to be Mario. I don't know where Vincent fitted into the scheme of things but I never saw him again. As for Joseph, he was apparently dropped from proceedings as he was unreliable and also prone to talk too much.

Mike returned from Malta confident that neither objective presented any insurmountable problems. However, he was unsure how to transfer the arms and specialist equipment to Malta. While some items could be legally imported or purchased locally, the rest would have to be smuggled in. Tony:

> I suggested we ferry in whatever we needed by boat, at night, and when several miles off the coast, transfer everything to a gemini or similar craft that was small and fast enough to avoid detection during the final approach. We were to land at Mistra, a secluded cove off Saint Paul's Bay, in the north-west of the island, and cache everything secretly so as to reduce any possibility of a double-cross.

By this time, Tony and Mike had been joined by a third man. His task, with Tony, was to sink the patrol boats at Marsamxett. They had already driven to the water's edge at nearby Ta'Xbiex to study their targets and find an easy, concealed entry into the sea opposite the moored vessels. Their plan was simple. The men would navigate the 250 metres to their objective underwater, attach shaped charges to several boats, set the timers, and swim back to where they had parked their hired car.

Our equipment was to have been quite basic except for one thing. I wanted to use ordinary Scuba. Night-time and a choppy sea would hide any tell-tale bubbles bursting on the surface, even if anybody was going to be looking for such a thing at 3 a.m. on a winter's morning! However, the others thought we should use oxygen rebreathers, which don't produce bubbles. It made sense, but there are problems with breathing pure oxygen. At depths in excess of 50 feet oxygen toxicity affects the central nervous system. This is known as an O_2 hit and can lead to various complications, loss of consciousness and death. An O_2 hit can also occur above 50 feet, so it was one more thing to be concerned about.

The charges were to be detonated at the same time as others placed by Mike, assisted by two colleagues from his Africa days. Verbal warnings were to be given before the explosions.

The choice of the second target was now undecided as the Maltese had complicated matters by increasing the list of objectives. It would eventually include the patrol boats (Marsamxett Creek); radio mast (Għargħur); military helicopters (Luqa); main ammunition depot (Mosta); Mediterranean Oilfield Services (Manoel Island); Telemalta building (Msida), as well as gas/oil and electricity installations, parliamentary and other political buildings, and various military barracks and outposts.

However, the operation began to fall apart during the final preparatory stages. The two men brought in by Mike had arrived in London and were anxiously awaiting instructions to join him in Malta. Tony and the third man to join the team were also waiting for the word to go. All four had invested time and money, so far, without receiving anything in return.

The only person to receive any payment was Mike. I suppose the rest of us, knowing that Mike had been paid expenses, felt sufficiently confident to risk our own funds, believing the investment to be worthwhile. However, Mike had met someone while in Malta, a guy quite unconnected with the plot, and hatched some kind of money-making scheme that resulted in his receiving an initial pay-out for goods that were never supplied. He then vanished from the scene. I know he pissed off quite a few of the local heavies. In fact, they managed to track down Mike in London and even considered having him killed. But Mike, who was always lucky, got away with it.

At about the same time it was announced that the operation had been postponed. The reasons are uncertain, but possibly resulted from Prime Minister Dom Mintoff's resignation on 22 December 1984. He was succeeded by his protégé, Doctor Karmenu Mifsud-Bonnici, who may have been considered more favourably by the Nationalists. It is also likely that the plot organizers failed to raise sufficient funds for what had become an increasingly ambitious project. The mercenaries they had hired were never paid and soon gave up hope of the operation being resurrected.

The years of socialist rule in Malta finally ended with a victory for the Nationalist Party under Doctor 'Eddie' Fenech Adami at the 1987 general election. The PN remained in power until the MLP was voted back into office in October 1996.

CHAPTER 8
SURINAM, 1986-91

Surinam lies between Guyana and French Guiana, on the northern coast of South America. Links with Europe began in the 16th century, although it was not until 1650-51 that a short-lived British colony was established on the Surinam River. It was soon taken over by the Dutch West India Company, and eventually Surinam became a colony of the Netherlands. The region flourished under Dutch rule, developing into a major exporter of bauxite, with the principal mines located at Moengo, in the north-west, and the Paranam area on the Surinam River.

The population of Surinam is approximately 35 per cent Creoles (of mixed Negro and other ancestry) and a similar number of Hindustanis who, together with Indonesians (16 per cent) and Chinese (two per cent), are descended from labourers and other immigrants who arrived in the late 19th and early 20th centuries. About 10 percent of Surinamese are Bush Negroes, descended from slaves who managed to escape into the interior where they preserved a tribal existence. Amerindians and others, including Europeans, account for the remainder of the population.

When Surinam became independent on 25 November 1975, the Netherlands promised a generous annual allowance, providing the new nation with one of the highest per-capita incomes in the developing world. But on 25 February 1980, the democratically elected government of Henck Arron was overthrown in a coup led by Desi Bouterse and Roy Horb, and replaced by the National Military Council. In August 1980, Bouterse deposed Ferrier, the President he had helped to install, and replaced him with Henck Chin A Sen, who was in turn prompted to resign after Bouterse

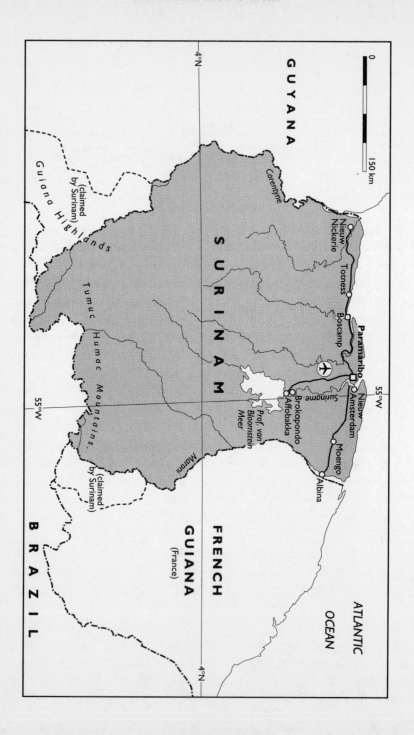

himself seized power in February 1982. Bouterse began to develop left-wing sympathies, forging ties with Grenada's Marxist Prime Minister Maurice Bishop and Fidel Castro of Cuba. Both the Cubans and their Soviet allies were allowed to open embassies in Surinam's capital, Paramaribo.

In October 1982, Bouterse was publicly humiliated when a reported 15,000 people staged a demonstration against his increasingly autocratic rule during a state visit by Maurice Bishop. Within six weeks, Bouterse had ordered the execution of 15 of his political foes.[1] The Netherlands promptly withdrew its subsidy, causing immediate economic problems for its former dependency. In February 1983, following a failed coup attempt, Bouterse's former ally, Roy Horb, was found hanged in his prison cell. In the wake of the invasion of Grenada by the United States in October 1983, Bouterse temporarily expelled all Cuban advisers, but by 1984 the Cubans had returned and were alleged to have been involved with the Libyans in running a terrorist training camp near Sipaliwini, on the border with Brazil. In addition, Libya had opened a 'cultural mission' in Paramaribo in exchange for a reported $100 million in aid.[2]

In July 1986, Ronnie Brunswijk, a former Bouterse bodyguard, initiated a revolt by attacking a military post at Stolkertsijver. By September, Brunswijk and his Surinam National Liberation Army (SNLA) was being assisted by at least three British mercenaries. Two were identified as John Richards (ex French Foreign Legion) and Carl Finch. The third is said to have parted company after discovering the severed head of a pro-government captive being boiled in the Britons' drinking water![3]

In mid-November, Finch and Richards also left, but by the following March Finch was back, along with two Britons named as Charlie Mosley and John Love. Other mercenaries, including deserters from the French Foreign Legion, are also thought to have arrived in Surinam in 1986-87, while at least one Belgian and two Americans were employed as military instructors (either in Surinam or neighbouring French Guiana) up to early 1984. Bouterse, too, was rumoured to have employed mercenaries in addition to those provided by Castro and Gaddafi.[4]

At the end of 1987, Ramsewak Shankar was elected President

and Arron Vice President and Prime Minister. However, Bouterse continued to retain overall control. In 1988, the Netherlands resumed its aid package, and in July of the following year Shankar and Brunswijk signed a peace accord. Nevertheless, Bouterse vowed that there would be no compromise with the rebels.

★ ★ ★

In late 1989, Alan 'Bowen' (see chapter 10), a former Royal Marine, was working the London 'security circuit'.

> One of the guys asked me if I was interested in doing a bit of mercenary work. I said, "yeah", and he introduced me to this Legionnaire, John [Richards]. He'd been out there a couple of times before. We had a meeting and he asked us a few questions about our backgrounds and he showed us a video, some pictures, copies of contracts, and said we were going to get £30,000 each to go to Surinam and help the Hindustanis train up their guerrilla army and then attack the Surinamese Army…
>
> We had a series of meetings to get to know each other. There was only one guy I knew. He was in the Marines with me, and all the rest were Legionnaires, apart from one who was Queen's Royal Irish Hussars, a 'tankie': though he pretended to be SAS, which was pretty obvious that he wasn't.[5]

Soon after, Bowen accompanied Richards to the Hague, home for the majority of Surinamese exiles. The former Legionnaire was often engaged in business meetings from which Bowen was barred, until the two were arrested by anti-terrorist police on suspicion of being IRA terrorists! They were released a day later, when the police realized their error, and both returned to London. A few weeks later, they flew to Paris and were joined by two French journalists whom Richards had invited to South America to record his exploits. There were now nine men in the team: Eric Deroo and his colleague; Briton Pat Baker; former French Foreign Legionnaires Oyvind Pedersen, from Norway, Britons John Richards, Mike Pemberton and Bill 'O'; and former Royal

Marines, Bowen and 'Finny'. The inclusion of the journalists was an unexpected and unwelcome development for the ex Marines.

Me and Finny had both burned our bridges by then, jacked the jobs we were doing, because we were going to make all this money in South America… So we had to go along with whatever [Richards] said.

We jumped on an Air France flight to Martinique, and by then we'd basically fucked these two journalists off, me and Finny – we didn't want anything to do with journalists, but all the Legionnaires loved it. They were all, like, you know, "Film me, film me".

I knew things were not right on the plane. I was sat next to Mick, one of the ex 2e REP [French Foreign Legion Parachute Regiment] guys. As we flew into Martinique, he said to me, "This is fucking great, this is. Here we are, going to some Mickey Mouse country, shoot some niggers and get paid for it."

They were all alright in London, but once we were on our way there, they suddenly became hardened killers.[6]

From Martinique, they flew on to Cayenne, in French Guiana, where they learned that the weapons they had been expecting had not materialized. Instead a contact provided money with which to buy shotguns from a local sports shop! Transport was a problem that was soon solved by renting an Avis transit van which sufficed for the day-long journey to Saint Laurent, where the wide and fast-flowing Marowijne/Maroni River marks the border with Surinam. Pat Baker negotiated with a local boatman who agreed to ferry the team across.

We crossed over … at the dead of night in two big pirogues. The river was about half a 'k' wide. As soon as we hit the jungle, me and Finny and Bill went all tactical, taking up fire positions on the edge of the jungle … and John starts lighting up fags, destroying everyone's night vision and we're all, like, fuck, what's going on? And he says, "Don't worry, there's no niggers here", and we stayed in this area for a couple of days doing a recce on a military garrison in the border town of

159

Albina, which was what we were being paid to do. We didn't know it until John told us. Then we had to tab inland to a town called Moengo where we were supposed to meet the Jungle Commando.[7]

By now, the two journalists had become very concerned about the entire project and decided to return home. Eric Deroo later described the behaviour of some of the men as particularly unnerving, especially once they were armed.[8]

Pat Baker, the former soldier who claimed to have served in the SAS, was experiencing problems keeping up with the others and announced that he was also leaving. The six remaining men continued to Moengo. By this time, Richards, Pemberton and Pedersen – all former 2e REP – had formed their own clique, with Bowen, Finny and Bill (the latter ex 2e REI – French Foreign Legion infantry) creating another. The Richards' faction displayed a recklessness that was considered by Bowen's group to be quite unprofessional. Bowen, Finny and Bill were, in turn, looked upon as being too serious in their careful and methodical approach towards the operation. It was a situation that would have disastrous repercussions.

At the Jungle Commando headquarters near Moengo, the mercenaries were welcomed by Ronnie Brunswijk, now involved in peace-talks with the government. It was decided that the mercenaries would not assist the Hindustanis at Nickerie, but instead would stay as military instructors for the Bush Negroes of the Jungle Commando, who were engaged in a long-running conflict with the minority Tacujana Indians.

We got stuck into the training with these Bush Negroes, which was pretty interesting, to say the least. They all had Brazilian-made FN FALs which have a cleaning kit in the pistol grip. These rifles were in an absolutely shit state. We grabbed the weapons of all these guys and stripped them down. You couldn't see through the barrels! They didn't seem to know that there was a cleaning kit inside the pistol grip. They were amazed. Their idea of cleaning these rifles was just to put some oil on the outside.

160

We asked these Jungle Commandos, "When did you last fire this rifle?"

"Oh, last week, I killed many, many enemy", they'd reply. But these rifles hadn't been fired in months, if not years.[9]

Initially, there were no problems in motivating Brunswijk's men, but gradually their enthusiasm dwindled. While Bowen, Finny and Bill continued to run training sessions for whoever was interested, the 2e REP faction posed in their Legion uniforms, prompting complaints from a French officer during his regular visits from French Guiana. Much of their time was spent in their billet at a former YWCA centre, and at Moengo's only bar, the 'Tasty Bite', re-named 'The Nasty Bite' by the mercenaries. They had now received a replacement for Pat Baker: Gary B, another Briton and former member of 2e REP was immediately accepted by Richards' group.

Eventually, the mercenaries had the opportunity of assessing the effectiveness of their training methods. Word was received that Moengu Tapu, a village between Moengo and Albina, had been occupied by the Tacujanas. Bowen, Finny and Bill decided to verify the report and prepared their troops for a fighting patrol. Moengu Tapu had previously been attacked by government forces, believed to have been assisted by Libyan helicopter gunships, and the inhabitants killed or forced to flee. When the mercenary-led patrol reached the village, it was found to deserted except for the Tacujanas.

So we settled the Jungle Commando on the high ground above the village, and we set up the ambush... We'd been teaching these guys for weeks how to lay an ambush and in practice they were the bee's knees, doing it by the numbers. Previously their idea of an ambush was to fire on automatic with their eyes closed, and then run away...

So we got down there. There were a few of these Tacujanas inside and outside this house and we thought, okay, we'll just pour loads of fire at this house and see if we can hit a few of them and then fuck the rest off. So, Finny initiated the ambush with an FN MAG and that was it. All the Jungle Commandos

with us fired a few rounds on automatic and then ran away!
The Tacujanas in the village started firing back at us – there
was only me, Finny and Bill taking all this fire from these
Tacujanas, so we had to do a strategic withdrawal.[10]

On their return to Moengo, the three Britons reported back to
Brunswijk and expressed their disappointment in his troops' poor
performance. "He basically said, well, you know, you have to train
them some more."[11]

So the training continued. Bowen and his two colleagues also
took it on themselves to establish some kind of defensive
procedure, placing guard posts on likely approach routes, selecting
ambush sites and positioning claymore mines. Many of the
'claymores' were manufactured by Bill with detonating cord and
plastic explosive from the bauxite mine at Moengo, and using nuts
and bolts for shrapnel. The ex Legionnaire also made crude, but
effective, hand grenades and booby traps. The monotony was
relieved by occasional patrols, but these rarely resulted in a contact
with the enemy: the boredom was beginning to have a noticeable
effect on the ex 2e REP men.

These Legionnaires ... they wanted to go and kill, you know.
They'd say, "We're here to kill fucking niggers." ... These guys
were strutting around town and beating the locals up. They
used to find guys asleep at their posts and say, "These guys
should be executed," because they'd fallen asleep, and we
would say, everybody knows that nobody is going to come up
that road, and they know that these jungle fighters aren't
going to go down that road, so there's all this watching for
fuck-all ... you can't start executing people just because you
don't like them. The situation between us got worse and
worse, so we kept to ourselves and they kept to themselves.[12]

No doubt irritated by the machismo of Richards and his crew,
Brunswijk decided to send them on an operation to assassinate the
Tacujana leader, Commander Thomas, whose base was in the
south of the country. As they prepared for departure, another row
developed.

While they were in the town, the Legionnaires liked these flashy sub-machine guns, Uzis and Ingrams, because they looked like Rambo gear. We stuck to the FALS, cleaned them all up, zeroed them in ... kept them with us all the time. But when they had to go on this operation, they wanted some FALS ... obviously, sub-machine guns were no good for what they were planning. They wanted our FALs because ours were clean and zeroed in, and they wanted all the grenades ... so we basically said, "Fuck off, go and get your own." They asked Ronnie, and Ronnie said, "No, you'll have to take some off my men." Well, they knew the state of the other rifles, so they were pretty pissed off.[13]

Before leaving, the mercenaries were provided with a local guide: he was contemptuously dismissed.

But these Legionnaires didn't even know how to read a map or compass. They were all corporals in the REP, and they thought, "We'll just walk down this trail here, and turn off at this branch here, and that'll take us to the village," – about 200 kilometres away! I said to them, "You can't go like that. The trails shown on the map might not exist anymore – the jungle grows so quickly – so take compasses and maps." These guys told me they didn't need maps and compasses. I repeated, "You've got to use them or you won't get there. You'll get lost and you'll die in the jungle." Then one of them admitted, "We can't read a map," which absolutely amazed me, because they were corporals in the Legion.

Mick put it like this: "We're fucking Paras. We're airborne. When we need to go somewhere, we parachute in, and then we get taken out after we've done the business. We don't have to learn how to map-read."

So, obviously, they got lost.[14]

For the mercenaries left at Moengo, a period of relative calm followed the departure of Richards and his associates. Then came news of an attack on an army outpost at Kraka in which several soldiers were killed or wounded. Bowen, Finny and Bill were ordered to report to Brunswijk at Moengo airport.

> There were about 30 Jungle Commandos armed to the teeth... We were armed with a couple of Uzis and an FN FAL, and I suggested to the boys we just put our weapons down, because, obviously, something was up. We didn't want to frighten these guys.[15]

They now learned how. Pemberton had been secretly recorded making a telephone call to his girlfriend, revealing his intention to kill Bill and the two former Royal Marines. Richards had been taped too, discussing a personal bank account in the Netherlands where he had deposited the mercenaries' pay – a reported £210,000.

And there was worse: Dutch and French intelligence agencies had apparently informed Brunswijk that Richards was planning his assassination. During a visit to the Hague with another, unknown, Englishman (Bowen) and a man identified as John Banks (see chapter 3), he had allegedly offered to kill the rebel leader for the Surinamese government. Bowen realized that these meetings had taken place while he was in Holland awaiting the return of Richards who, he thought, was meeting their employers. The tapes were supported by documentation confirming the dates, times and locations of Richards' meetings.

Only too aware of the danger they faced if implicated, the three Britons made every effort to distance themselves from Richards. Fortunately, Brunswijk had noticed the rift between the two mercenary groups and was prepared to believe that Bowen, Finny and Bill knew nothing about Richards' true motives for being in Surinam. He then announced his decision to execute Richards and his men.

> He said he was going to kill them and then hand the bodies over to the government. We said, "Fucking right, fucking do it."... There weren't going to be any complaints from us because we thought they were all arseholes. So, you can imagine our surprise when they all came walking into the bar a couple of days later.[16]

It transpired that the patrol had chanced upon an army outpost which they decided to attack, killing at least seven soldiers and wounding 14 others.[17] Bowen recalled how excited Pemberton was.

> He was going, "Fucking hell! Did you see it on the news? That was me. I killed every one of them."
> I said, "Yeah? How was that, Mick?"[18]

Pemberton explained how he had approached a building alone after his comrades expressed their doubts about mounting an attack. It was early in the morning, and the occupants were still fast asleep. Pemberton threw in some grenades before rushing in and shooting the soldiers in their beds. He was fired on by a soldier from another hut, but after a single burst the soldier's weapon either jammed or he ran out of ammunition. Pemberton shot him dead. The mercenaries called out for anybody left alive to come out with their hands up. Those who did were lined up and shot.

Brunswijk's men apprehended the mercenaries shortly after their return. According to Bowen, he, Finny and Bill, assisted by an unsuspecting Pemberton, captured Richards as he was leaving his billet.

> He knew something was going on and he tried to bring his rifle up... We jumped him, disarmed him and then Mick gave him the butt in the head a couple of times. We dragged him over to the centre of the village and handed him over to Ronnie... While we were there, the other three [ex]legionnaires were also disarmed...
> They questioned John and, at first he denied everything about ... all the intelligence from the Hague and the French. He denied everything, so they played the tapes and then he said, "Okay, okay, but I would never have done it, Ronnie, I was just trying to get money out of them for nothing."[19]

Bowen also questioned Richards.

> I said, "What about our money?"
> He said, "What money?"

"You know," I said. "We've got tape recordings of the phone calls you made to your contact in the Hague."

He replied, "Okay, no problem. When we go back, I'll give you your money."

I asked, "Why didn't you put it into our accounts like you were supposed to have done?"

He said, "Look, it doesn't matter, I can give you the money when we get back."[20]

Bowen claims that he and Finny persuaded Brunswijk to release Richards' companions, who were escorted to the river and sent back to French Guiana. Richards was then taken into the jungle and executed. On 27 June 1995, Carlton Television's investigative series *The Cook Report* claimed to reveal how Richards had died. Pemberton and Baker accused Bowen of participating in the killing. According to Pemberton:

Alan confessed to me that he killed John. He was the one that contacted me and told me that John was dead, and I asked him straightaway ... who did it, and he said, "We did," obviously meaning himself, Finny and Bill. He then explained to me exactly how it happened, and that was maybe a couple of days after they returned from Surinam, which was, maybe, a week or so after John's death.[21]

Baker claimed to have received a telephone call from Bowen and Finny.

"They were still in Surinam... Alan said to me... "We've done the bastard. John's dead." Also at the same time, Finny was shouting down the phone, "We've killed the bastard! We've killed the bastard!"[22]

During a secretly filmed conversation with Pemberton, Bowen also implicated himself, Finny and Bill.

Well, I tell you what happened with John... Ronnie says, "Kill him"... you know and Finny and Bill are going, "Yeah, ... kill him" ... and when they took him off to the jungle ... they tied him up, I felt ... terrible ... because he ... deserved it, and tied him against a tree and he said, "What's happening to me, Alan?", and I said, "Oh, you're just going to get bitten by the mosquitoes all night, and then in the morning Ronnie's going to question you and you'll tell him everything he wants to know ... and then I sort of walked past and Finny and Bill were there... Finny had a Mossberg as well, and I said, "I can't do it. I'm not that hard. I can't do it."... He said, "Okay, just ... get over there" ... and then all of a sudden ... I turned around and heard John go, "No, no," and then, bang, bang ... Bill's ... FAL jammed straight away ... so he ... cocked it again and Finny was going, whack, you know ... pumping them into John ... and I see Bill go, "... piece of shit", like, and [indicates throwing weapon down] grabbed the ... shotgun off Finny and said, "No, give it to me," and went, bang, bang ... I saw the rounds, the shells hitting John. He was ... twisting around and ... whacking around ... all his chest was ... and his guts were hanging out and ... he was on his stomach ... and I walked over and I said, "Yeah, you're dead ... and as I walked away I heard this, "Ohhh, why are you doing this to me?"... So, I just ... put the ... barrel on his head and went ... and blew half his ... head off.[23]

After Richards' execution, Bowen, Finny and Bill settled back into their training routine, interrupted only by the occasional minor action.

Brunswijk eventually paid each of the men £9,000 for their services, after which Bowen crossed into French Guiana to assess the situation in preparation for the mercenaries' departure from Surinam. He was promptly apprehended by the French.

And they chained me to a wall in the colonial prison – fucking chained me against a wall – and then this intelligence officer (who had been in Surinam, criticizing the Legionnaires) came in and barked some orders. They unchained me and he brought a couple of beers in, and said, "You're free. You can go back to your hotel. But, first, come out for a drink with me after this." He brought me some chicken sandwiches because … I'd caught malaria and was like a fucking skeleton.

He asked me exactly what had happened over there. So I told him basically the same as what I'm telling you, and he actually said, "Why don't you come and join the Legion?" He was alright. He said, "When are the other two coming across?" I told him, "They'll be across in the next couple of days." And he said, "Okay. Go back to your hotel. Don't stray too far because there's loads of Surinamese agents… If they know you're here, they'll be looking for you and they'll kill you."

So, I stayed in the hotel room and then Finny and Bill arrived two days later.[24]

They were obliged to surrender their passports to the French authorities and were arrested; though according to Bowen, "They were dead polite about it."[25] After being told that they were to be deported, the mercenaries were driven to Cayenne and, largely for the benefit of the press, placed in police cells.

As soon as the journalists had gone, they opened the cells – handcuffs off – "Sorry about that, lads." You know, they held up a 747 for an hour so we could see ourselves on TV, and this intelligence officer said, "Listen, boys … you're being deported now for political reasons, but if you ever want to come back … you're welcome."

Anyway, we were deported back to France. We thought we were going to be collared in France, deported back to England, collared by Special Branch and dumped in the shit. Nothing happened. Nothing at all. They deported us: and we went first class as well![26]

★   ★   ★

Bowen later met one of their financiers in the Hague, who confirmed that Richards had been paid in full for all the mercenaries. The money, still unclaimed, remains in an account in Holland.

Pemberton was questioned about his taped telephone calls, but denied he had ever discussed killing Bowen or anybody else.

After *The Cook Report*, Bowen and Finny tried to find out just how much Pemberton and Baker were paid for their involvement in the programme. Apparently, neither received a penny. Bowen remains mystified as to their motives.

The British Police, not unnaturally, showed an interest in Richards' death. Bowen denied all involvement and was later advised through his solicitor that no charges were pending.

★   ★   ★

In the summer of 1991, Bowen was invited back to Cayenne by Perry, a 'Chinese-Surinamese businessman'. Unable to take up the offer immediately, Bowen asked 'Gus' (see chapter 12) another former Royal Marine, if he would travel in his place, promising that he would join him as soon as he could. Bowen was thus kept informed of events until he met up with Gus a few weeks later when he was presented with another opportunity to train the Jungle Commando. As it was in Perry's interests to put an end to Ronnie Brunswijk's influence, he was also asked to consider assassinating the rebel leader.

The possibility of a long-term contract was an attractive proposition. Gus was left to conduct a feasibility study amongst the rebels in Surinam, while Bowen discussed the matter over with Perry in Cayenne. Bowen envisaged that the operation would require no more than a dozen or so mercenaries. But there was a problem: Perry claimed to have insufficient funds. Undaunted, Bowen suggested a solution: "I came up with a plan of liberating the money from a bank in Moengo – an unauthorized loan. We had every intention of paying it back once we had won the war but ... I think he got cold feet then."[27]

The following day, Perry introduced Bowen to a Frenchman who, he insisted, was in a position to help. Although he suspected the man of being some kind of intelligence or police agent, Bowen was persuaded by Perry to repeat his plan. The stranger left, assuring Bowen that he would be contacted again as soon as possible.

At 0900 hours the next morning, Bowen was apprehended at his hotel by four French officials who explained that it was currently inadvisable to re-start the war in Surinam. He was then escorted to the airport and deported for the second time. Gus, who was still in the jungle across the border, was arrested shortly afterwards and flown back to Europe.

Within months, both men were back in uniform, serving alongside the Croats in the former Yugoslavia.

CHAPTER 9
OPERATION PHOENIX, COLOMBIA 1988-91

Colombia is considered to be one of the most dangerous places in the world – a land where often indiscriminate violence and murder have prevailed throughout much of this century. Thousands have perished in numerous local revolts, which culminated in 1948 with a major insurrection and an era of anarchy and civil strife known as The Violence. It ended in 1958, when the federalist Liberal and centralist Conservative parties agreed to alternative periods in office, an arrangement that lasted nearly 30 years. But Colombia's troubles continued, with the formation of several left-wing guerrilla movements. During the late 1980s, there was an escalation of killings, this time by right-wing death squads, some allegedly linked to the army and police, others to drug cartels.

Colombia's politics are hopelessly entangled with the country's illegal (but immensely lucrative) narcotics industry. Those who once earned a meagre income from working their land now realize its potential for producing more profitable crops. The situation has created so-called drug barons, incredibly wealthy and powerful men who preside over their own fiefs protected by ruthless private armies. Amongst the more influential figures in the Colombian underworld during the mid-1980s were José Gonzalo Rodríguez Gacha and Pablo Escobar Gaviria of the notorious Medellín-based drug cartel.

★　★　★

After serving together in Angola in 1976, Peter McAleese (see chapters 2, 3 and 4) and Dave Tomkins (see chapter 3) had gone

171

their separate ways; the former continuing to offer his services as a professional soldier and the latter establishing himself as an arms dealer. In June 1988, McAleese received a telephone call from his old friend. A meeting was arranged, also attended by a Colombian known as Ricardo, during which Tomkins explained that he had been contacted by a colleague acting on behalf of Colombian officials interested in recruiting mercenaries to attack a local headquarters of the Revolutionary Armed Forces of Colombia (FARC), an organization supported by Cuba and funded primarily by the narcotics trade. FARC was responsible for a number of terrorist incidents in its ongoing campaign against the government, and yet the authorities were reluctant to resort to military action, preferring to resolve the issue by debate. The security forces, frustrated with the proceedings, had instructed several officers, including Ricardo, to find an alternative solution to the problem.[1]

McAleese agreed to accompany the pair to Colombia to assess the situation. All three arrived in Bogotá on 1 July. A few days later, several men (at least two of whom were ex army officers) were introduced, and aerial reconnaissances organized of the target building, *Casa Verde*, in the Sumapaz Valley. It served as a rebel HQ and a way station for mule trains which supplied 400–600 guerrillas in another camp ten kilometres away.

On 9 July, Tomkins returned to England to handle the logistics of the operation. McAleese remained in Colombia for another two weeks to prepare a plan of attack before leaving to recruit another nine mercenaries. Four were hired in Britain and the rest in South Africa: all were former soldiers who had served in Rhodesia and/or the SADF. They seemed satisfied with the explanation that they would be working for the Colombian Army with the possible backing of the secret police, which may have been the case. But at a US government investigation in Washington on 27 February 1991, which Tomkins attended at the cartel's request testified:

> While in Bogotá, I was advised that the finance for these operations was being provided by a Colombian narcotics trafficker called Gonzalo Rodríguez Gacha. We were assured that this alliance was a necessary and temporary

arrangement, as funds could not have been taken from the military budget without compromising the operations.[2]

Among those who cross-examined Tomkins was Senator Joseph Lieberman who asked:

"Did you have any sense during your involvement here whether there was a quid pro quo between Colombian military personnel you were dealing with and Rodríguez Gacha for his financing of this FARC operation?"

"Yes, I am sure there was," replied Tomkins.

"You presumed that there was some kind of protection that was going to be given to Gacha as a result of his willingness to finance this?"

"Yes, I am sure there probably was."[3]

Whoever actually paid their wages, and Tomkins and McAleese allegedly received approximately $2,000 a week[4], was of little interest to the mercenaries. As far as Tomkins was concerned:

Whether the finances were generated from cocaine ... didn't bother us – didn't bother me anyway – we were told it was a secret operation. The government per se were not aware of it ... the army, at a very high level, and I mean very high level ... sanctioned it.[5]

Tomkins returned to Colombia with an advance party to inspect suitable training areas: McAleese joined him on 18 August after recruiting the South African element, and the rest of the team arrived over the weekend. Shortly afterwards, they were taken 200 kilometres through the mountains of the eastern Cordilleras to Puerto Boyaca in the Magdalena Medio region, where they were ferried across a lake to a small island known locally as *Isla de la Fantasia* and accommodated in a villa near a small bungalow occupied by a couple employed as caterers.

McAleese organized a fitness programme for the men while they waited for the arrival of their arms and ammunition. So far, the only weapons they had been given were some old H&K G3 rifles. After a few days, the liaison officer, known as Julio, delivered sufficient G3s to equip the rest of the team, enabling McAleese to amend the training schedule to include weapon training, immediate action drills, fire and movement, battle skills, patrolling and navigation exercises.

One day, during shooting practice on the mainland, the mercenaries were interrupted by the arrival of four Landcruisers carrying heavily armed Colombians. Ricardo emerged with another man while their escort hastily set up radio communications. The stranger was non other than José Gonzalo Rodríguez Gacha. McAleese later claimed that at the time he was unaware of who Gacha was, but assumed him to be "a big Mafia man".[6] After satisfying himself that all was well, Gacha departed. Two nights later, McAleese was escorted to a Spanish-style villa where he again met Gacha, who listened attentively as McAleese explained his plan of attack. Gacha asked if it would be possible for the mercenaries to assault the secretariat at the main guerrilla base several miles from the *Casa Verde*. McAleese was confident that this could be achieved, but not with 11 men. Consequently, the team was reinforced with 50 or so trainees from the Association of Farmers and Ranchers of the Middle Magdalena (ACDEGAM), a civic group that provided various community services to the local populace, and also served as Gacha's private army.

It became necessary to move to a bigger camp, and this was followed by three more moves: by this time conditions had deteriorated considerably since *Isla de la Fantasia* and the mercenaries were finding it increasingly difficult to maintain their initial enthusiasm. The problem was compounded by the lack of suitable arms and equipment. Tomkins recalled that:

Our training programmes were restricted by the equipment we received... [The Colombians] were useless really: the average guy who already had a weapon could barely field-strip it... You would find guys with the wrong calibre round in their magazine... On the demolitions side, where I was involved, I was looking for C4 or any military-type plastic explosive, cordtex and detonators etc., but they came up with commercial dynamite ... and you would get things like, well, here are four detonators. Only four, you know, and cordtex – detonating cord – 30 feet, and that was it. I was thinking, "Jesus Christ almighty! Do you people not understand what you are asking us to do?... It can't be done with this crap."[7]

When McAleese returned to Bogotá to discuss matters with a higher authority, it soon became evident that there was considerable confusion regarding the precise nature of the mercenaries' mission. Training had by now produced a reasonably efficient local force, but to what end? Furthermore, although additional weapons and equipment had been ordered, nothing had materialized. According to Tomkins:

Gacha ... seemed to be the principal paymaster... We put out a listing of all the stores required. This amounted to about seven tons... It was passed to my guy who had originally introduced me to the Colombians who said, yes, I can get this. But, rather than confining it to that, Gacha must have thought, this is good, and he ordered 58 tons of equipment – not for us – for him and his bandits... But this created a huge logistical problem. We were still unaware of most of this at the time because we were still stuck in the boonies... It only became apparent later, as Christmas drew near and we still weren't going anywhere.[8]

There seemed no point prolonging the operation. McAleese requested that his men be allowed to return to Bogotá, where the team was duly paid off and disbanded. McAleese and Tomkins were the last to leave on Friday 18 November, four and a half months after first setting foot in Colombia.

★   ★   ★

In February 1989 Tomkins was contacted by a Colombian army officer, known to him from the previous year, with an offer of further employment.

175

On the 13th of the second, 1989, I attended a meeting in London with two Colombian nationals. I was requested to recruit another team for an operation against Pablo Gaviria Escobar... I was advised that the sponsors were a group of businessmen whose assets were being destroyed in a bombing campaign, and members of their staff murdered by his men. I was assured that no government interference would hinder this operation. I was advised that the principals were not wanted in Colombia for any crimes, and were prominent figures with visible legitimate assets. I accepted the contract.[9]

Tomkins and McAleese flew into Cali on 24 February. They were greeted genially by their old contact Ricardo and, after settling into a spacious town apartment, briefed on the new mission.

Escobar rarely remained in the same place for long. But he owned a luxurious villa between Puerto Triumpho and Medellín – *Hacienda Napoles*, set in a huge jungle clearing, surrounded by security fencing and guard towers, and defended by some 80 men. The mercenaries' new task was to attack the villa as soon as intelligence learned of Escobar's next visit there.

It was the sort of challenge that appealed to McAleese, who immediately began work on a plan, leaving Tomkins to recruit the team. Of the original nine mercenaries, five were able to return to Colombia. They were joined by five ex regular soldiers, two of whom had served in South Africa, and a former Territorial. The men were accommodated in two apartments in Cali before moving into a luxurious villa in spacious surroundings outside the town.

McAleese conducted several overflights of *Hacienda Napoles*, enabling him to prepare a briefing for his men, though for security reasons none were informed at this stage who or where the target was. Nevertheless, for Australian Terry Tagney, it was all too much and at his own request he was dropped from the mission. The remainder continued training. In contrast to the previous operation, this time there was no shortage of equipment.

We asked for helicopters, we got helicopters. Whatever we asked for, we got. This was a real smooth bunch... Their organizational capability far surpassed that of the bandits...

If they wanted something, they sent an order by fax or telex to their agents in the United States, and it arrived on the next freighter or aircraft, albeit disguised as something else.[10]

In time, the mercenaries were joined by 'Tiger', a police narcotics officer, and Toyco, a major in the Air Force, who were to pilot their recently acquired Hughes 500 and Bell 204 helicopters. They were soon put to use, ferrying the men to and from another more suitable training area at La Gagua on the Rio Manguido. Then early in May, Tomkins received word that James Adams of *The Sunday Times* was following up on disclosures about the earlier operation by a former Colombian official. When it became apparent that Adams also knew of the latest venture, Tomkins and McAleese were left with no option but to meet the reporter in Panama City where it was agreed that he would delay publishing his story in return for an exclusive once the current task had been accomplished.

Arriving back at La Gagua, McAleese continued with his preparations for Operation Phoenix Two, gathering together his men and the helicopter crews for a detailed briefing and full dress rehearsal. Essentially, the plan devised was as follows: after deploying Tomkins and interpreters, Almaro and Ramon, all of whom formed part of a five-man support group, McAleese would control events from the Hughes 500 piloted by Tiger. Toyco, flying the Bell 204, was to ferry in the two remaining members of the support group, and two four-man assault/house-clearing groups. Their task was to attack *Hacienda Napoles* and kill Pablo Escobar. Enemy forces totalled an estimated 80 men armed with M60 or FN general purpose machine guns, AR-15 rifles, Uzi and Ingram SMGs and handguns.

The mercenaries were issued with M16 or AR-15 rifles. Those in the assault group were also equipped with 9 mm pistols, red and green smoke grenades for use as heli-landing aids, and 'knock-knocks' – charges designed for gaining entry through locked doors. The support group carried 9 mm pistols, 66 mm M72 LAWs and hand grenades. Everybody was provided with a personal radio with earpiece and microphone. Dress consisted of boots, camouflage uniform and a balaclava with a phosphorescent yellow cross on top for easy identification from the air. McAleese had managed to acquire an Israeli bullet-proof vest for himself, while the remainder wore custom-made combat vests.[11] Each man was also equipped with a shock pack and escape kit, the latter consisting primarily of civilian clothes, a compass and several thousand dollars worth of pesos.

Additional air support was provided by a Cessna aircraft installed with a repeater station to boost communications (codenamed Telstar by the team); a fixed-wing 12-seater Cessna Sky Caravan to evacuate the force on completion, and a Bell 214 Jetranger helicopter for use as back-up and in case of casualty evacuation.

During the assault phase, the mercenaries were to overfly *Hacienda Napoles* while McAleese, manning a pintle-mounted GPMG in the Hughes, and supported by those in the Bell, opened fire on three guard towers overlooking the area. After neutralizing any immediate threat, the Hughes would hover at roof-top height above the hacienda to enable Tomkins to drop specially prepared satchel charges on either side of the building. These were designed to kill or disable anyone inside. A nearby gate-house was to be destroyed in similar fashion. The Hughes would then cover the deployment of the assault troops. As soon as the Bell 204 was clear, the Hughes would come in with its support element, before orbiting the scene as McAleese's command helicopter-gunship.

The main task of those in the support group was to 'fire in' the assault troops during their sweep through the villa, and then cover their colleagues' withdrawal. After confirming that Pablo Escobar was dead, the mercenaries were to reorganize at the landing ground for uplift to a nearby airstrip where they would transfer to the waiting Sky Caravan.

McAleese and his men carried out five dress-rehearsals using live ammunition and a mock-up of the target until finally, at 1100 hours on Saturday 3 June, word was received that Escobar was at his villa.

The support flight took off from an airstrip at Cali and proceeded to rendezvous with the Hughes and Bell 204, whose route passed over two mountain ranges rising to 4,500 metres. The first was easily negotiated, though by this time the morning's fine weather had given way to rapidly thickening cloud, with visibility deteriorating further as the helicopters neared the second obstacle. While the more powerful Bell maintained position above the Hughes, Tiger suddenly noticed what appeared to be a sunlit gap in the clouds ahead, and immediately headed towards it. McAleese later recalled:

> Suddenly the sunlight vanished, the gap disappeared like the reflection it was, we flew into the clouds and straight at the trees. Tiger shouted and pulled at the controls but it was too late. The Hughes smashed into the green canopy, the perspex bubble shattered and the whole aircraft twisted upside down with the power of the rotor blades caught in the branches. I felt a terrible wrenching pain in my back. The noise of the screaming engine, breaking metal and splintering branches filled my ears. Disorientated, I remember falling, the momentum of the helicopter plunging it through the trees towards the steep slope beneath. Eventually, we stopped moving. I was hanging head down, held in my seat by my safety belt.[12]

Tomkins remembered:

> The weather was atrocious. It was terrible – rain, thunder, clouds like shit – couldn't see anything. You would look out of the chopper and it was flying in clouds. Occasionally it would break and you would see the other chopper... As we approached the mountain ... [the] Hughes 500 ... was having a job, presumably because of the weight of ammunition and machine guns and God knows what else we had on it, and the clouds were everywhere – rolling thunder clouds, and we were trying to get over the peak or through the peak and ... there was no warning at all, none whatsoever. Tiger ... just went for this gap between the ridges and the clouds rolled in and he just kept going at what he assumed was there... The next minute we were all over the fucking mountain about 65 feet from the top, and at 8,200 feet the last time I looked at the altimeter, and we splattered in – just came to a grinding halt... The first thing that I remember was the sheer fucking panic to get out

179

… because I was upside down… You're thinking very quickly. Thoughts were irrational … I was still in the chopper … and I was waiting for it to explode as they do in Hollywood, but of course we were on fumes anyway when it crashed, but I knew there were all the bombs on board. The satchel charges, whilst they in themselves were fairly safe, were armed with M1A2-15 second delay fuses. I didn't know what had happened to them. There could have been any damage to them … I was waiting for the explosion – and I just saw this fucking opening, which was the door, with branches and bushes coming through it, and I just hit it and scrabbled my way through … we were in the tree-tops… My first instinct was my own survival … and I'm falling, crawling, falling … and I suppose I got 50 feet down … before I stopped and looked around … I suppose seconds had gone past … and I know I'm out of it but I'm waiting for the bang which doesn't come and now, all of a sudden, rational thoughts are coming: We're nearly out of gas. It hasn't blown. I can see the tail smoking. Then I see Peter staggering about. Somebody else has come out of a bush covered in claret. I know I've been hurt. I'm covered in blood. I think, I'm afraid to put my hand on my head because I know my head's split open. As far as I'm concerned, my head is in two parts and I'm going to feel my brain, and I had a tiny little cut … but I tell you that fucker bled like you wouldn't believe. I think I got it when the chopper stopped. My rifle was in front of me, resting in the corner and I think it drove me forward and the sight stuck in my head because the barrel was bent.[13]

Tomkins was now able to assess the situation.

I didn't go into shock at all, funnily enough … not at all… There was one body missing, which was Tiger, so we crawled back in … and he was in a terrible state. Not apparent at that stage… There wasn't any blood. I was surprised. But the shock to his system, the damage, must have stopped everything working. He was dying. We were looking for shock packs … everything was strewn all over the place… We tried to find something which we could give him a jab with... He was a bit twisted up ... and he had come round and was mumbling, *mi pierna*, which is, my leg, and once we got some morphine – we managed to find one syringe – we began looking for a vein. I looked at his (left) arm ... and it looked like it was cut from shoulder to wrist, right to the bone, and both sides had folded out ... like it had been filleted. I imagine he had gone forward through the screen which was all jagged perspex... He mumbled and we tried to move him and ... he'd been cut virtually from the spine right the way around and he was just about parted in two... He was grey and he was obviously ... just barely alive. He started mumbling in Spanish, I think he was praying... We stuck every bit of morphine that we could get into him. Couldn't get a vein – we just banged it straight into his neck and called the other Spanish guy down and said, stay with him, speak to him in Spanish, whatever... He was dead in minutes.[14]

Now, there was further cause for concern, as the extent of McAleese's injuries became apparent.

Peter started to go into shock and he recognized it... We tried to get a shock pack into him but his veins also started to collapse, so we slashed it open and he drank it, instead. We had moved away from the chopper, down slightly ... [to] this bit of clear space underneath the canopy... We laid him down there... I defused all the explosive charges and we lit a fire using C4 from the satchel charges.[15]

Ironically, those who managed to escape serious injury had been perched atop ammunition and explosives carried in place of passenger seating, whereas Tiger and McAleese – one dead, the other disabled – were both provided with seats and safety straps.

Those who were able now began to search for a workable radio with which to signal the Bell 204. With its occupants still unaware of their comrades' plight the helicopter had continued to a refuelling point just short of the objective. Eventually, a radio was located and communications re-established via 'Telstar', enabling the Bell to be directed towards the crash site. Unable to land close by, Toyco opted to put down at a suitable LZ below the mountain, next to a cascading stream. The survivors were instructed to make their way to a section of the stream 500 metres below their location, while a rescue party attempted to follow its course uphill. Tomkins decided to set off on his own, leaving Almaro and Ramon with McAleese. After struggling through the bush for about half an hour, Tomkins was joined by the two Colombians who had left McAleese after making him comfortable, confident that they could easily relocate him by re-tracing their route. As Tomkins could see little point in returning to the crash site at this stage, all three continued downhill in an attempt to cover as much ground as possible before nightfall. Later, the ex SAS in the team would describe the terrain as "the worst fucking jungle they had ever come across in their lives".[16]

Darkness descends with little warning in the jungle. That evening, Tomkins and his two companions resigned themselves to a freezing night on the mountainside. A short distance away, the injured McAleese also waited patiently for daybreak.

At dawn, Toyco's helicopter was heard to start up and leave. The other mercenaries had been prevented from reaching the crash site and were concerned about being discovered by Escobar's men who were sure to be sweeping the area. Later that morning, Tomkins, Almaro and Ramon were surprised to see two old men approaching through the dense foliage. The pair tended a small potato field close to where Toyco had landed the previous afternoon. Unaware of who the strangers were, they had readily agreed when asked to continue the search and now led the thankful survivors to their crude shelter.

Less than twenty minutes had passed when one of the guides cheerfully announced the approach of an army patrol. In his domain, Escobar controlled everyone and everything, and there was no reason to think that the local government forces would be exempt. Tomkins and his companions had no option but to force their startled hosts to take them back uphill where they remained until the patrol departed.

The following day, the three were evacuated by a helicopter, which also brought a rescue team for McAleese. He would endure two more nights on the mountain and a laborious and painful descent before being airlifted to a waiting Cessna for the flight back to Cali. Tomkins described his condition upon arriving at their apartment.

> He was in a terrible state. In fact, I helped him shower... He was covered in mud and dirt and blood and bits from the trees. He was freezing cold. We showered him and got him dressed and got him X-ray'd... He looked like he had been battered with a baseball bat from head to foot... He couldn't move.[17]

Although severely bruised, McAleese was fortunate to have escaped with just cracked ribs. The body of Tiger, who was reported to have died during a classified mission, was eventually recovered and buried with honours.

On 18 June 1989, Tomkins returned home to replace lost items of equipment and also to recruit another four team members, including two helicopter pilots. The five arrived in Colombia on 5 July. Six weeks later, a series of murders, including that of Luis Carlos Galan, the country's leading presidential candidate, resulted in tough government action against the suspected perpetrators. Escobar's known assets, including *Hacienda Napoles*, were sequestrated. The drug baron went into hiding in an effort to avoid capture, and in so doing unwittingly foiled the mercenaries' assassination plans. Shortly afterwards, on 3 September, the team dispersed and once again returned to their respective countries.

On 13 August 1989, James Adams published his report in *The Sunday Times,* spread across two pages and titled: 'Dogs of War Stalk Drugs Baron'. Two of the mercenaries, Terry Tagney and Ned Owen, also sold their stories to the media. Operation Phoenix was thus well and truly compromised.

Or was it?

★   ★   ★

In June 1991, Colombia's President César Gaviria Trujillo promised to end the extradition of drug traffickers and to impose reduced prison sentences on those who surrendered. Escobar was amongst those who took advantage of the offer. He was held in a secure area in the hills overlooking his home town of Envigado, protected on the inside by six of his top lieutenants, and with external security provided by 40 guards, half of whom were said to have been personally selected by Escobar himself. As other drug traffickers joined Escobar in his 'prison', Tomkins was offered a third contract – this time to kill all those being held at Envigado.

A lot of money was offered ... so we said, yeah, if it's right, if we get all the things we need and we plan it right, but we need intelligence.[18]

It was soon concluded that an operation was feasible and an audacious plan began to take shape. Essentially, an A-37B Dragonfly strike aircraft was to be used to bomb the target. An assault team would then storm the building and ensure that Escobar and his colleagues were dead.

Tomkins was tasked with acquiring the aircraft, an obsolete type used during the Vietnam War. A dismantled A-37 was located in France, but it was considered too costly and time-consuming to render it airworthy.

Then I got a call from a dealer. He had found somebody who could get me one – but it turned out to be a US Custom's 'sting operation'... Somebody who was in trouble had decided to sacrifice me to save himself, though I was unaware of this at the time, so the whole plan still went ahead. I flew out to Miami and eventually got to see the thing.[19]

Months of negotiations and paperwork followed while Tomkins vainly attempted to clear the aircraft for export, until

Somebody got word to me that I was being set up and said, go, get out now. So, I managed to slip the net.[20]

The operation might still have gone ahead were it not for the arrests of a number of Colombians and Costa Ricans who were accused of stealing bombs from the Costa Rican airforce – for the proposed strike on Envigado!

The Colombian government subsequently arranged to transfer Escobar to a more secure unit, in response to claims that he was continuing to conduct drug operations from Envigado. He and several other prisoners were able to break out shortly before the move.

★   ★   ★

José Gonzalo Rodríguez Gacha, the principal financier of Operation Phoenix One, was shot and killed by Colombian police on 15 December 1989.

Pablo Escobar Gaviria died in a shoot-out with government forces on 2 December 1993.

It has since been claimed that Britain's Special Air Service had been assisting the Colombians in their anti-drugs campaign since April 1989. It is also alleged that the involvement in Colombia of Peter McAleese was an unwelcome intrusion and that, for a time, he had been considered for assassination by Her Majesty's Government.[21]

CHAPTER 10
"LOVELY PEOPLE":
YUGOSLAVIA, 1991-95

Everybody in the former Yugoslavia is acutely aware of their ethnic and religious origins, their tumultuous history, and the relevance of it all to the present situation. The liberation of Belgrade by the Russians in October 1944 ended three and a half years of Nazi occupation in Yugoslavia. Under the leadership of Josip Broz Tito, Yugoslavia's multi-ethnic communities maintained an uneasy but peaceful coexistence for nearly 36 years; a period of stability that was the prelude to the worst violence seen in Europe since World War II.

After Tito's death in 1980, a growing sense of nationalism swept the country and Yugoslavia's old problems re-emerged. By 1990 the situation had produced several prominent leaders, threatening the position of President Slobodan Milošević and the majority of Serbs who supported the traditional nationalist concept of a Greater Serbia. On 25 June 1991 the north-west region of Slovenia declared independence, and tanks and armoured vehicles of the Yugoslav People's Army (JNA) were deployed in response to what was seen by many Serbs as an act of treason. Opposing forces consisted of lightly armed but well organized and determined Territorials. In a series of clashes, the JNA, whose troops often seemed confused and uncertain about their role, put up only a token resistance. Tanks and other equipment were seized and added to the Territorials' rapidly growing arsenal and in the confusion Slovenian conscripts deserted. Within ten days the JNA were defeated and, in accordance with the Brioni Accord acknowledging Slovenia's liberation from the control of Belgrade, withdrew from Slovenia. According to the Slovenian Red Cross, 60 people had been killed.

"LOVELY PEOPLE',: YUGOSLAVIA, 1991-95

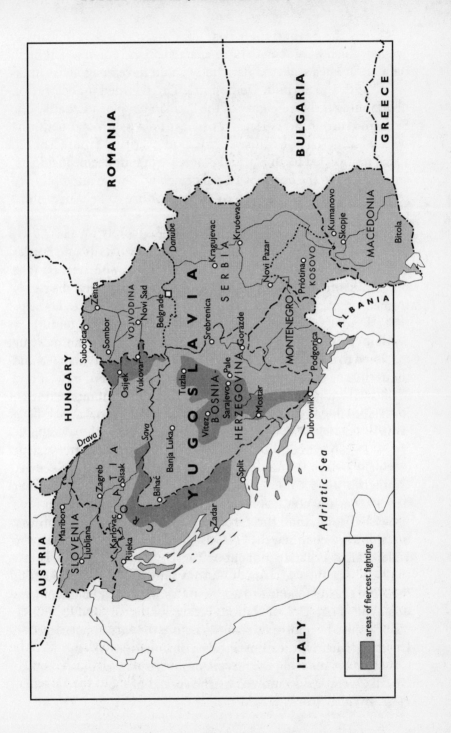

187

Across the border, the Croats had been closely monitoring events, which were soon to be re-enacted on their own soil, though on a far greater scale than anybody could have imagined. On 25 July 1990, the Serbian Democratic Party issued a declaration proclaiming the sovereignty of the Serbian people in Croatia. The Serbian Autonomous Region of Krajina was proclaimed nine weeks later. When Krajina decided on partition from Croatia, rising tension led to an alarming increase in internecine incidents, culminating in the death of 12 policemen who were attempting to rescue colleagues abducted by Serbs at Borovo Selo in eastern Croatia's Slavonia region.

When Croatia declared independence on 25 June 1991, conditions in Slavonia rapidly deteriorated into daily gun battles between Croats and Serbs, the latter supported by the predominantly Serb-led JNA. Throughout the country, the newly formed Croatian National Guard Corps (ZNG) began to lay siege to Federal barracks, capturing a large quantity of military equipment including tanks and heavy weapons. The fighting escalated to open warfare: towns and villages were devastated and thousands of people made homeless in a succession of mortar and artillery barrages, bombings, tank assaults and infantry attacks. Both sides dug in as they attempted to consolidate what had been won.

On 18 November, Vukovar fell to Serbian forces after a siege lasting 87 days. Nine days later the United Nations Security Council agreed to send a peacekeeping force to the former Yugoslavia on condition that the latest of many cease-fires prevailed, and that the Croats lifted their siege of military installations, enabling the JNA to withdraw. Two days later, the Federal army began to pull out of Zagreb.

Elsewhere, the war went on. It took until 21 February 1992 for the UN Security Council to approve Resolution 743 allowing the deployment of a United Nations Protection Force (UNPROFOR), but it would be another six weeks before the first units arrived in Croatia. Meanwhile, hostilities continued, with the Croats succeeding in relieving Dubrovnik in June; but thereafter, events in Croatia were overshadowed by the spread of the war to Bosnia-Herzegovina.

The fighting in Slovenia was over almost before the West could really grasp what was happening. Croatia was different: what had begun as a few localized incidents quickly escalated into widespread violence before erupting into full-scale war. Soon, foreign volunteers, attracted by rumours of a non-existent 'International Brigade', began to arrive singly and in small groups. Some turned up with little more than the clothes they wore; others brought their own uniforms, and a few, notably Americans, their own weapons.

Kaj, a Dane, arrived as a tourist in peacetime Yugoslavia. When Croatia declared independence he decided to stay and assist the Croats, putting to use experience acquired with the Danish army. Kaj was soon involved in a number of operations including intelligence-gathering missions in Serb-dominated areas. His method was simple. Driving a Danish-registered van, Kaj told anybody who stopped him that he was a tourist visiting Serbian friends – a ploy not without risks. On one occasion at a Serbian road-block, he watched as a driver was dragged from his vehicle and beaten to death. The Dane felt certain that he too would be killed, but his passport saved him. The experience did not put a stop to his excursions. Ironically, the 'tourist' eventually compromised himself by appearing, in uniform, in an interview on Croatian television.

Kaj may well have been the first 'International'. Nobody will ever know how many followed: hundreds, certainly. Among the first British volunteers was Dave Fersen, who admitted to being absent without leave from the French Foreign Legion, which he joined after serving as a radio operator in the Royal Navy. Dave arrived in Zagreb in August 1991. After enquiring as to where the fighting was, he travelled by train and bus to Petrinja and joined the forces of the Croatian Interior Ministry (MUP) a few days later. Fersen was unimpressed by what he saw in Croatia.

> The MUP are more organized than the [National] Guard and a bit more professional. They told me they were anti-terrorist but when we went out looking for Serbs in Sisak – we were going from house to house – they didn't have a clue. Not a clue. Bang on a door – four of them would be stood under a

light … I couldn't believe it. There were snipers in Sisak and they all stood by the door, banging on it.[1]

After five or six weeks in Petrinja and Sisak, Fersen took part in the capture of a JNA radar installation.

There were about 15 of us, all MUP. We got there along irrigation ditches. The plan was for an armoured car to drive through the front gate as we were attacking. It was supposed to arrive at 7.00 o'clock, but by 7.30 there was no sign of it. So, we crawled right up to the perimeter fence and this dog started barking… I got everybody down, brought up my sniper rifle and saw this Yugoslav officer looking through his binoculars in the direction the dog was indicating. I could have shot him but, the thing was, everybody was sitting about, a stone-throw from the base, just picking their noses. What can you do?

If I shot him – well, we would have been right in it. We didn't know the strength of the base or what weapons they had. I had a LAW [Light Anti-Tank Weapon] and my mate behind me had an RPG-2 [40 mm Rocket Propelled Grenade]. He wanted me to go on, but there was a bunker with a 20-millimetre cannon. He wanted me to go up there, but I wasn't going to risk that because they'd already got on to me. So he got his RPG ready and we stood up. He fired his RPG and I tried to fire the LAW three times. Nothing. I threw it away and that was it.

Then we just let them have it for about three hours. We couldn't see anything – just throwing grenades and firing tromblons [*trombloni*: rifle grenades] and shooting at them – and they radioed in for a plane. By now it was quite dark and foggy and the plane came over and dropped its flares and bombs, but it was about a kilometre off, and as it went over they fired a flare from the base. They did it the wrong way round, so we were lucky.[2]

The Croats withdrew and returned the following day, this time with ten times as many troops and three vehicles. An armoured car approached the camp entrance and the commander demanded that the garrison surrender. The Serbs promptly requested air support and, soon after, two MiGs arrived, firing rockets and machine guns. Somehow, the Croats and their vehicles escaped being hit, but their commander, still at the gate, was fatally wounded by a mine.

The Croats again pulled back. A couple of days later Fersen was one of 10 men who returned in time to witness the evacuation of the base.

> Two helicopters and five MiGs came over. The helicopters came in and fired and cleared a landing zone. They flew over us, landed, and picked up the blokes and then flew low right over us... My mate stood up and let rip with an AK. I went, "Get down!"... The helicopters scared me... With a MiG, if you're spread out, its not going to see you. But a helicopter can just hover and sit on you. I was shitting it.[3]

When the helicopters departed, the MiGs turned their attention on Petrinja. In the meantime, Fersen and his comrades were able to enter the army base where they took possession of some anti-aircraft guns and more than 50 rifles. Fersen remained in the Petrinja-Sisak area for six weeks before becoming a lieutenant in a 'Special Battalion' based at Kumrovec, north-west of Zagreb. By November, however, he had had enough, and left: "Because of the money basically. I don't mind being shot at, but at least I've got to get some money for it."[4]

As an officer, Fersen was paid 16,000 dinars a month – about £140. Most of the 'Internationals' were fortunate if they received 11,000 dinars, but this did not deter the flow of eager volunteers.[5] According to Fersen, 23 American-Croats arrived from New York equipped with their own uniforms and helmets, radio sets and SWAT vests!

What was the attraction of serving as an 'International' in Croatia? Certainly not the money. When questioned, many foreign volunteers claimed they were ideologically motivated: they had seen the television and newspaper reports which, from the beginning, portrayed the Serbs as 'the bad guys' and the Croats as the defenceless underdogs. The message was simple: Croatia needed help. What Croatia received was a handful of professional soldiers and an influx of pseudo-mercenaries with little or no formal military training. Among the former were those who had seen active service and (whether or not they cared to admit it) saw in Croatia an opportunity to experience the adrenaline rush that only combat provides; while the latter group included impressionable youngsters whose notion of war owed much to Hollywood. Some looked on Croatia as some kind of romantic crusade, while almost all of them enjoyed the macho 'merc' image. But anybody could look the part.

Karl Whitburn, from Birmingham, was a member of the ZNG 110 Brigade based near Karlovac in late 1991. The former electrician and pizza-delivery-man clearly regretted his decision to come to Croatia: he was horrified by stories from the front line, and particularly concerned about what to expect if captured by the dreaded *Četnici*[6] "What they do is, first of all, cut your eyes out, cut off your ears, nose and then your balls."[7]

After returning from patrol one day, 23-year-old Whitburn left his assault rifle with his comrades in the house cellar that served as their bunker, changed into civilian clothes and returned to Zagreb and his Croatian girlfriend. Nobody tried to stop him.

Amongst the little group who remained in Karlovac were 22-year-old Ben Bronsten, from Brighton; 'Fran', a 26 year old Frenchman; and 19-year-old Andrew, from Truro, who was adamant that "We're definitely not mercenaries. I mean, strange mercenaries, with no money – well, about a hundred quid a month."[8]

'John', a Londoner, was at 33 considerably senior to his colleagues, and probably because of that tended to exert a degree of influence over them. He too intended to stay, but had drawn up a contingency plan in case he and his men needed to pull out.

We are worried about the political situation because we're getting no information at all. These guys won't tell us anything. All we can pick up is what's on the Croatian news, which is highly censored. So, we're very, very nervous about that. We certainly don't intend to get involved in a civil war. But the thing is, we could find ourselves not knowing about it... If the worst comes to the worse, we'll try to march into Slovenia, which is only 25 kilometres away... The only other way is straight up into Austria or Hungary... We're in a situation now where we don't know if we can leave.[9]

Certainly, at the time there was a degree of friction between some Croatian politicians, notably President Tuđman and Doboslav Paraga, leader of the extreme right Croatian Party of Rights (HSP), represented in the field by the Croatian Defence Force (HOS). While Tuđman retained control over the majority of Croatian forces, Paraga's HOS, although numerically inferior, were arguably more motivated, undoubtedly more aggressive, and commanded a great deal of respect, bordering on fear, within the military and political arena. Unlike the ZNG and MUP, HOS commanders were wary of most 'Internationals'. The few who were accepted tended to be those with some military experience.

'John Ward', who is believed to have served in The Parachute Regiment (TA), and Raymond Jeffrey, formerly of the Scots Guards, were probably the first mercenaries to join the HOS. They claim that soon after their arrival in Zagreb, a meeting was arranged with Paraga. According to Jeffrey:

> That day we wore our combat clothing. We took a taxi to the HOS building and made our proposal. We explained the need for a reconnaissance of the front line positions in order to assess the situation so that we could advise on what was required, on how to jack up the troops.[10]

Jeffrey and Ward were sent to Topusko, south of the capital, and subsequently presented their plan for an all-round defence of the town. Paraga was obviously impressed and hired both men as military advisers. Ward was assigned the rank of major, and his colleague became a captain. Ward:

> We then worked in the area of Topusko where we saw a bit of fighting. The Chetniks would attack the defensive positions and put up a few rounds, and when return fire came down they would about-turn and run away. Then the mortaring and

machine-gunning would start. We never saw a lot of that during the day … it always seemed to occur at last light… We never, ever, got any contacts at night.[11]

After a few weeks the two were joined by former Royal Engineer, 'Dave Tomkins'.[12] It was not uncommon for the mercenaries to be ordered into action with troops who, only minutes before, had been undergoing instruction in basic weapon handling. Fortunately, the opposition usually offered only token resistance, and sometimes none at all. One day, Ward led an ambush against eight enemy tanks. He recalled:

> They were lying on the road … so we just opened up on the lead tank with RPGs, and rattled the tank which started brewing, and the guys in the other tanks just opened the hatches and fled. It was as quick as that.[13]

Ward claimed that eventually

> We got that well known down there and were that trusted that people began sending for us. Tuđman's people were asking for us: Can the guys come down and look at this? So, we were maybe two days here and a day there… It was like a wee fun shoot, as Raymond once put it…[14]

But their popularity was not appreciated by everybody. An Australian-Croat, known as Falcon, developed an intense hatred of the mercenaries. Matters came to a head when one of Falcon's clique who joined the trio died in suspicious circumstances. Shortly after, Falcon and 16 of his men confronted the Scots. All three immediately armed themselves. It was a stand-off, with neither side keen to shoot first. Prudently, the outnumbered mercenaries decided to withdraw to the relative safety of HOS headquarters where they were entrusted with reorganizing security for Paraga, remaining until a pay dispute prompted their departure. Ward also admits they were all more than a little frustrated with the way the war was being conducted, describing the overall situation as being "like One flew over the cuckoo's nest with AK47s".[15]

Reg Walker joined the HOS at about the same time that John Ward and Ray Jeffrey left. He claimed to have served in the British army until 1983, following which he managed his own security business. As for his reasons for being in Croatia:

> If I die, I'll go into a HOS grave. I'm happy because I know I'm not a fucking hypocrite. I got off my arse and did something, the same as a lot of other geezers over here who got sick to death months ago, when they showed pictures of some of the women and children who were slaughtered outside Karlovac.[16]

Walker was particularly incensed at the apparent reluctance of Britain to involve itself:

> Where is our government? Where is our fucking government…? I voted Tory all my life and I am now ashamed of my government's lack of action. This isn't bloody Africa or the Far East. This isn't the other side of the world. This is part of Europe… This is, or was, a civilized country.[17]

Towards the end of 1991 Croatia retained a tenuous hold on what remained of eastern Slavonia. Vinkovci, a few kilometres from the shattered ruins of Vukovar, which had recently fallen to the Serbs, was defended by various police and army units. Nineteen-year-old Neil Valentine, who said he had spent "a few months in the Guards when I was about 16" was in Croatia because "I've always had a dislike for Communists, and that's basically what [the Serbs] are. Then I opened a paper and saw they had foreigners, that they were letting them in to help. So, I just got a plane ticket and went the next day."[18] In fact, Valentine flew into Belgrade, where bemused officials re-directed the politically naive youngster to Croatia! During his five weeks in Vinkovci Valentine had had ample opportunity to learn to differentiate between incoming artillery, mortar and tank fire, but had seen very little combat.

> We've had a couple of little scraps but nothing major … near Mirkovci, a couple of us went out in the middle of the night

because they had a sniper and a machine gun there. We just went 100 metres up the road from our guard-post and the sniper was very close, so we had a good shot at him for two minutes. I had a '66' [more probably a 64mm *zolja* LAW] so my mate gave me covering fire from the side of the road. I was behind this concrete box between the pavement and the road, so I jumped to the side of the road to get a clear shot. The sniper was only 70 metres from us but I think he was sort of distracted by the other guy. He was shooting at him, and the machine gun, which was about 150 metres away, was also shooting at him. But, because it was raining, the 66 didn't work. I tried for about 20 seconds, then moved back, dried it off, jumped to one side and tried again. Then I moved back, ran over to my mate and gave it to him and said, "You try it. I'll cover you." He did the same and it didn't work. While he was doing that, the sniper jumped out of the window and ran down the road.

I don't think we actually got him. The machine gun was shooting at us – around us – but we had a go at him… But there were so many trees on both sides of the road that our bullets were just bouncing off them. And since then, about two weeks ago, we haven't had any snipers come close to us, not really. They're shooting long distance now.[19]

On the outskirts of Vinkovci is the hamlet of Mala Bosna. In the winter of 1991 it was held by a handful of HOS, including 51-year-old Briton, Brian Madden, who claimed to have served with the Green Jackets in Sarawak and Aden, and with the Australian army in Vietnam. Now he was helping to defend a few houses one kilometre from Serbian territory. He was fatalistic about his prospects: "I'll stay as long as they want me. I've got nothing else to do. Nothing to do, and the rest of my life to do it in."[20]

Madden's commander at Mala Bosna probably spoke for most of his countrymen when he expressed his gratitude for such foreign allies: "We appreciate it. These lovely people – Nice guys."[21]

Keith Phillips, a former Royal Marine, had worked in airport security before boredom drove him to take advantage of a voluntary redundancy scheme at a time when he was already considering going to Croatia. He was approaching 40 and felt that it would probably be his last chance to do what he did best. Soon after, Phillips travelled by rail to Zagreb and introduced himself to an official at the Ministry of Defence. Satisfied with his credentials, the Croats assigned him to an anti-aircraft unit on the island of Pag but with little happening there, Phillips again grew bored and transferred to the MUP. Subsequently, he was recruited by a 'Special Police Anti Terrorist' group known after their commanding officer as 'Đuro's Men'. According to Phillips, the unit had taken part in more than 100 actions since its formation a year previously and not a single man had been lost. Phillips believed that this was partly due to the attitude of their CO. "We've got a real good boss. He's an incredible man. He won't send his men out on anything that he thinks is unsafe."[22] The task of 'Đuro's Men' was to carry out "jobs that the army don't want to do ... and it's normally behind enemy lines: diversion tactics, confusion. What I try to do is make them feel uneasy, because if they're looking behind them all the time, our guys have got a chance, the army have a chance to hit them from the front."[23]

Phillips maintained that his role was that of instructor and was reluctant to discuss his own involvement in any fighting, preferring instead to highlight the actions of his colleagues. They, in turn, spoke of how, in between training, Phillips accompanied the men into battle. One episode in particular did much to enhance his reputation. Over open sights, Phillips had used an FN rifle to shoot a Serb standing on a tank some 700 to 800 metres distant. The Croats were suitably impressed with such marksmanship. So was Phillips who, in fact, had been aiming at the tank itself, merely hoping that the round hitting the armour would be sufficient to deter the enemy!

Phillips is one of the few 'Internationals' to be granted Croatian citizenship. When last heard of, he had left the police to join the army, and was living in Zadar with a local girl.

For a while, Phillips and two Australian-Croats were the only overseas volunteers serving in the 150-strong police unit. Others who arrived tended not to stay long. These included Bryn Hankin, a 22-year-old former Scots Guardsman (who, according to Phillips, "cracked up") and a mysterious Frenchman, 19-year-old

Guillaume Bonhomme, who apparently was later caught returning from Serbian territory where he claimed to have been searching for his brother who was fighting for the Serbs! Another strange character was Brian, who professed to be a former captain in the United States Marine Corps and "still part of the military organization. My boss is a one star in the Navy and we go back a long way – all the way to Beirut."[24]

It was not at all clear why Brian was in Croatia, though it was later alleged that he absconded with a fortune in Croatian funds.[25] If so, he is one of a minority to have made any money out of the situation.

★　★　★

During late 1991, the Serbs in Bosnia-Herzegovina had made clear their support for a "Serbian Republic ... within the framework of Yugoslavia".[26] But at the end of February 1992, within weeks of recognition of Slovenia and Croatia by the European Community, a referendum resulted in a vote in favour of autonomy for Bosnia-Herzegovina. The Bosnian Serbs, most of whom had boycotted the referendum, responded by erecting barricades in the capital, Sarajevo. Within weeks, the situation had become critical: in scenes reminiscent of those in Slovenia and Croatia, Sarajevo's army barracks were besieged and looted. The city's terrible bombardment commenced on 6 April.

As the situation deteriorated, the UN withdrew its headquarters from the capital, and Sarajevo became a focal point for media coverage of the war, which spread rapidly throughout Bosnia-Herzegovina. With the onset of winter the situation in Sarajevo worsened: water and electricity services were severely disrupted, and there was a desperate shortage of food and medicines. From the hills around the city, Serbian gunners kept up a constant barrage, with snipers adding to the misery and mayhem.

Elsewhere, all three sides fought to retain what each considered to be their territory: in areas that were untenable, the inhabitants were killed or forced to flee and their property destroyed, leaving a no-man's land with vigilant troops quick to shoot at anybody risking entry. In the early stages, the Serbs' superior firepower enabled them to achieve significant gains in spite of a united Muslim-Croat effort. Later the alliance collapsed as territorial claims were disputed and the Bosnian Muslim army had to contend with both the Bosnian Serbs and Croats, each reinforced by their compatriots from across the border.

A number of 'Internationals' later offered their services to the Bosnian Croats and/or Muslims. Towards the end of 1991, Dobroslav Paraga had been arrested for allegedly inciting armed insurrection. Ultimately, the HOS ceased to exist as a cohesive force in Croatia, only to re-emerge at a later date in Bosnia. Tony Kendall fought with the HOS in Bosnia for several months until late 1992. In September, he was based at Ljesvojac, awaiting the arrival of a number of predominantly Turkish Mujahideen who were to be attached to the HOS as a diversion group. Kendall recalled:

Initially I did have conflicting opinions towards fighting alongside so-called 'Islamic fundamentalists', preconceived notions that I should guard my back at all times. At least in my case I need not have been too concerned, for they were both surprised and pleased to find another 'stranger' out in Bosnia fighting against the Serbs.

The majority of them had previous military or combat experience. In fact the group leader, a pensive, controlled man named Sollaiman who gave the impression of speaking more with his eyes than with his voice, had fought, along with Mahmut, another Mujahideen man, against the Soviets a few years earlier in Afghanistan...

They settled in fast, soon displaying sound weapon handling skills, personal hygiene and a professional, sober approach to warfare – characteristics that were so thin on the ground in our part of Bosnia...

After a week's acclimatisation in no-man's land, which involved the usual push and shove small arms exchange of fire, it was decided by the powers that be that our combined unit would be sent into offensive action by 104 Brigade, on the 19th of September 1992. We would be tasked with spearheading an assault into the well-fortified positions of our Chetnik counterparts at the other side of the village.

We were rallied into position at 0530. Our unit, about 50-strong, being split into two, an equal amount of Mujahideen and Croats in both squads. The Mujahideen had hoped to be fighting independently. On the day this was not the case.

I was part of the first group, located amongst the forward ruins of our territory in no-man's land, about 45-50 metres from the first Chetnik *mitrailleuse* position (heavy machine gun, believed to be .05 Browning). The second squad was 70 metres to our left flank, in a wooded area, waiting in ex HVO [Croatian Defence Council] bunkers. HVO opened up with a mortar barrage at 0630. Myself and Mahmut, the Afghan veteran, were detailed to go along with Miran, a crazy but nonetheless experienced Slovene who had been continuously fighting since the war kicked off back in Croatia. Miran was bringing up the OSA, a formidable anti-tank weapon. Both Mahmut and I were given the responsibility of providing him with cover and support whilst he selected and took out any threatening Chetnik armour.

Within no time of the HVO barrage starting, as expected, we heard the gut churning growl of a heavy engine. Then came the thick, grey billowing tell-tale smoke from the exhaust. Miran chose a suicidally dangerous vantage point amongst the roofless rafters that once passed as somebody's attic. Belly down either side of Miran, we watched and waited as the thick line of exhaust smoke drew nearer, manoeuvering its way through the shell-damaged debris in the Serbian held part of the village. The tank was about 120 metres away when Miran identified it as a T-55. By now our position was compromised and we were drawing a multitude of incoming small arms fire, as well as a hail of rifle launched *trombloni*.

Silly as it sounds, I was more concerned about falling through the many gaping holes in the roof, than of being hit by rifle fire. Miran had found his mark, just giving us enough time to prepare for the pressurised back-blast. He fired the OSA. The HEAT [High Explosive Anti Tank] projectile fell slightly wide of the target, kicking up a cloud of dust and smoke as it penetrated and demolished nearby structures. However, luck was on our side as this near miss must have provoked a degree of thought from the tank crew. Within seconds they were back-pedalling for cover and beating a tactical withdrawal. I often found that the Serbs were reluctant to aggressively commit their AFVs [Armoured Fighting Vehicles], preferring instead to use them as mobile artillery pieces from afar.

The next six hours were spent enduring at close range a relentless artillery duel – from both sides... Finally, we were told to make ready as we would be 'going in' within the next 10 minutes. One final chance to check RPGs, grenades, magazines, knives etc. We were all mustered close together, which seemed remarkably crazy and very reminiscent of World War One philosophy. Those 10 minutes seemed to drag on forever, people apprehensively clock-watching, psyching up. We all knew that not everyone would be coming back... Then with one minute to go our unit CO pops up to tell us that our assault has been called off.

The volumes of artillery fire had been totally useless at softening up the positions we were due to clear. The Chetniks, fearing an all-out attack, had massed reinforcements; whilst out of our original number of 50, we had suffered 10 casualties from shrapnel alone, and we hadn't taken an inch of Serbian territory. Among the injured were Philip, my English-speaking Croatian friend, and Mohammed from Gambia, one of only a couple of black men to join the fighting in all of Bosnia.[27]

Such events had a marked effect on unit morale, and the Mujahideen began to lose confidence in their HOS commanders. This was not improved by the cultural and religious differences between the devout Muslim 'strangers' and their more liberal Bosnian allies, which was to be a problem in many areas where the Mujahideen served. Despite this, Kendall, together with Mahmut

stayed with HOS for another couple of months, always anticipating the arrival of more Mujahideen. As often

happens in Bosnia, promises are easily made with no intention
of being kept. Within the next few weeks more European
volunteers drifted in to join our ranks. HOS formed us into a
separate group, often sending us to the most dangerous
positions where our Croatian hosts were reluctant to be. After
a total of three months solid combat at the front, I eventually
returned home to England.[28]

Croatia had largely been an artillery war, against which the Croats
could do little. Bosnia quickly developed into a much bloodier full-
scale conflict in which there was no place for inexperienced
pseudo-mercenaries.

Alan 'Bowen' (see chapter 8) arrived in Croatia in October 1991,
serving with the ZNG 'Young Lions' in Nuštar and with 110
Brigade around Karlovac, until being wounded by a mortar round
in nearby Turanj. After his recovery, Bowen continued to fight for
the Croats in Bosnia. Initially, he served in a Bosnian-Croat special
forces unit known as *Bojna Frankopan*, together with German ex
Legionnaire, Thomas Lister, and Paul, formerly of the Royal Green
Jackets. Paul was unique in that he was probably the only black
volunteer to have fought in both Croatia and Bosnia. Later, Bowen
joined the Bosnian Muslims, serving in a diversion group along
with several other 'strangers' – mainly Britons. In November 1992,
the unit was involved in a day-long battle near the village of Lokve,
close to Mount Igman.

A rapid build-up of Serbian forces in nearby Kasatiči resulted in
the Muslims rushing reinforcements to Lokve, where Bowen and
two other Britons joined three more of their countrymen already in
position and under fire in trenches between two small hills, Gaja
and Borak.

We made our way under the barrage, through the trenches
and arrived to find Bill observing the Chetnik hill opposite
with some binoculars.

"Incoming!" he shouted. Everybody ducked deep into the
trenches. There was a ripping sound as the shell passed
overhead. It impacted in some trees 100 metres behind us.
When I looked myself, I saw three T-55s about two kilometres

away. They were firing intermittently at different points along our lines.[29]

After a near miss from a Sagger wire-guided missile, the tanks withdrew. At about 1100 hours the mortar barrage intensified and a tank was heard approaching from Kasatiči.

It was an ominous sign, we decided, because where tanks went, infantry went also... We hurriedly prepared ourselves. A 60mm recoilless rifle was wheeled up, LAWs were armed and RPG-7s loaded. The tank came closer and closer. Any second now and it would appear. Then it stopped at no more than 100 metres away. It was hull down in some dead ground.

We waited nervously, anxious for something to happen. Then from the bush ahead of us we heard a noise that could only be described as sounding like a herd of elephants. "Jesus!" I said. Everybody aimed their rifles towards the noise. Then the machine-guns on the flanks of our trenches which Bill had sited with interlocking arcs of fire earlier, opened up simultaneously. It was the signal for the whole front to erupt. The heavy Browning .50 cals on the hills could be heard above the terrific noise of the battle, thudding away, turning the area ahead of us into a lethal killing ground. Hundreds of rounds were zipping overhead. The Chetniks were firing too high, which meant they couldn't see us. We could see fleeting glimpses of them running through the trees, just enough to fire controlled bursts at. After 30 minutes the firing gradually died down to periodic machine gun bursts.[30]

It was still uncertain whether the Serbs intended to launch an all-out assault, or were merely testing the defences, which had only recently been improved on the advice of the British mercenaries. Zig-zag trenches interspersed with bunkers had been constructed, and heavy machine guns strategically sited. However, in spite of their recommendation, the local commander had neglected to mine the area in front of the positions. Had he followed the Britons' advice, the Serbs might have given up after their initial attack, but when enemy mortar fire intensified it became clear that the battle was not yet over. The tank in front of Bowen's position opened up with its Browning, while Serbian infantry fired rifle grenades. Suddenly,

The mortaring stopped and the real fighting began. The Chetniks had gotten closer this time. Everybody was firing on automatic. The enemy were everywhere in front of us. The heavy machine gun on Borak to our right was thudding away, scything the area in front of us. Everybody was screaming insults at the Chetniks and firing at the same time. Then the HMG on Borak stopped firing. Seconds later rounds started coming down into our trenches. 'Shit!', shouted Howie. Dave and I switched our fire to Borak, firing over the heads of Bill and Howie who had ducked down in the trench to avoid the incoming rounds. The Browning started firing again and the rounds stopped coming our way so we continued firing in front of us. I saw a group of enemy about 120 metres away drop into dead ground. I grabbed one of the *zolje* and fired it at the trees behind them hoping to hit them with the blast, but the *zolja* missed the trees and travelled on down to Kasatiči. The firing lasted another 10 minutes then died down to the odd shot. Then the mortaring started again...

It seemed an eternity before the fighting restarted. First, Gaja erupted with machine gun fire. Seconds later, Borak came under attack. Then, right on cue, the tank ahead of us fired its main gun, followed by its Browning. The shell hit the trees behind us whilst the HMG rounds raked the trench parapet. A Muslim in the trench with Dave was hit in the shoulder by a rifle round and fell. Dave immediately started to aid him while the rest of us returned fire. Again the machine guns on the flanks swept the woods ahead of us. The Chetniks were close this time. We could see them dashing into cover over 30 metres ahead. The whole area was being saturated with small arms fire. It was unbelievable how anything could be alive in the woods. We continued firing at anything that moved... One of the Muslims fired an RPG-7 into the trees. The rocket exploded at about chest height, possibly hitting some enemy. Then two more rockets fired by one of our men on Borak hit the woods. Again the attack faltered. Over the sound of the machine guns we could clearly hear screaming from the woods. Three Chetniks broke from the wood on our left, crossing a piece of open ground hoping to reach Borak, but they were quickly dealt with by the MG42s on the hill. The enemy had by now lost heart. They had tried to break through our lines three times and each time had been beaten back.[31]

In fact, the Serbs had nearly broken through the lines at Borak, which explained how Bowen and his comrades had come under fire from that position. During the day, four Muslims were killed and nine wounded. Many more Serbs also died. Reports that the Serbs also employed mercenaries were substantiated after the battle.

At the HQ in Lokve itself, the bodies of 18 Chetniks, left behind in the enemy's' rush to get off the hills, were lying waiting to be buried. These must have been too close to our trenches for their comrades to recover. Papers on the bodies showed some to be Russian and Romanian mercenaries.[32]

★   ★   ★

In January 1993, fighting erupted again in Croatia when the Croats launched an offensive to recapture key positions around Zadar. In May an attempt to end the conflict in Bosnia-Herzegovina failed with the collapse of the much publicized Vance-Owen plan. In April, Srebrenica had been declared a UN protected 'safe area'. Under continued international pressure, and faced with the prospect of a military alliance between Bosnian Serbs and Croats, Bosnian President Alija Izetbegović agreed to the establishment of five more safe areas for Muslims in Bosnia.[33] Meanwhile, renewed fighting around Travnik culminated in Croats fleeing their erstwhile Muslim allies to seek refuge with the Serbs.

Hostilities continued through the summer and autumn of 1993. North-east of Sarajevo, Žuć was subjected to a devastating artillery barrage. South-west of the city, Muslims and Serbs battled for possession of Mounts Igman and Bjelasnica, from which the victorious Serbs would later be forced to withdraw to escape the threat of NATO airstrikes. Elsewhere, the Muslims achieved considerable success, taking control of several important towns. As Bosnia-Herzegovina entered its second winter of the war, the fighting showed little sign of abating, until the detonation of a mortar bomb over Sarajevo's market place that killed 69 and wounded more than 200 people. Although it could not be proved who was responsible, the renewed threat of NATO intervention persuaded the Serbs to pull back their heavy weapons from the vicinity of Sarajevo. By the end of February 1994, after having been under attack for 22 months, the capital was finally able to return to some semblance of normality, though the siege was to continue until September 1995.

In April 1993 Operation Deny Flight was launched to enforce a UN no-fly zone over Bosnia. On 28 February 1994, NATO carried out its first offensive action in its 45-year history, when American F-16 fighters destroyed four Serbian aircraft operating in defiance of the ban.

In March 1994 a tentative peace was negotiated between Croats and Muslims, subsequent to forming a joint federation. Towards the end of the month, there were reports of fierce fighting between Muslim and Serbian forces in central Bosnia. In the east, the UN-designated safe area of Goražde continued to come under attack by the Serbs. Relations between UN forces and the Serbs deteriorated in April with the bombing of Serbian positions by NATO aircraft and the retaliatory abduction of UN personnel. By 24 April, following the death of a British 'joint commission observer' (reported to be an SAS forward air controller) and the loss of a British Sea Harrier, from which the pilot safely ejected, the threat of further air strikes persuaded the Serbs to halt their offensive, and a fragile peace followed.

Talks aimed at securing a comprehensive cease-fire began in Geneva on 6 June 1994, and on the 8th a one-month cessation was agreed. Within days, however, fighting was reported in the north-west Bihać enclave, between Zenica and Tuzla, around Brčko, and in the area of Vozuća in the Ozren mountains. Commander of the UN forces in south-west Bosnia, Brigadier Andrew Ridgway, stated on 28 June, "There is no peace in Bosnia and no cease-fire, not even a cessation of hostilities... There will be at least 20 years of war."[34] The war did continue – for another 16 months.

Fighting was particularly fierce around the Bihać pocket where, in November 1994, a Bosnian victory was turned around by a massive Serbian counter-attack, supported by several thousand Muslims loyal to the renegade Muslim leader Fikret Abdić.

In May 1995 Croatian forces again went on the offensive and this time seized control of western Slavonia. Meanwhile, the Bosnian Muslims achieved a significant victory on Mount Vlasić. However, in July, Serbian forces took Srebrenica before closing in on Žepa. The following month, the Croats launched a massive offensive and overran much of western Krajina, including the capital, Knin.

On 28 August, another mortar bomb detonated near Sarajevo's market square killing 37 people. The UN carried out a crater analysis, announced the perpetrators to be Serbs, and launched warplanes against Serbian targets across Bosnia. The assault ended only when the Serbs grudgingly withdrew their heavy weapons from around Sarajevo. In other parts of the country, Croatian and Muslim forces took advantage of the situation and carried out a series of attacks against the Serbs.

★   ★   ★

Towards the end of 1995, Alan Bowen was presented with further evidence of mercenaries operating with the Serbs when, "we killed a Chinese volunteer on Treskavica. I saw the body myself."[35] Treskavica was the scene of one of the last major actions of the war when Muslims captured the heights overlooking the strategically important town of Trnovo. Bowen was part of a force of about 400 men tasked with establishing a new front line in order to prevent the enemy from rushing up reinforcements during the battle.

It was only supposed to be a one-day action and the front line troops would come and take over our positions. We went there with just ammunition and claymores and rockets... We ended up being there for 17 days with minimal food, no warm clothing… It was so cold at night that we had to light fires or we would have frozen to death… You had to be by the fire … and they would be trying to zero in on the fires, but you had no choice.[36]

The only accessible route in was dominated by the Serbs, making it impossible for the Muslims to relieve their comrades on Treskavica. The already desperate plight of the defenders was aggravated further when one man vanished during the night, only to be discovered dead and partially eaten by wolves.

Around 20 Muslims died on Treskavica, and many more were wounded. Amongst those killed was General Zaim Imamović, described by Bowen as "a legend in Bosnia. He was a real soldier's man, a really nice guy."[37] In spite of continuous artillery, mortar and machine gun fire and near suicidal assaults by determined Serbian troops, the Muslims succeeded in holding the heights.

We took those hills and afterwards and there were dead Chetniks all over the place. I'll give them that. They stood and fought. They didn't run away. They fucking stood and fought to the last man.[38]

★   ★   ★

In October 1995 the warring parties finally agreed to an American-brokered ceasefire and, on 21 November 1995, a peace agreement was at last signed, bringing to an end Europe's most protracted conflict since World War II.

CHAPTER 11
FOREIGN LEGIONS

Ayo Gurkhali: The Gurkhas

Gurkha – the word conjures up an image of a slight, but immensely tough, fighting man, armed with the *kukri*, the curved blade that is synonymous with these soldiers. How accurate is this perception? And who exactly are the Gurkhas?

The original definition of a Gurkha was a man of Mongolian stock from the ancient principality of Gorkha, 50 miles west of Kathmandu, whose ruler, Prithwi Narain Shah, founded Nepal in 1768. Today, a Gurkha can be any of the martial classes of Nepal, although the term is more usually associated with those in the service of the British army. Gurkhas are represented by various tribes. Many are practising Hindus with a strong undercurrent of animism, and some are Buddhists. Their association with Britain dates to the latter part of the 18th century when the East India Company was furthering its aims in India, and Prithwi Narain Shah was also expanding his domain. After the death of Prithwi Narain Shah, his successor's uncle, General Amarsing Thapa, attempted to extend Nepal's borders westward, but an attempt to push further east resulted in war with Tibet. In 1814-15, the Gorkhas' determination to expand brought them into conflict with the East India Company. Such was the Gorkhas' aggression in battle that the British took the remarkable step of inviting their adversaries to join forces with them, establishing a relationship that has endured to this day.

The Gurkhas remained loyal to Britain during the Indian Mutiny of 1857 and went on to serve in Burma, Afghanistan,

India, Malaya, Malta, Cyprus, Tibet and China. During World War I, Gurkhas fought on all the major battle fronts, earning two Victoria Crosses. From 1918 to 1939, they saw action in Afghanistan and on India's North-West Frontier. In World War II, ten VCs were awarded as further testament to their courage and ferocity.

The Gurkhas continued to be deployed in trouble spots during the post-war period, but faced a crisis on 8 August 1947, one week before India was to become independent, when it was announced that of the ten Gurkha regiments, four had been selected for service in the British army, while the remainder would exist as part of the Indian army. A referendum was held to provide the soldiers with the option to transfer from one army to the other. A few months later, there was another referendum, although this time those in the Indian army were not given the opportunity to serve in HM forces.

There followed a re-organization of the British Gurkha regiments, all of which were now under-strength. Indeed, operational requirements necessitated the deployment of recruits still in training. The Gurkhas in British service were to see active service in Malaya and Borneo, where a thirteenth VC was won. Lieutenant Colonel J P Cross served with the 1st and 7th Gurkha Rifles before becoming commandant of the Border Scouts during Confrontation in Borneo. Describing jungle conditions there, he later wrote:

> The brunt of the fighting fell on Gurkha troops. This was guerrilla warfare, when the enemy struck and faded, ambushed and withdrew, terrorised then dispersed. The Gurkhas did everything that the guerrillas did, but did it better: an achievement that resulted from their inherent martial qualities, previous operational experience of jungle warfare and a very high standard of self-discipline – an unbeatable combination. The men had to live in the jungle for weeks on end, clearing an area of enemy, holding it and dominating it. Everything that the soldier needed for this was carried on his back. Ambushes were frequently used. This involved an eye for country, noting the minutest details for tell-tale signs, track discipline, marksmanship and self

discipline – no cooking, no washing with soap, often having no hot meals, making no noise and leaving behind no signs. To do otherwise meant failure. When a man is hunted for any length of time he becomes animal-like in his sharpened senses. To win a war under such circumstances, a soldier needs more of what is normally required of him, especially in country where the jungle is thicker, vaster and hillier than it had been even in Malaya and against an enemy harder than there had been during the Malayan emergency. It was even harder when the Gurkhas were engaged in cross-border operations. Without abnormal stamina, fortitude and quick reactions, and without the complete acceptance of discomfort and danger at all times, no victory would have been possible.[1]

In the mid-1960s, defence cuts resulted in the Brigade of Gurkhas being substantially reduced: by the mid-1980s, the principal combat strength lay in five infantry battalions, with three additional support units, and various depots and smaller contingents.

Until 1997 the Gurkhas' main role was to prevent Chinese immigrants from illegally entering the British colony of Hong Kong, and to ensure stability along the Sino-Hong Kong border. The Gurkhas were also deployed on active service in 1982 following the Argentine invasion of the Falkland Islands, and later in the Gulf.

There is still no shortage of volunteers eager to serve the Crown. Of some 6,000 hopefuls who applied in 1996, about 700 met the minimum entry requirements, and, after rigorous tests, these were whittled down to just 160 recruits.[2]

Towards the end of 1996, as the Gurkhas wound down their presence in Hong Kong in preparation for its reversion to Chinese rule, a British broadsheet reported: "Those going to Britain are happy they will be getting a rise. In Hong Kong the Gurkhas were always paid significantly less than British soldiers in the garrison. The bad news is that they will not be allowed to travel with their families. It seems that the Army does not mind Gurkhas having something approaching a normal life as long as they do not do so on British soil."[3]

It was a warranted indictment. Although a long-standing agreement between Britain, India and Nepal decreed that Britain's Gurkhas were paid a similar basic wage as their counterparts in the Indian army, there was no excuse to treat such loyal and devoted soldiers any more differently from their colleagues in Her Majesty's Forces. Public outrage led to a welcome volte-face from the British Government when the armed forces minister, Nicholas Soames, announced that Gurkha soldiers withdrawn from Hong Kong could bring their families to Britain after all. Equally well received was news of a pay review which should result in Gurkhas receiving a comparable amount to their British counterparts.

By mid-1997, the Brigade of Gurkhas consisted of one infantry battalion serving in the UK as part of 5 Airborne Brigade, and another in Brunei, with squadrons in the transport, signals and engineers corps. In addition, three Gurkha Reinforcement Companies (GRCs) were created as an interim measure with the aim of filling the gaps in the British army caused by a shortage of recruits.

In Hong Kong, there was little opportunity for Gurkhas to participate in the same large-scale exercises as those conducted in Europe and elsewhere. Today, many are having to re-train as air mobile troops and to adapt to other aspects of modern warfare. The Gurkhas' long-term prospects are by no means certain. Service cut-backs and the rapid decline of British influence abroad do not auger well for the armed forces generally, but for the moment at least, Britain continues to employ this select body of men whose dedication to soldiering for its own sake is perhaps best summed up by Lieutenant Colonel Bijaykumar Rawat, the first Nepali to command an infantry battalion.

> Where do my loyalties lie? To the King of Nepal or to Her Majesty the Queen? As long as I'm in the British army, I remain loyal to Her Majesty...
>
> Our track record speaks for itself. The British army, particularly the infantry, has many problems. We don't. Unlike the average British soldier, the Gurkhas who join do so with total commitment.[4]

Honneur et Fidélité: La Légion Etrangère

As a consequence of P.C. Wren's *Beau Geste*, and several high-profile actions since 1945, the French Foreign Legion is the best-known mercenary formation in the world. Once a legendary haven for those seeking to escape their past, today's Legion can afford to be very selective about who it recruits. The disintegration of the Soviet army and drastic cuts in eastern European defence budgets have released a new generation of hardened soldiers, keen to serve under the French tricolour, and while some of the 'Belgian' recruits are Frenchmen born and bred, many Legionnaires are volunteers from all over the world, paid to fight and die for France.

The Legion's tremendous *esprit de corps* owes much to its heroic past. In July 1830, King Charles X was deposed and replaced by Louis-Philippe who authorized the formation of a 'legion of foreigners' to supplement his overstretched forces and, no doubt, to safeguard his own tenuous position. The initial intake included veterans of the Napoleonic Wars and volunteers from other troubled nations in Europe. By September 1831, five battalions had been sent to Algeria, then in the early stages of colonization by France.

In 1833 the dying King Ferdinand VII of Spain willed the throne to his infant daughter, Isabella, under the regency of her mother, Maria Cristina, setting the scene for a bitter conflict between the Queen and her brother-in-law, Don Carlos. In June 1834, Portugal, Britain and France intervened on behalf of the monarchy. What followed was a particularly savage and uncompromising civil war between the 'Carlists' and 'Cristinos'. Of the 5,000 Legionnaires who arrived in Spain in August 1835, fewer than 500 returned to France nearly two and a half years later.

During its period in Spain, the Legion underwent some important changes, switching from an infantry corps to an all-arms force with its own support and reconnaissance units, artillery and sappers, and several cavalry squadrons. Single-nationality battalions were dispensed with, so that everybody was required to serve together, united by a common language: French.

Even as the Legion was being fought to a standstill in Spain, recruiting was underway for new battalions destined for Algeria

213

where, by 1841, the Legion fielded two regiments. Between 1854 and the early 1900s, the Legion also fought in the Crimea, against the Austrians in Italy, and in Mexico where, during the Battle of Camerone on 30 April 1863, 65 Legionnaires withstood a series of attacks by an estimated 2,000 Mexicans, at the end of which just three Legionnaires remained standing. The anniversary of the battle is remembered each year by all units of the Foreign Legion.

The Legion also fought in the Franco-Prussian War, in Indo-China, Dahomey, the French Sudan, Madagascar, and in South Oran. In World War I the Legion saw active service from the Western Front to the Dardanelles, and still managed to protect French interests in Morocco where hostilities continued into the 1930s. Units also served in Syria in 1925.

During World War II, Legionnaires fought in Norway, France, Eritrea, Libya, Egypt, Tunisia, Italy, Germany, and in Indo-China where the Legion continued to serve following the Japanese surrender; this time against the local communist guerrillas. During nine years of fighting, 10,483 officers and men died. The last major battle, at Dien Bien Phu, ended in defeat for the Legion after an eight-week offensive by the Viet Minh: France withdrew from Indo-China soon after.

On 1 November 1953, the Algerian National Liberation Army (FLN) launched the first in a series of terrorist attacks in Constantine Province, initiating a war that eventually led to independence for Algeria and resulted in an uprising by Legionnaires and French paratroopers, disillusioned by politicians who seemed to have ignored their achievements in the field.

Englishman Simon Murray joined the French Foreign Legion in February 1960 at the age of 19. After basic and parachute training he was assigned to the 3rd Company, 2nd Foreign Parachute Regiment (2e REP) based at Camp Pehaut, near Phillipeville. A few days later, on 7 November 1960, he joined his regiment and commenced operations in the Djebel Aurès and Djebel Chélia. On 1 December, he was involved in his first contact when the Regiment's 2nd Company came under attack. The 3rd Company was ordered to provide covering fire. Eventually, the 1st and 4th Companies, supported by Alouette helicopter gunships, were ordered to clear the enemy positions. Fifty three Arabs were killed in return for nine dead Legionnaires and 30 wounded. Later that afternoon, the 3rd Company was ordered to clear a nearby valley, forcing any enemy towards an opening where a company of 13th Demi Brigade was deployed as a stop group. Murray provides a graphic description of the moment when he is finally confronted by the enemy:

> To my left was Martinek and beyond him Auriemma, and to my right about five yards away was Theo. I could see none of them but I could clearly hear their movements as they struggled through the bushes. In front of me was a small clearing, not more than 15 yards across, and as I edged towards it, I thought I saw the bushes move beyond me.
>
> There was a sudden scream of "*Attention!*" from Martinek and a sharp staccato burst of machine-gun fire – bullets really whistle when they pass close by. In the same second I was flat on the ground, literally squirting bullets into the bushes in front where I had seen the movement, using my gun like a hose to water roses. Theo, Martinek and Auriemma were all firing madly too, and suddenly from Theo a yell "*Grenade!*" Firing stopped with a sudden bang – all heads down and arms across the eyes – a sizzling silence while breath was held, and then the almighty blast shattered the eardrums as it careered round the valley in a bounding echo.
>
> It was an offensive grenade thrown by Theo. No shrapnel, just a blast to put the enemy heads into the earth, and as the blast was still ringing in our ears, we were all once more pouring rounds into the bushes. The sound of machine guns chasing the echo of the grenade blast was like the dying cackle of wicked demons.
>
> Screams of "*En avant. En avant.*" from the rear urged us forward – and it was over. In the bushes were three young Arabs, so full of bullets they looked like the pockmarks of some rash on their faces.[1]

That evening Murray witnessed the brutalizing effects of war after he and two others were detailed to fetch the heads of the dead Arabs so that they might be identified. In the event, only two heads were collected. The third was unrecognizable. After they were photographed, they were flung into the bushes.

There then followed an incident that I will recall to my dying day with a shudder, but which at the time caused an uproar of laughter. Some Spaniards in the 2nd Section had prepared a small cauldron of soup by adding water to the dehydrated soup packets in our rations. The *équipe* had eaten and there appeared to be a considerable amount left in the pot, so they called over a German and invited him to fill his tin mug. Just as he was about to put the cup full of soup to his lips one of the Spaniards, with a mighty guffaw, reached his hand into the cauldron and pulled out by the hair one of the Arab heads, which he had retrieved from the bushes. On looking up at the noise, one could see the scene and follow the story at a glance – the Spaniard stood there with the ghastly head dripping soup, dangling by the hair from his outstretched hand, while the German stood aghast, white as a sheet, frozen for a second, and then promptly turned and threw up. This gave rise to another guffaw from the Spaniard and his chums. There is no accounting for people's sense of humour, though I must confess at the time I laughed like hell; so did we all – that is, except the fellow who had received the soup. He never actually touched a drop. It was the nearness of the thing that made him ill, as it does when you narrowly miss a bad accident in a motor car.[2]

In January 1961, a referendum in France and Algeria resulted in a majority vote in favour of negotiations between President Charles de Gaulle and the FLN. In the meantime, military operations continued.

On 22 April, several Legion and airborne units mutinied in support of French colonists in Algeria. Murray's regiment took control of Algiers airport and stood by in anticipation of a parachute drop on Paris itself. Confusion and uncertainty prevailed until the 26th, when Murray recorded that

Challe and Salan [senior officers in the uprising] have fled –

the party is over and all is lost. Some of our officers have also disappeared. We began the long slow trek back to Philippeville.

The 1st Legion Para Regiment has been officially disbanded. They have blown up their barracks at Zeralda. It was the most magnificent *quartier* in the French army, which they built themselves from scratch, brick by brick, in the tradition of the Legion.[3]

The war continued until a cease-fire came into effect on 18 March 1962, by which time the violence had spread to Algeria's principal cities. The following month another referendum was held, resulting in an overwhelming call for independence. Algeria became independent two months later, on 2 July.

In 1969, the Legion began the first of a number of deployments in Chad. More recently it has also seen action in Zaïre when, on 19 and 20 May 1978, 2e REP jumped into Kolwezi, in Shaba Province (formerly Katanga) to rescue European residents caught up in the violence perpetrated by Katangese rebels returning from exile in Angola to re-conquer their homeland. In 1982, 2e REP was the first Legion unit to serve with the multinational peacekeeping force in the Lebanon, and in the 1990s Legionnaires saw service in the Gulf War and in the former Yugoslavia.

Today, the Legion trains for rapid action operations. Although part of the French army, it remains a small, self-contained professional force of around 8,500 men. It is a unique organization which retains much of the mystique that still appeals to the many adventurers, romantics and escapists who continue to enlist. According to one British Legionnaire

People come here because they're looking for adventure. They're young guys who have heard of the Foreign Legion, who have read about it. The second reason are those who have financial problems. They can be gamblers, they can be people who have accumulated a great number of debts. The others who have minor criminal problems, that is, they may have done a few burglaries and if they're caught this time, they could go inside for a couple of years... There are those, of course, for sentimental reasons, who have come here, who have left a girl friend. They've been very stung by their romantic failure. And you also get the ex servicemen of course.[4]

John, an American, fought in Vietnam before signing on with the Legion.

> You got some guy who's well-balanced, who wants a wife and two kids, with a little white picket fence and all this crap, you know, man, we don't need him. We need the kind of guy who ain't got any idea what he's going to do tomorrow. 'Cos if you've got a guy who's got his head functioning correctly, he don't need us. We take all these other weirdos and stick them together and make something out of it, and it works. That works well. But why someone stays here, man, is 'cos he's found something that makes his life worth living a little bit longer for.[5]

Somehow, the slow, arrogant march of the Legionnaire, his exotic uniform, his style and panache symbolise the character of France. As the attempted putsch in Algeria demonstrated, loyalty may be to the Legion first, but it is also impossible for the Legionnaire not to share an affinity with his adopted country, as Joe, a young Mexican American, explained:

> In the beginning it's hard, because it's not your country, it's not your flag. After you been here for a long time, you begin to understand what is France and you begin to love this country.[6]

Viva la muerte! La Legión Española

The early 1900s witnessed the emergence of one of Spain's most dedicated soldiers. Lieutenant Colonel José Millán Astray Terreros was a hardened veteran of 24 years' military service when, at the age of 41, he formed a special force for service against hostile tribesmen in the Spanish Protectorate of Morocco. Modelled on the French Foreign Legion, the unit was inaugurated on 4

September 1920, as *La Tercio de Extranjeros*: The Regiment of Foreigners.[1] Initially, the Legion comprised three *banderas* (battalions), four depot companies, a command and an administrative headquarters, but in the early years the structure altered as *banderas* and *tercios* (regiments) were formed, disbanded and reformed. The unit also went through various changes of identity: in 1925 it became *Tercio de Maroc* (later simplified to *Tercio*) and in 1937 was again renamed as *La Legion*, comprising the 1st and 2nd *Tercios*.

In the 1920s the Legion was constantly in action against Moroccan insurgents, suffering more than 8,000 casualties between June 1921 and June 1927. In 1934 it was deployed in mainland Spain to quell a violent insurrection launched by the militant miners' unions. Two years later, the Spanish army mounted a coup against the left-wing government in Madrid which led to three years of bitter civil war in which the Legion suffered 37,393 dead, wounded and missing.

The Legion then returned to Morocco and a relatively uneventful existence until the Moroccan declaration of independence in 1956. Thereafter, it was deployed against insurgents of the Sahara Liberation Army (SLA). In February 1958, the threat to the neighbouring French Saharan territories of Algeria and Mauritania prompted France to join with Spain in operations against the SLA. The rebels were defeated the following month. In 1961, the 1st and 2nd *Tercios* moved to Melilla and Ceuta, while the 3rd and 4th *Tercios* (formed in 1939 and 1950 respectively) retained their bases in the Spanish Sahara, where sporadic disturbances continued throughout the early 1970s. On 28 February 1976, Spain decolonized its Sahara territory, but retained the coastal enclaves of Melilla and Ceuta.

By the mid-1980s, the Legion comprised four *tercios*, all named after military heroes of the 16th and 17th centuries: the 1st *Tercio* was '*Gran Capitán*' (based at Melilla); 2nd '*Duque de Alba*' (Ceuta); 3rd '*Don Juan de Austria*' (Canary Islands), and the 4th '*Alejandro de Farnesio*' (Ronda). As Spain prepared to join NATO in the late 1980s, there were further changes that included the formation of an airborne unit – the Legion Special Operations Battalion (BOEL). In the mid-1980s the Legion discontinued its recruitment of foreigners, whose contribution had remained fairly consistent at around 10 percent, but chose to retain those who were already serving.

In 1983, Tim W (see chapter 4), formerly of the British army and South African Defence Force, arrived in Ronda in the Spanish Province of Málaga and presented himself at the Legion barracks there. Within an hour, he was taken to the mountain town of Montejaque where, the next day, he was interviewed and subjected to a cursory medical examination. Passed as fit, he signed the standard three-year contract offered to all foreign volunteers and received his kit issue. In the middle of his second night in the Legion Tim was awakened and, along with several other recruits, informed that they were to leave for North Africa.

> I got the train down to Algeciras. The ferry took about an hour, an hour and a half, over to Ceuta. From there I went to the Legion Headquarters, called the *Serio*... From there I was assigned to the 5th *Bandera*... We were allotted companies, and I got the 6th, along with another foreigner – a Pakistani – and a Spanish national serviceman.[2]

The enlistment procedure seemed surprisingly straightforward:

> The thing that struck me about it is how easy it would be to join the Legion if you were a criminal or on the run ... because there is absolutely no checking up. You don't even need a passport to join. You just have to give them a signed declaration of who you are.[3]

In this respect there was very little difference between the Legion of the mid-1980s and the tradition of anonymity established by Millán Astray, who was concerned only with a man's fighting ability. Willingness to sacrifice oneself for the Legion and Spain was the prime requisite for the 1920s Legionnaire. It was a spirit that apparently continued to prevail.

> There is a lot of emphasis on learning what they call the *espíritus* – the Creed – of the Legion. There are 12 you have to

learn off by heart, and two or three of these are recited every night… I had to learn them all under threat of violence.[4]

The Creed of the Legion is a legacy of its founder and provides an insight into the mentality of the man and the ethos of his creation.

The spirit of the Legionnaire is unique and without equal; blind and fiercely combative, seeking always to close in on the enemy with the bayonet.

The spirit of comradeship, with the sacred oath never to abandon a man in the field even if all perish.

The spirit of friendship, sworn between each two men.

The spirit of unity and succour. At the cry of "To me the Legion", wherever they may be, all will go to the rescue and, with or without reason, defend the Legionnaire who called for aid.

The spirit of marching. A Legionnaire will never say he is tired until he collapses with exhaustion; the corps will be the swiftest and toughest.

The spirit of perseverance and endurance. He will never complain of fatigue, nor of pain, nor of hunger, nor of thirst, nor of drowsiness; he will do all tasks, will dig, will haul cannons, vehicles; he will man outposts, escort convoys, he will work on whatever he is ordered.

The spirit of seeking battle. The Legion, from the lone man to the entire Legion, will hasten always to where firing is heard, by day, by night, always, always, even though not ordered to do so.

The spirit of discipline: Fulfill one's duty, obedience until death.

The spirit of combat: The Legion will demand always, always, to fight without turning, without counting the days, nor the months, nor the years.

The spirit of death: To die in combat is the greatest honour. One does not die more than once. Death comes without pain and to die is not as horrible as it appears. More horrible is to live as a coward.

The flag of the Legion will be the most glorious because it will be stained with the blood of its Legionnaires.

All Legionnaires are brave; each nation is famous for its courage; here it is necessary to demonstrate which people are the most valiant.

Recruits also had to learn traditional Legion songs, and familiarize themselves with the unit's short and bloody history. Easiest to remember was the Legion's battle cry, *Viva la Muerte!* – 'Long live Death!'

Until NATO's acceptance of Spain, Legion instructors relied on brutal intimidation of the hapless recruits to instil basic military skills. A typical example was weapons training where a recruit was required to demonstrate his marksmanship by shooting at a standard Figure 11 target. A poor shot was often rewarded with a beating about the head! It was rarely explained where he had gone wrong, let alone how to correct his error. No doubt because of his previous military service, Tim was fortunate to qualify as a trained Legionnaire in just 10 days as opposed to the more typical three months. He soon learned that discipline was severely maintained even after training. Originally, the Legion had a punishment squad attached to each *bandera* where miscreants were subjected to constant hard labour under the most appalling conditions. Sixty years on, a term in a Legion jail was still a terrifying prospect. Military prisons are notoriously unpleasant, but those of the Legion were particularly barbaric. According to Tim:

> [Jail] was frightening... There used to be a big black guy running the jail, another foreigner... All the Spanish hated him. He used to beat them about in jail. They slept outside, on a concrete floor, with just a blanket over them... When the guards felt like it, they threw buckets of water over them, or beat them up.[5]

Chris Nash, another Englishman, joined the Legion when he was just 17. His experiences have left him with bitter and painful memories.

> The Spanish idea of discipline is based on fear... If the strict code of discipline is broken, the offender is liable to

imprisonment. This involves extremely hard labour. At the time I was in the Legion you could, in certain circumstances, be shot.[6]

Soon after enlisting Nash was arrested and, without explanation, assigned to *La Sección de Trabajo* – the Work Section.

I found myself digging holes from 0400 to 1900 hours, and it was not until I was released that I realised just how long I had been sentenced for and why. I was actually given 60 days hard labour for going into an out-of-bounds area that I did not even know was out-of-bounds… I was the only non-Spaniard in the prison at the time, and I was the only one who got unrealistic amounts of food and water, and the only one who was consistently beaten by a certain Spanish corporal who was always drunk.[7]

The NCO continued to taunt Nash until, finally, the young Englishman could take no more.

This cunt, he used to come and stand behind me. Only me, straight at me … and he would breathe all over me, and I would never look at him, and he would hit me on the back… He was a nasty piece of work, and in the end I lost my fucking temper with him. I didn't care any more. All the skin was off my hands … raw skin, blister upon blister upon blister, until there was no skin there at all … I went for him with a pick, but it slipped out of my hands and it didn't get him how I wanted it to … it pushed him over. I thought I was going to get done then… I just didn't care anymore, but surprisingly enough he got up and shook my hand, and after that day I had no trouble with him. He said he was testing me all along, but that's bollocks. I scared him because I went to kill him, and that's all there is to it.[8]

The corporal later mysteriously vanished while on a ship destined for North Africa.

Nash served a total of 11 months imprisonment, mostly in *Fuerte Militar Maria Cristina*, the Legion's military prison. For much of the time he was held in solitary confinement, known as 'the box'.

> It's about the size of a wardrobe. You can't stand up in it. You can't lie down in it. You just squat, and it stinks of piss and shit and fucking blood, and it's just mud walls all around you.[9]

The guards ensured that Nash remained disorientated by serving his meals at irregular intervals. He soon lost all sense of time. Not that it really mattered as prisoners never knew how long they would be inside the box anyway.

In the field, the Legion devoted much time to that great test of stamina, the route march. Legionnaires covered long distances over very rugged terrain, though at a relatively gentle pace interspersed with frequent rest-stops. The combat effectiveness of the Legionnaire was limited by his reliance on his officer and lack of training in advanced weaponry and modern warfare. Tactics consisted primarily of skirmishing in line abreast and, occasionally, flanking attacks. In this regard, the Legion was surprisingly parochial, and not far removed from the methods used against its original enemy in 1920s Morocco.

By the early 1980s the Legion had acknowledged the need for better-trained troops with the introduction of a Special Operations Unit (OLEU) and Special Operations Sections (SOE). The former was essentially a commando group consisting primarily of Spaniards, while the latter were specialist platoons within the *banderas* In between his brushes with authority, Chris Nash was assigned to the SOE.

> SOE are very fit, very fit. Incredibly so, in fact. They're also very well disciplined. An officer only has to snap his fingers and you jump to it... SOE has a more professional attitude towards it all. There are certain rules and regulations that you won't bend like, smoke a cigarette ... and you're out of SOE... They'll give you a good hiding and kick you out. If you drink to excess, you're out... SOE are shit-hot as far as discipline and physical fitness are concerned ... and weapons training.[10]

While in the SOE Nash took part in mainly routine border patrols in Morocco, but on one occasion he was involved in an unofficial raid in reprisal for a number of Legionnaires who became critically ill after eating food believed to have been poisoned by the Moroccans.

> I knew something was going down when all of SOE were mustered for a briefing… About 30 to 32 members of SOE, including myself, went over the border illegally – just picked up the barbed wire fence and drove in. There was nothing to stop you.
>
> I got the impression that the target was purely a random choice … but I later heard that undercover agents from the Legion had obtained information leading to those responsible for poisoning the food… We drove into the village in two big American-made trucks and a couple of Land Rovers, all armed with SMGs and plastic grenades [shrapnel-filled bombs in plastic casing]. We went into this village and ransacked little houses. They shot little kids and that. Some of them got a bit carried away and started doing the old business, a bit of rape here and there – but they were going for the young males. They are a nasty piece of work…
>
> My group consisted of eight men and a sergeant. We just kicked down the doors went into the houses, smashed the women if they started getting out of order, and wasted the blokes… We weren't even shot at. It was murder, if you like.[11]

Tim W, who also served in SOE, recalled only the boredom and monotony of repetitive training, guard duties and inspections, and the temporary respite of the *maison* (canteen) and weekend excursions into town. After one year in the Legion, he went absent without leave and returned to England.

By the time he was released from *Maria Cristina*, Chris Nash had served nearly three years in the Legion and was looking forward to his discharge. He was in for a rude shock.

> When I came out, my Captain wanted to see me. He said there was something I didn't read in my contract. There was no

contract – I didn't sign a fucking contract in the first place, but he was saying, "There's something we ought to point out… When you joined the Legion, you signed on for three years, but if you go to *Seccion de Trabajo*, you have to serve twice that amount again." In other words, I had to do four months more. And, if you go to *Maria Cristina* … you have to do triple that time again. So, I was looking at another 27 months, plus four months.[12]

Nash promptly went AWOL and made his way to Casablanca disguised for part of the journey as a Moroccan. At Casablanca, he boarded an Air France flight to Paris, arriving in England soon after.

In October 1991, Nash took a great risk by returning to Melilla. He was accompanied by journalist, Richard Grant, whose account of the trip was published in a popular men's magazine a few months later.[13] Even after eight years, Nash found the sight of *Maria Cristina* disconcerting. Just as disturbing was a reunion with a former comrade, a Frenchman of 28, who was the same age as Nash but looked years older. He had forgotten how to converse in English, and even found it difficult to remember his own language. He now spoke only the gutter Spanish of the Legionnaire. After 11 years in *La Legión*, he knew no other life. No doubt, Millán Astray would have been proud of him.

CHAPTER 12
INTO THE 21st CENTURY

Thirty-five years ago, the emergence of organized groups of mercenaries in the Congo caused consternation in a world no longer accustomed to 'private armies'. But the Congo was an anomaly in that, for years afterwards it remained the only major mercenary venture to have achieved its purpose. Individuals and small teams contrived to operate in Africa and elsewhere, but never on the same scale or with the same degree of success as Mike Hoare and 5 Commando (see chapter 1).

This book describes some of the operations in which mercenaries have been involved since the 1960s. It would take several volumes to adequately describe all such events, which include the Yemen (1960s), Lebanon (1970s and early 1980s), Nicaragua (1980s) and Afghanistan (1980s).

In addition to these major conflicts, there have been more minor operations, such as that involving former Royal Marine 'Gus' (see chapter 8), who took charge of the forces of Sheikh Saqr Bin Mohammed Al-Qasimi of Sharjah and Ras-Al Khamani in the United Arab Emirates in the early 1980s. Gus was later involved in a 'training mission' for RENAMO guerrillas in Mozambique. In March 1986, there was an abortive operation which led to the arrest and imprisonment in Brazil of eight Americans en route to overthrow Flight Lieutenant Jerry Rawlings of Ghana. (Four later escaped and the rest were released following extradition to Argentina.) In October 1987, there were reports of German, French, Australian and New Zealand pilots flying Mirage F-1s for Iraq against Iranian targets. An estimated 400 , mainly Tamil, mercenaries, tried and failed to oust President Maumoon Abdul

Gayoom of the Maldives in November 1988. In February 1990, at least two New Zealand helicopter pilots were revealed to be working for a company under contract to the Papua New Guinea Defence Force (PNGDF) in Bougainville.

Seven years later, Bougainville made headline news when it was disclosed that "The PNG government has contracted Sandline International, a Bahamian registered company with representative offices in London and Washington DC to assist it in its operations against rebels in the island of Bougainville who have been fighting the authorities."[1] The report went on to explain that Sandline had sub-contracted work in PNG to Executive Outcomes (EO), a South African company. Three weeks later, at least 40 employees were apprehended by members of the PNGDF loyal to Brigadier General Jerry Singirok, who had been dismissed as Defence Force Commander after he condemned his government's decision to use foreign military 'advisers' and called for the resignation of Prime Minister, Sir Julius Chan. Amongst those held was Tim Spicer, a former Lieutenant Colonel in the Scots Guards, and chief executive officer of Sandline International. All were later released.

For decades, governments have provided military training and facilities to overseas clients. British tax-payers would no doubt be appalled to learn just what they have helped to fund. Sometimes, however, costs are met by the client, as in the case of salaries for British service personnel on loan to the Sultan of Oman's armed forces.

It was inevitable that, sooner or later, suitably qualified individuals would also realize that they could supply such services. The benefits were obvious. A private company would not necessarily be hindered by factors that sometimes restrict official organizations; it could tender for contracts considered too sensitive for direct government involvement; it could also operate on behalf of commercial corporations with a vested interest in restoring order in certain volatile regions.

In the late 1960s, Colonel David Stirling, founder of the Special Air Service in World War II, formed Watchguard International to provide specialist military services for those governments able to afford them. Another firm associated with retired SAS officers was KMS (supposedly an abbreviation of Keeni-Meeni Services, *Keeni*

Meeni being an SAS term for undercover operations in Aden in the 1960s). In the 1980s, KMS reportedly operated on behalf of the Sultan of Oman, the Sri Lankan government and the Contras in Honduras/Nicaragua, and was allegedly involved in Afghanistan. Another company, Gurkha Security Guards (GSG) Limited, attracted considerable media attention following the disappearance of one employee, Andy Myers, and the death of another, Bob MacKenzie (see chapters 2 and 4), in Sierra Leone in February 1995.

America's Military Personnel and Resources Incorporated (MPRI), officially a private enterprise but thought to be affiliated with the CIA and/or other US intelligence agencies, is behind the training of Croatian and Bosnian Muslim forces in the former Yugoslavia and has been linked with operations in Zaïre in early 1997. MPRI employs senior ex US military and intelligence personnel. Its main competitor, Executive Outcomes, tends to recruit from black and white former SADF officers and men who can readily adapt to a role not dissimilar to that for which they were originally trained.

Executive Outcomes, formed in 1989, is managed by Eeben Barlow, a former officer in the SADF's 32 Battalion and military intelligence. The company provides services ranging from mechanized infantry and armour to amphibious and air force training and support. In 1993, EO secured its first major contract, to help the Angolan government in its ongoing campaign against UNITA; and for the next two years veterans of South Africa's border war found themselves assisting a former enemy against their erstwhile allies, who were eventually prompted to re-enter negotiations for a peace settlement.

The Angola contract ended at the end of 1995, by which time EO had already been hired by the National Provisional Ruling Council of Sierra Leone to put down a rebellion by the Revolutionary United Front (RUF) subsequent to the involvement of GSG earlier in the year. Between May 1995 and its withdrawal from Sierra Leone in February 1997, EO succeeded in driving the RUF from the capital, Freetown, and was instrumental in seizing important economic and strategic assets, including the diamond mining region of Kono, in the eastern Province. Within twelve months of EO's arrival in Sierra Leone, the country was able to hold its first multi-party elections for nearly 20 years. In a shrewd move, guaranteed to weaken the resolve of even the most hard-nosed cynic, the company involved itself in a 'hearts and minds' campaign, working with aid agencies and government officials to rehabilitate child soldiers, many of whom were dependent on alcohol and narcotics. EO also helped to resettle displaced persons and provided security, logistics and intelligence for humanitarian organizations.

In just seven years, Executive Outcomes had developed into a multi-million-pound business with powerful allies, believed to include South Africa's Strategic Resource Corporation (SRC), Heritage Oil and Gas, and Britain's Branch Energy (since taken over by the Canadian-based company DiamondWorks). The existence of EO is symptomatic of the failure of the international community and local leaders to prevent the economic, social and political breakdown of many states in Africa. But, as events in Papua New Guinea have shown, EO is keen to extend its area of operations. Further indication is provided by an unconfirmed report that the company orchestrated a highly successful hostage rescue operation in Indonesia in 1996, generally believed to be the work of Britain's Special Air Service.

The privatization of war is a concept that may become a feature of 21st-century conflicts, and if recent successes are indicative of its future performance, EO will no doubt remain at the forefront of those companies seeking to cash in on this extremely lucrative business.

★ ★ ★

As EO wound down its activities in Sierra Leone, another mercenary operation was underway in Zaïre. President Mobutu Sése Séko whose take-over of the Congo in the 1960s owed much to the achievements of 5 Commando (see chapter 1) had sought the assistance of mercenary troops to safeguard his regime from an uprising by predominantly Zaïrean Banyamulenge Tutsi rebels led by Laurent Kabila, an opponent of Mobutu since the former's own pro-Lumumbaist days in the early 1960s.

It was not the first time that Mobutu had been threatened. Kabila is thought to have been involved in a bid to overthrow the government in 1977, and in 1978 there was a coup attempt by Katangese exiles and other dissidents who crossed into Zaïre from neighbouring Angola. That both efforts failed is due primarily to foreign (notably French) intervention. But opposition to Mobutu increased as the economic situation in Zaïre continued to deteriorate, largely as a result of government mismanagement and corruption. In 1989, the US State Department estimated the President's personal wealth at over five billion dollars, equivalent to the national debt of his country.[2]

On 30 October 1996, fighting was reported in eastern Zaïre as Banyamulenge Tutsis seized Uvira before sweeping through areas inhabited mainly by refugees and remnants of the defeated Hutu forces which had taken refuge across the border following the genocide of Tutsis during the 1994 Rwandan civil war. The rebel forces were supported by Rwanda and Uganda, just two of the countries troubled by insurgents who had operated from safe havens provided by Mobutu. In the coming months, thousands of displaced Hutus would perish. Hutu soldiers and *interahamwe* Hutu militiamen were accused of using civilians as a human shield against rebel attacks, and there were confusing reports of Hutus being murdered by both Hutu extremists and rebel forces. Aid workers attempting to alleviate the suffering were sometimes impeded by Zaïreans and rebels opposed to relief efforts that benefited their enemies.

As the Alliance of Democratic Forces for Liberation Congo-Zaïre (ADFL) advanced deeper into Zaïre, a number of white mercenaries arrived to bolster the demoralized Zaïrean Army. It was claimed that three combat aircraft, pilots and technicians, and "at least 80 mercenaries" (presumably ground forces) were provided in a covert operation by French intelligence in January 1997.[3] Another source maintained that some of those hired were recruited by Congo veteran Christian Tavernier (see chapter 1), who was then apparently arrested and jailed in Kinshasa on suspicion of defrauding the government of funds intended for the war effort. He was later released and fled to Brazzaville.[4] While most of the mercenaries seem to have been Serbs, reports also indicated the presence of other nationalities particularly French, Belgians and, later, Moroccans, none of whom were able to prevent the rebel advance.[5]

President Mobutu was often absent from Zaïre during this critical period. It was common knowledge that he was suffering from cancer and alternated much of his time between hospitals and his villa in the south of France. He was in France when, in mid-March 1997, it was announced that Zaïre's third largest city, Kisangani (formerly Stanleyville), had fallen. On the 21st, the ailing President finally returned to his homeland. By this time, the rebels were in control of an estimated 30 percent of the country; his army was disintegrating, and parliament had just passed a vote of no confidence in the Prime Minister, Leon Kengo wa Dondo. In desperation Mobutu declared his willingness to "share power" with Kabila. The offer was promptly rejected. However, representatives from both sides agreed to attend a summit in Togo with other African leaders and Kofi Annan, the United Nations Secretary General, which led to further negotiations between Alliance and government envoys in South Africa.

In the meantime, France, Belgium, Britain and America prepared to intervene militarily in case it became necessary to evacuate their nationals in Zaïre, particularly if the rebels attacked Kinshasa (formerly Léopoldville). On 2 April, Etienne Tshiksekedi, a long-time rival of the President, was appointed as the new Prime Minister. He immediately excluded Mobutu's supporters from his Cabinet, reserving six ministries for Kabila's rebels, an offer that was rejected by a rebel official. The following week, he was dismissed and replaced by General Likulia Balongo, which led to riots in Kinshasa. At the same time, rebel forces entered Lubumbashi (formerly Elizabethville) and America called for Mobutu to resign. Kinshasa was now the only city still in government hands. On 22 April, France, Mobutu's last Western ally, distanced itself from the Zaïrean President by calling for a transitional government. Twelve days later, Mobutu and Kabila met aboard a South African warship, the *Outeniqua,* for talks hosted by South Africa's President Nelson Mandela and chaired by UN Special Envoy, Mohammed Sahnoun. Neither party was able to reach an agreement. When a second meeting was arranged for Wednesday 14 May, Kabila failed to attend.

Mobutu returned to Kinshasa, to be advised by senior officers that they could not and would not defend the city. On the 16th, the President left for Gbadolite, his jungle palace in the north, on the first stage of his journey into exile. The rebels marched into the capital the next day, whereupon Kabila assumed control of the country which was immediately renamed the Democratic Republic of the Congo. Kabila, a former enemy of Mobutu's former Western allies, was now viewed as a preferable alternative by the governments of those same nations upon which Mobutu's rise and fall had so depended.

In September 1997, four months after he was obliged to flee the Congo, Mobutu Sése Séko succumbed to his illness and died in exile in the Moroccan capital, Rabat.

★   ★   ★

Recent events seem to favour properly funded, well-equipped and expertly led mercenary operations such as those conducted by Executive Outcomes in Angola and Sierra Leone. The same cannot be said for the more traditional methods which were successful in the past, but proved disasterous in the Congo in 1997, although such failures will hardly deter those individuals seeking to fight in someone else's war.

NOTES

CHAPTER 1
A CALL TO ARMS: THE CONGO AND
5 COMMANDO, 1960-68

1. In January, 1961, the Léopoldville government disposed of Lumumba by the simple expedient of flying him to Elizabethville. According to Anthony Mockler writing in *The New Mercenaries* (Sidgwick & Jackson, HB), 1985, pp 43-44, Lumumba was probably struck with a bayonet by Tshombe's Minister of the Interior, Godéfroid Munongo, and then shot in the head by a Belgian mercenary named Ruys. However, Jerry Puren, in *Mercenary Commander* (Galago, HB), 1986, p 21 believes that Munongo would not have disposed of such a valuable political pawn, and infers that the killing was carried out on the orders of Colonel Mobutu.
2. Jerry Puren, *Mercenary Commander*, p 52.
3. Pierre Mulele was eventually executed on the orders of then President Mobutu.
4. Jerry Puren, *Mercenary Commander*, pp 189-90.
5. Mike Hoare, *Congo Mercenary* (Robert Hale), 1967. Republished as *Mercenary* (Corgi, PB), 1968.
6. Mike Hoare, *Mercenary* (Corgi, PB), 1980, pp 44-50.
7. Mike Hoare, *Mercenary*, p 79.
8. Mike Hoare, *Mercenary*, p 233.
9. Amongst the Cuban 'advisers' assisting the rebels at this time was the revolutionary leader, Che Guevara.
10. Kimba and three other former Cabinet Ministers were executed on 2 June 1966, for their alleged involvement in a plot to kill Mobutu.
11. An account of the uprising is provided by Anthony Mockler, *The New Mercenaries*, pp 82-83. Further details are to be found in the account by Jerry Puren, *Mercenary Commander*, pp 225-29.

12. In April 1986, Schramme was sentenced in absentia by a Belgian court to 20 years' imprisonment for the murder of Quintin.
13. Although the perpetrators have never been identified, it is assumed that the CIA financed and planned Tshombe's abduction.
14. Jerry Puren, *Mercenary Commander*, pp 266-67.

CHAPTER 2
RHODESIA, 1966-79

1. Barbara Cole, *The Elite, The Story of the Rhodesian Special Air Service* (Three Knights, HB), 1984, pp 31-35; and David Martin and Phyllis Johnson, *The Struggle for Zimbabwe* (Faber and Faber, HB), 1981, p 9.
2. Barbara Cole, *The Elite*, pp 45-53.
3. Rhodesian Army recruiting brochure *This is The Army*, p 2.
4. Anthony Rogers, adapted from 'Fireforce Ops with the Rhodesian Light Infantry', *Combat and Survival*, June 1989.
5. Letter dated 9 September 1985, from Dave Armstrong to the family of John Coey. An account of this action by Barbara Cole in *The Elite*, pp 85-89, differs slightly in the sequence of events as she mentions only two wounded, as opposed to the four indicated by Armstrong.
6. Dave Armstrong, letter to the family of John Coey.
7. Account provided by Derek Andrews in February 1997.
8. Derek Andrews, February 1997.
9. Barbara Cole, *The Elite*, pp 176-80.
10. Robert Mackenzie, 'Fast Strike on Chimoio II', *Soldier of Fortune* February 1994.
11. Robert Mackenzie, 'Fast Strike on Chimoio II'.
12. Peter McAleese, *No Mean Soldier* (Orion, HB), 1993, p 109.
13. John Foran, letter to the author, 3 April 1990.
14. John Foran, April 1990.
15. Tony Y, letter dated 12 December 1978.
16. Guerrilla casualty figures from Al J Venter's *The Chopper Boys* (Greenhill Books, HB), 1994, p 122. RLI casualties from the author's diaries.
17. Author's personal diary.

CHAPTER 3
ANGOLAN FIASCO:
'COLONEL CALLAN'S' MERCENARIES, 1975-76

1.	In fact the operation, codename 'Savannah' , actually began two months earlier, in August 1975, when South African forces entered southern Angola to safeguard national interests in the Calueque/Ruacana hydroelectric complex.
2.	The role in Angola of 'Colonel Callan' and his mercenaries has been described in several publications. Certainly the most detailed account (though not necessarily wholly accurate) is that by Chris Dempster, Dave Tomkins and Michel Parry, *Fire Power* (Corgi, PB), 1978. Other books referred to include that by Wilfred Burchett and Derek Roebuck, *The Whores of War* (Penguin, PB), 1977; Peter Tickler, *The Modern Mercenary* (Patrick Stephens, HB), 1987; Peter McAleese and Mark Bles, *No Mean Soldier* (Orion, HB), 1993; Anthony Mockler, *The New Mercenaries* (Sidgwick & Jackson, HB), 1985.
3.	Another account, attributed to 'Brummie' Barker, gives the date of McAleese's departure to Santo Antonio do Zaïre as 21 January: Wilfred Burchett and Derek Roebuck, *The Whores of War*, p 91.
4.	Dave Tomkins, interviewed 2 December 1996.
5.	This is one, unconfirmed, version of how Ako Joseph Nai became separated from the other mercenaries. He later surrendered, or was captured, and provided a statement for the court during Callan's trial.
6.	John 'Spider' Kelly, interviewed 13 November 1996. A somewhat different version of the meeting between Callan and Banks is provided in the account by Chris Dempster, Dave Tomkins and Michel Parry, *Fire Power*, pp 293-95.
7.	Wilfred Burchett and Derek Roebuck, *The Whores of War*, pp 102-3.
8.	Wilfred Burchett and Derek Roebuck, *The Whores of War*, pp 103-4.
9.	Wilfred Burchett and Derek Roebuck, *The Whores of War*, p 104.
10.	In their book, *Fire Power*, p 330, Chris Dempster, Dave Tomkins and Michel Parry state that the report of Tômboco having fallen was a "false alarm". Anthony Mockler, in his account, *The New Mercenaries*, pp 192-93, wrote "Callan had found the 'enemy column' that had captured Tômboco to be a comparatively small affair. He had run headlong into it – a tank, a troop carrier and some MPLA infantry – with his 'killer group'. According to Tom Chambers, a member of Callan's group who claimed to have fought

previously for the Nigerians in Biafra, Callan had reacted more quickly. The group had routed the enemy, killing 20; and then Callan personally, to Chambers' horror, had shot eight prisoners. Leaving a small detachment in possession of Tômboco, they had made their way back to the 'palace' at São Salvador for the night."

11. According to Wilfred Burchett and Derek Roebuck, *The Whores of War*, p 105, the executed man was David Wileman. Other accounts name Michael Wileman as one of those executed.

12. Wilfred Burchett and Derek Roebuck, *The Whores of War*, p 105.

13. As many as 14 men, including the one killed personally by Callan, may have died.

14. In his account, *The Modern Mercenary*, p 173, Peter Tickler quotes Colin Evans as stating that the mercenaries destroyed three tanks and killed 163 enemy troops. In the account by Chris Dempster, Dave Tomkins and Michel Parry, *Fire Power*, pp 352-54, Dempster says Callan told him that four tanks were knocked out and an estimated 200 enemy were killed or wounded in return for 11 mercenaries wounded. (Three more were killed and eight wounded by a land mine prior to the ambush).

15. Peter Tickler, *The Modern Mercenary*, pp 173-74. In the account by Chris Dempster, Dave Tomkins and Michel Parry, *Fire Power*, pp 363-67, Dempster relates how 'Sammy' Copeland told him that Callan's team carried out four hit-and-run attacks.

16. Chris Dempster, Dave Tomkins and Michael Parry in *Fire Power*, p 367, claim that according to Copeland, 'Ginger' died during the night from loss of blood. In Wilfred Burchett and Derek Roebuck, *The Whores of War*, p 125, Kevin Marchant recalled, 'Ginger, who had a broken leg, had asked us to leave him where he was and we left him. When Callan heard this, about 20 minutes after the explosion, he sent a group to go and fetch Ginger. There were four or five men. I never heard or saw any more of them.'

17. João Antonio and his wife later gave evidence during the trial of those captured.

18. Kevin Marchant, quoted in Wilfred Burchett and Derek Roebuck, *The Whores of War*, pp 130-31.

19. Chris Dempster, Dave Tomkins and Michel Parry in *Fire Power* are unclear about the precise dating of events. A case in point is the death of Vic Gawthrop, an alleged MI6 agent, who is reported to have died during a patrol led by 'Canada' Newby on 10 February (p 423) and, apparently, while on patrol with Callan a week or so earlier (p 350). Wilfred Burchett and Derek Roebuck in *The Whores of War*, p 48, stated that Vic Gawthrop's brother, Brian, another Angola mercenary, confirmed the date as 9 February.

CHAPTER 4
FROM RHODESIA TO SOUTH AFRICA:
SADF, 1975-82

RECCES: RECONNAISSANCE COMMANDOS, 1980-83

1.   Jean C, taped account, c. early 1997.
2.   Jean C, 1997.
3.   Jean C, 1997.
4.   Jean C, 1997.
5.   Jean C, 1997.
6.   Jean C, 1997.
7.   Jean C, 1997.
8.   Portuguese and ANC casualty figures provided by Gavin Cawthra, *Brutal Force, The Apartheid War Machine* (IADF, PB), 1986, p 163. According to Helmoed-Romer Heitmann, *The South African War Machine* (Bison Books, HB), 1985, p 178, "The SADF estimated that 30 ANC personnel had been killed in the raid, while the Mozambique Government claimed that 11 ANC members and one civilian had died."
9.   Jean C, taped account, c. early 1997.
10.   Paul, taped account, 9 May 1997.
11.   Paul, May 1997.
12.   Paul, May 1997.
13.   Paul, May 1997. Much later, Paul was offered another, more plausible explanation. According to a source said to be involved with processing the material, the crates contained British South Africa Police secret files.
14.   Paul, May 1997.
15.   Gordon Harland, interviewed 27 February 1997.

OS TERRIVIS – THE TERRIFYING ONES:
32 BATTALION, 1975-89

1.   AI J Venter, 'Firefight!', *SCOPE* magazine, 11 September 1981.
2.   Colonel Jan Breytenbach, *They Live By The Sword* (Lemur Books, HB), 1990, p 171.
3.   Nigel W, interviewed c.1984-85.
4.   Letter from Tim W to the author, c.1985-86.
5.   Tim W, interviewed c.1985-86.
6.   Nigel W, interviewed c.1984-85. Since Nigel gave his interview much has been published about 32 Battalion, including two books

by Colonel Jan Breytenbach (see selected bibliography listing at the end of this book). Even so, relatively little is available about the contribution made by former members of the Rhodesian Security Forces who served in the unit.

7. During the major (publicized) deployments by the SADF, such as Operation Protea in 1981, those in 32 Battalion usually wore regulation South African uniforms and carried standard issue weapons.

8. Nigel W, interviewed c.1984-85.

9. Nigel W, c.1984-85.

PHILISTINES:
PATHFINDER COMPANY,
44 PARACHUTE BRIGADE, 1980-82

1. Sean Wyatt, taped account provided to the author, 31 July 1992.
2. Sean Wyatt, July 1992.
3. Sean Wyatt, July 1992.
4. Account provided by Sean Wyatt in January 1990.
5. Sean Wyatt taped account, July 1992
6. Ken Gaudet, 'Angolan Firefight', *Soldier of Fortune* magazine, September 1987.
7. Ken Gaudet, 'Angolan Firefight'.
8. Ken Gaudet, 'Angolan Firefight'.
9. Ken Gaudet in 'Angolan Firefight' states that two South Africans were killed and five wounded; 71 SWAPO killed, five captured and an unknown number wounded. Peter McAleese and Mark Bles, *No Mean Soldier* (Orion, HB), 1993, p 163, indicate that the SADF lost three killed and five wounded. In 'Combat', an article by Al Venter in *SCOPE* magazine, 13 March 1981, two South Africans and 66 enemy troops are stated to have died. Colonel Jan Breytenbach, *They Live By The Sword* (Lemur Books, HB), 1990, p 185, mentions 96 SWAPO fatalities.
10. The DSIR was responsible for the development of the more esoteric vehicles used in South Africa's bush war. The Pathfinders' patrol vehicle, known as the 'Jackal', also included refinements such as a strengthened chassis, extra fuel tanks (which, together with those already installed, were fitted with multi-mesh aluminium to deter a possible explosion from incendiary rounds), and a gun platform. Doors and windshields were removed and a mesh grill fitted to protect the engine compartment. The 2.5 Mercedes Unimogs, used as supply vehicles, were also specially adapted and armed.

11.   Graham Gillmore, edited manuscript.
12.   Graham Gillmore, edited manuscript.
13.   Account provided by Derek Andrews in February 1997.
14.   Graham Gillmore, edited manuscript.
15.   Derek Andrews, February 1997.
16.   Tim W, interviewed c.1985-86.

CHAPTER 5
COUP AND COUNTER COUP:
COMOROS, 1975-95

1.   Mike Hoare, *Congo Mercenary* (Robert Hale), 1967, reprinted as *Mercenary* (Corgi) 1968.
2.   The *Antinea*, formerly *Cap Fagnet*, was purchased by Denard with the help of Commandant Guillaume (the only French Naval officer to have been imprisoned for his involvement in the Secret Army Organisation (OAS) opposed to President Charles De Gaulle's policy in Algeria).
3.   Hugues de Tappie, interviewed 11 December, 1996.
4.   Hugues de Tappie, December, 1996.
5.   Hugues de Tappie, December, 1996.
6.   Hugues de Tappie, December, 1996.
7.   Hugues de Tappie, December, 1996.
8.   Patrick Ollivier, interviewed 11 December, 1996.
9.   Samantha Weinberg, *Last of the Pirates* (Jonathan Cape, HB), 1994 pp 83 and 104.
10.   Hugues de Tappie, December, 1996.
11.   Samantha Weinberg, *Last of the Pirates*, p 92, identifies Commandant 'Charles' as Belgian Roger Ghys, a veteran of the Congo.
12.   Samantha Weinberg, *Last of the Pirates*, pp 108-9. Additional information provided by Patrick Ollivier, 28 May, 1997.
13.   Hugues de Tappie, December, 1996.
14.   *The Sunday Telegraph*, 31 January 1993.

CHAPTER 6
COMEDY OF ERRORS:
SEYCHELLES, 1981

1.   Mike Webb: a Briton and former officer in the RLI.

2.   Roger, taped account provided to the author, 1986.
3.   Anthony Mockler, *The New Mercenaries*, (Sidgwick & Jackson, HB), 1985, pp 265-69.
4.   Mike Hoare, *The Seychelles Affair* (Corgi, PB), 1987, pp 39-41.
5.   Anthony Mockler, *The New Mercenaries*, pp 268-69.
6.   Anthony Mockler, *The New Mercenaries*, pp 274-76, and Mike Hoare, *The Seychelles Affair*, Chapter 3.
7.   Roger, taped account provided to the author, 1986.
8.   According to Anthony Mockler, *The New Mercenaries*, p 300, the mercenary concerned was Kevin Beck. Mike Hoare, *The Seychelles Affair*, pp 112-15, claims that one of his men was stopped and searched after another passenger, who had joined their aircraft during its stop-over at the Comoros, was found to be carrying fruit in contravention of Customs regulations.
9.   Discrepancies regularly occur between Mike Hoare's interpretation of events and other accounts. The circumstances of Johan Fritz's death is one example.
10.   Roger, taped account provided to the author, 1986.
11.   In *The Seychelles Affair*, p 87, Hoare briefly describes how an AK47 was made to fit in the base of a holdall after the butt was removed. He demonstrates a curious ignorance of basic weapon handling in dismissing the importance of the butt, "which in any case was of the folding para type".
12.   Roger did not personally witness this event. Hoare states that, "The commander popped up firing blindly in all directions. Answering fire hit him in the chest and he slumped down dead." (*The Seychelles Affair*, p 123.) Anthony Mockler, *The New Mercenaries*, p 304, claims that the vehicle commander, Lieutenant David Antat, was shot by his own men when he refused to surrender.
13.   Mike Hoare, *The Seychelles Affair*, pp 125-26.
14.   Roger, taped account provided to the author, 1986.
15.   Roger, 1986.
16.   Roger, 1986.
17.   Steve Berry, quoted in the *Daily Mail*, 27 November 1981.
18.   Roger, taped account provided to the author, 1986.
19.   Roger, 1986.
20.   Roger, 1986.
21.   Roger, 1986.
22.   Roger, 1986.
23.   Roger, 1986. In commenting about Dolinchek, Roger stated that "Somebody told me he was a representative from the South African government. In fact, he wasn't. He worked for the NIS ... but he wasn't there in an official capacity."

24. Roger, taped account provided to the author, 1986.
25. Roger, 1986.
26. The trial is described in some detail by Mike Hoare in *The Seychelles Affair*, and in Anthony Mockler's *The New Mercenaries*.
27. Anthony Mockler, *The New Mercenaries*, pp 332-33.
28. Anthony Mockler, *The New Mercenaries*, p 336.
29. Roger, taped account provided to the author, 1986.
30. Roger, 1986.
31. Roger, 1986.
32. Roger, 1986.

CHAPTER 7
MALTA, 1984-85

1. *The Times* (of Malta), 1 August 1981.
2. Quote by 'Tony', whose account forms the basis of this chapter. Additional information was provided by two other former team members.
3. 'Mario' is thought to have been a member of an alleged Nationalist hit-squad that existed in the early 1980s. The seven-man team was unofficially sanctioned by a Nationalist MP, and also guaranteed free legal aid if required. Two men were targeted by the group. One was allowed to live; the other was killed, though his death resulted from a personal feud rather than a planned execution.

CHAPTER 8
SURINAM, 1986-91

1. *Time* magazine, 30 May 1983.
2. Patrick Chauvel, 'Mercs in Surinam', *Soldier of Fortune*, June 1987.
3. Patrick Chauvel, 'Mercs in Surinam'.
4. Patrick Chauvel, 'Mercs in Surinam'. Additional information also from *Soldier of Fortune*: 'Merc Rip-Off in Surinam' by Dr John, August 1984; 'A Slow Boat to a Slow War', by Robert K Brown, August 1987; 'Case of the Missing Mercs', by Patrick Chauvel, December 1987.
5. Alan 'Bowen', interviewed 15 November 1996.
6. Alan 'Bowen', November 1996.
7. Alan 'Bowen', November 1996.
8. Eric Deroo, in *The Cook Report*, Carlton Television, 27 June 1995.
9. Alan 'Bowen', interviewed 15 November 1996.
10. Alan 'Bowen', November 1996.

11. Alan 'Bowen', November 1996.
12. Alan 'Bowen', November 1996.
13. Alan 'Bowen', November 1996.
14. Alan 'Bowen', November 1996.
15. Alan 'Bowen', November 1996.
16. Alan 'Bowen', November 1996.
17. According to Ronnie Brunswijk in *The Cook Report*, 27 June 1995, the mercenaries killed "about nine".
18. Alan 'Bowen', interviewed 15 November 1996.
19. Alan 'Bowen', November 1996.
20. Alan 'Bowen', November 1996.
21. Mick Pemberton, in *The Cook Report*, 27 June 1995.
22. Pat Baker, in *The Cook Report*, 27 June 1995.
23. Alan 'Bowen', *The Cook Report*, 27 June 1995.
24. Alan 'Bowen', interviewed 15 November, 1996
25. Alan 'Bowen', November 1996.
26. Alan 'Bowen', November 1996.
27. Alan 'Bowen', interviewed February, 1997.

CHAPTER 9
OPERATION 'PHOENIX':
COLOMBIA, 1988-91

1. Much of the background for this chapter originates from chapters 11 and 12 of *No Mean Soldier* (Orion, HB), 1993, by Peter McAleese and Mark Bles, and from an interview with Dave Tomkins in December 1996.
2. *Arms Trafficking, Mercenaries and Drug Cartels*, Hearing before the Permanent Subcommittee on Investigations of the Committee on Governmental Affairs, United States Senate, 102nd Congress, First Session, 27 and 28 February 1991, p 20.
3. *Arms Trafficking, Mercenaries and Drug Cartels*, p 29.
4. *Arms Trafficking, Mercenaries and Drug Cartels*, p 27.
5. Interview with Dave Tomkins, 2 December 1996. An indication of the seniority of Colombian Army officers involved in the operation may be provided in the following exchange between Tomkins and Senator William Roth in Washington, DC on 27 February 1991 (*Arms Trafficking, Mercenaries and Drug Cartels*, p 26). Senator Roth: "You have said that a British citizen arranged an initial meeting between you and a Colombian general and his son that led to your involvement in conducting paramilitary training sessions in Colombia. Who was the Colombian general with whom you

243

negotiated?" Tomkins: "I have made no mention in my statement about a Colombian general." Senator Roth: "However, I believe that is what you told the staff in their interview of you, is that not correct?" Tomkins: "You mean in the United Kingdom?" Senator Roth: "Yes, that is correct." Tomkins: "That may very well have been correct." Senator Roth: "If that was the statement you made in your interview in England, would you please identify who that general was?" Tomkins: "No, sir, I will not identify him." Senator Roth: "Why not?" Tomkins: "Client confidentiality."

6.   Peter McAleese and Mark Bles, *No Mean Soldier*, pp 217-18.
7.   Dave Tomkins, interviewed 2 December 1996
8.   Dave Tomkins, December 1996. The arms shipment is thought to have been delivered to Gacha in December 1988.
9.   *Arms Trafficking, Mercenaries and Drug Cartels*, p 21.
10. Dave Tomkins, interviewed 2 December 1996.
11. McAleese's bullet-proof vest was probably left by a previous training mission undertaken by Yair Klein, a retired Israeli Defence Force colonel, and head of *Hod Hahanit* (Spearhead), a specialist security company based in Tel Aviv. Klein and his team conducted two, possibly three, training courses for ACDEGAM between March 1988 and early 1989. Klein was subsequently implicated in a plot to supply weapons to Gacha after the discovery in Colombia of 232 Galils from an Israeli arms shipment originally destined for Antigua and Barbuda.
12. Peter McAleese and Mark Bles, *No Mean Soldier*, pp 250-51.
13. Dave Tomkins,interviewed 2 December 1996
14. Dave Tomkins, December 1996.
15. Dave Tomkins, December 1996.
16. Dave Tomkins, December 1996.
17. Dave Tomkins, December 1996.
18. Dave Tomkins, December 1996.
19. Dave Tomkins, December 1996.
20. Dave Tomkins, December 1996.
21. *SAS, The Soldier's Story*, Carlton Television, 4 July 1996.

CHAPTER 10
"LOVELY PEOPLE":
YUGOSLAVIA, 1991-95

1.   Dave Fersen, interviewed 15 November 1991.
2.   Dave Fersen, November 1991.
3.   Dave Fersen, November 1991.

NOTES

4. Dave Fersen, November 1991.
5. By November, 1991, the dinar had been greatly devalued. Although the official exchange rate was about 38 dinars to £1.00, the local currency was worthless outside the country. Many people went by the black market rate, which fluctuated at around 114 dinars to £1.00.
6. The original Chetnik was a member of a 19th-century Serbian royalist militia. In 1991, the term was used to describe a Serbian irregular and, eventually, any Serbian soldier. Serbs, remembering Ante Pavelić's pro-Nazi Independent State of Croatia, in turn referred to Croats as *Ustaše*.
7. Karl Whitburn, interviewed in Zagreb, 30 November 1991.
8. Andrew, interviewed in Karlovac, 1 December 1991.
9. 'John', interviewed in Karlovac, 1 December 1991.
10. Raymond Jeffrey, interviewed 10 November 1991.
11. 'John Ward', interviewed 10 November 1991.
12. Not the Dave Tomkins who served with 'Colonel Callan' in Angola in 1976.
13. 'John Ward', interviewed 10 November 1991.
14. 'John Ward', November 1991.
15. 'John Ward', November 1991.
16. Reg Walker, interviewed in Zagreb, 1 December 1991.
17. Reg Walker, December 1991.
18. Neil Valentine, December 1991.
19. Neil Valentine, December 1991.
20. Brian Madden, interviewed in Mala Bosna, 5 December 1991.
21. Local HOS commander, interviewed in Vinkovci, 4 December 1991.
22. Keith Phillips, interviewed in Nin, February 1992
23. Keith Phillips, February 1992
24. Brian, interviewed in Nin, February 1992
25. Information passed on to the author during a subsequent trip to Croatia.
26. *Review of International Affairs* (Belgrade), Vol XLIV, 1014, p 11.
27. Tony Kendall, 'Bosnia War', *Combat and Survival*, February 1995.
28. Tony Kendall, 'Bosnia War'.
29. Alan 'Bowen', 'The Battle for Borak', *Combat and Survival*, June 1993.
30. Alan 'Bowen', 'The Battle for Borak'.
31. Alan 'Bowen', 'The Battle for Borak'.
32. Alan 'Bowen', interviewed 15 November 1996.
33. The 'safe areas' were Srebrenica, Žepa, Goražde, Bihać, Tuzla and Sarajevo.

34. *The Times*, 29 June 1994.
35. Alan 'Bowen', interviewd 15 November 1996.
36. Alan 'Bowen', November 1996.
37. Alan 'Bowen', November 1996.
38. Alan 'Bowen', November 1996.

CHAPTER 11
FOREIGN LEGIONS
INTO THE 21st CENTURY

AYO GURKHALI! THE GURKHAS

1. Lieutenant Colonel J P Cross, writing in the introduction to *Gurkhas*, Sandro Tucci (Hamish Hamilton, HB), 1985, p 21.
2. East, BBC Television, 22 May 1997.
3. The *Independent*, 2 November 1996.
4. *The Guardian*, 2 November 1996.

HONNEUR ET FIDÉLITÉ: LA LÉGION ETRANGÈRE

1. Simon Murray, *Legionnaire* (Sidgwick & Jackson, HB), 1980, pp 99-100.
2. Simon Murray, *Legionnaire*, p 102.
3. Simon Murray, *Legionnaire*, p 139.
4. *Legion of the Damned*, Orana Films Pty Ltd, ABC television, 24 March 1991.
5. *Legion of the Damned*.
6. *Legion of the Damned*.

VIVA LA MUERTE! LA LEGION ESPANOLA

1. Much of the history of the Spanish Legion, up to 1976, is drawn from *The Spanish Foreign Legion*, by John Scurr (Osprey, P/B), 1985.
2. Tim W, interviewed c. 1985-86.
3. Tim W, c. 1985-86.
4. Tim W, c. 1985-86.
5. Tim W, c. 1985-86.
6. Chris Nash, letter to the author, 10 January 1986.
7. Chris Nash, January 1986.
8. Chris Nash, interviewed, April 1987.
9. Chris Nash, April 1987.
10. Chris Nash, April 1987.

11. Chris Nash, April 1987.
12. Chris Nash, April 1987.
13. Richard Grant, 'In Search of the Fiancé's of Death' *Esquire*, March 1992.

CHAPTER 12
INTO THE 21st CENTURY

1. The *Independent*, 25 February 1997.
2. The *Independent*, 5 May 1997.
3. *The Guardian*, 3 May 1997, named its sources for this information as, "American intelligence reports and an official in a company French intelligence used as cover". The *Independent*, 7 May, 1997, claimed that, "A French businessman", involved in the operation, "does appear to have been linked to the [French] President's special African adviser, Fernand Wibaux. But diplomats in Paris believe that Mr Wibaux was acting without the backing of the Prime Minister and Foreign Ministry and even against the wishes of the President's chief-of-staff, Dominique Villepin."
4. Information via former French mercenary, Patrick Ollivier, 4 April and 27 May 1997.
5. Contemporary media reports suggest that up to 300 mercenaries were in the country by early January. On 24 February 1997, *Newsweek* claimed that there were, "an estimated 200 Krajina Serbs, a few Ukrainian pilots and a handful of Frenchmen and Belgians" operating in Zaïre. Serbian, French and Moroccan mercenaries were said to have been at Kisangani when it was taken by the rebels in mid-March 1997. During heavy fighting around Kenge in early May, government forces were allegedly supported by, "several hundred fighters from UNITA", according to The *Independent*, 8 May 1997.

SELECTED BIBLIOGRAPHY

Geoffrey Bond, *The Incredibles, The story of The 1st Battalion, The Rhodesian Light Infantry* (Sarum Imprint), 1977.

Jan Breytenbach, *Forged in Battle* (Saayman and Weber), 1986.

Colonel Jan Breytenbach, *They Live By The Sword, 32 'Buffalo' Battalion – South Africa's Foreign Legion* (Lemur Books), 1990.

Wilfred Burchett and Derek Roebuck, *The Whores of War, Mercenaries Today* (Penguin Books) 1977.

Gavin Cawthra, *Brutal Force, The Apartheid War Machine* (International Defence and Aid Fund for Southern Africa), 1986.

Chris Cocks, *Fireforce, One Man's War In The Rhodesian Light Infantry* (Galago), 1988.

John Alan Coey, *A Martyr Speaks* (New Puritan Library), 1988.

Barbara Cole, *The Elite, The story of the Rhodesian Special Air Service* (Three Knights), 1984.

Chris Dempster and Dave Tomkins with Michel Parry, *Fire Power* (Corgi Books), 1978.

Mike Hoare, *Mercenary* (Corgi Books), 1968.

Mike Hoare, *The Seychelles Affair* (Corgi Books), 1987.

Peter McAleese with Mark Bles, *No Mean Soldier, The Autobiography of a Professional Fighting Man* (Orion), 1993.

Anthony Mockler, *The New Mecenaries, The History of the Mercenary from the Congo to the Seychelles* (Sidgwick and Jackson), 1985.

Simon Murray, *Legionnaire, An Englishman in the French Foreign Legion* (Sidgwick and Jackson), 1978.

Robert Pitta, Jeff Fannell, Simon McCouaig, *South African Special Forces* (Osprey), 1993.

Colonel Jerry Puren as told to Brian Pottinger, *Mercenary Commander* (Galago), 1986.

Lieutenant Colonel Ron Reid Daly CLM DMM MBE as told to Peter Stiff, *Selous Scouts, Top Secret War* (Galago), 1982.

Anthony Rogers, Ken Guest and Jim Hooper, *Flashpoint! At the Front Line of Today's Wars* (Arms and Armour Press), 1994.

Peter Tickler, *The Modern Mercenary, Dog of War, or Soldier of Honour?* (Patrick Stephens), 1987.

Samantha Weinberg, *Last of the Pirates, The Search for Bob Denard* (Jonathan Cape), 1994.

REPORTS AND OTHER WORKS

Fire Force Exposed, the Rhodesian security forces and their role in defending white supremacy (Anti-Apartheid Movement), 1979.

Arms Trafficking, Mercenaries and Drug Cartels (US Government Printing Office), 1991.

PERIODICALS

Combat and Militaria (Aceville Publications), various issues.

Combat and Survival (originally Aerospace Publishing, currently MAI Publishing), various issues.

Raids (Histoire et Collections), various issues.

Soldier of Fortune, (Omega Group Limited/Soldier of Fortune Magazine), various issues.

INDEX

2 Commando, 40
5 Commando, 17-18, 19, 20-1, 22, 23-4, 27, 28, 227, 230
6 Commando, 21, 23-4, 28-30
10 Commando, 28
14 Commando, 22
32 Battalion, 91-8
44 Parachute Brigade, 98-114
51 Commando, 18-19, 20
52 Commando, 18-19, 20-1
53 Commando, 19, 20
54 Commando, 18-19, 20-1
55 Commando, 19, 21
56 Commando, 19
57 Commando, 19, 21, 23
58 Commando, 20

Aba, 22, 23
Abdallah Abderemane, Ahmed, 116, 118, 122-3, 125
Abdallah Mohammed, 122
Abderemane, Ahmed Abdallah, 116, 118, 122-3, 125
Abdić, Fikret, 207
Abedi, Wasochi, 26
Acker, Gary, 76-7
Adami, Dr 'Eddie' Fenech, 154
Adams, James, 177, 183
Aden, 229
Adoula, Cyrille, 13, 14
Afghanistan, 123, 202, 210, 227
African National Congress (ANC), 83-4
Ahmed, Mohammed, 122

Ahmed Abdallah Abderemane, 116, 118, 122-3, 125
Aitken, Ken, 67-70
Aketi, 20
Akoo, Joe see Nai, Ako Joseph
Al-Qasimi, Sheik Saqr Bin Mohammed, 227
Albertville, 16-17, 27
Albina, 160, 161
Algeria, 13, 213, 214-17, 219
Ali, Sultan Said, 116
Almaro (interpreter), 177, 182
Altena Farm, 34
Ambriz, 58
Andrew (of Truro), 192
Andrews, Sgt Derek, 42, 107, 113
Angola, 14, 15, 30, 56-77, 86, 90-8, 102, 105, 114, 118, 217, 229, 230, 236-7
Anjouan, see Comoros Islands
Annan, Kofi, 232
Antat, Lieut. David, 241
Antigua, 244
Antonio, João, 72, 237
Armstrong, Dave, 40, 42, 235
Arron, Henck, 155, 158
Aru, 22
Aspin, Leslie, 59-60
Astray, Millán, 220
Auriemma (in Algeria), 215
Aves, Paul, 71, 75

Bahembi tribe, 24
Baker, Pat, 158, 159-61,

166, 169
Balongo, Gen. Likulia, 232
Bambi, 114
Banks, John, 59-60, 65-6, 75, 77, 164
Baraka, 25-7
Barbuda, 244
Barker, Derek 'Brummie', 63, 74, 76, 236
Barlow, Eeben, 229
Barr, Cpl. Dave, 101, 111, 113
Barrett, Col. Gareth, 81
Basson, Koos, 54
Battlegroup Alpha, 92
    Bravo, 92
    Foxbat, 92
Beck, Kevin, 241
Beech, Sgt Bob, 114
Belford, Donald, 58
Belgian Congo, 11-31, 227
    Kasai Province, 11
    Katanga Province, 11, 13-14, 30
    Orientale Province, 22, 24
    see also Zaïre
Belgrade, 186, 195
Bendera, 24
Benin, 118, 125
Berry, Staff Sgt Dave, 114
Bestbier, Col. Frank, 114
Biafra, 32
Bihać, 206, 245
Bill (in Croatia), 202
Binion, Cpl. Pete, 54-5
Bishop, Prime Minister Maurice, 157
Bjelasnica, Mount, 205
Bles, Mark, 239
Blume, Maj., 16
Boddy, Tony, 71, 72
Boende, 18-19

Bogotá, 172, 175
Bondo, 23, 24
Bonhomme, Guillaume, 197-8
Borneo, 210
Borovo Selo, 188
Bosnia-Herzegovina, 188, 198-208
Botes, Des, 132
Botes, Capt. Piet, 99-100
Botswana, 35, 85, 105
Bougainville, 228
Bouterse, Desi, 155, 157-8
'Bowen', Alan, 158-61, 163-70, 202-5, 207-8
Bracco, 30
Brazil, 227
Brazzaville, 231
Brčko, 206
Breytenbach, Col. Jan, 78, 92-4, 98-9, 106, 111-14
Brian, 198, 239
Bridge, Eric, 17
Brindley, Gordon, 101
British South Africa Police, 36, 238
Bronsten, Ben, 192
Brooks, Aubrey, 132-4, 136, 138-41, 143
Brunei, 212
Brunswijk, Ronnie, 157-8, 160-7, 169, 243
Bufkin, Dave, 74-5
Bukavu, 29-31
Bulgaria, 89
Bunia, 21, 22
Burchett, Wilfred, 236-7
Burundi, 24
Busmey, L/Cpl. J, 102
Buta, 23, 24
Butcher, Brian 'Butch', 67-70
Butembo, 19
B, Gary, 161

C, Jean, 78, 80, 84
Cabinda, 118
Caetano, Marcello, 56
Cahama, 111
Cali, 176, 178, 183
Callan, Tony, 58-9, 61-6, 70-3, 76, 236-7
Camerone, Battle of, 214
Cameroon, 124
Camille, Eddie, 130
Canary Islands, 118, 219
Canini River, 107-10
Caprivi Strip, 85
Carey, Barney, 130-3, 136-41, 143
Carlos, Don, 213
Carmona, 58

Casa Verde, 172, 174
Casablanca, 226
Cassinga, 92
Castro, Fidel, 155
Cayenne, 159, 168, 169
Četnici, 192
Ceuta, 219
Chad, 123-5, 217
Challe (in Algeria), 216
Chambers, Tom, 236-7
Chan, Prime Minister Sir Julius, 228
'Charles', Comdt, 123, 240
Cheik, Said Mohammed, 116
Cheraquera, 114
Chetequera, 92
Chimoio, 45-6, 49
Chin A Sen, Henck, 155
China, 148
Chipenda, Daniel, 91-2
Chivemba, 113
Christodoulou, 'Shotgun' Charley, 58-9, 61-2, 64, 72-3, 75-6
Clarke, 'KD', 101
Coetivy Island, 129
Coey, Cpl. John, 41, 235
Cole, Barbara, 235
Cole, Capt. Peter, 81
Colombia, 171-85, 244
Comoros Islands, 116-26, 132, 241
Congo, see Belgian Congo
Copeland, 'Sammy', 62, 66-8, 71-2, 74, 237
Courtenay, Paul, 49-50
Crimea, 214, 199, 200, 202
Croatia, 188, 205, 229, 245
Cross, Lieut. Col. JP, 211
Croukamp, Sgt Maj. Dennis, 101, 105, 107
Cuamato, 102, 104
Cuba, 157, 172
Cuimba, 69, 76
Cullinan, 138

Dalgleish, Ken, 132-4, 142, 146
Damba, 63, 65, 66-8
Dave (Croatia), 204
'Dave' (Zimbabwe), 88-9
Davies, Philip, 71
de Beer, Cpl. Jannie, 40, 41
de Gaulle, President Charles, 13, 217
Deby, Idriss, 125
Delport, Col. Mucho, 98
Democratic Republic of the

Congo, 233
Dempster, Chris, 61-4, 66-8, 70-1, 73-4, 236-7
Denard, 'Col.' Robert, 14, 24, 28-31, 116, 118-23, 124, 125, 126, 129, 132
Deroo, Eric, 158, 160
Dien Bien Phu, 214
Dingwall, Jean, 144-5
Djaffer, Prince Said Mohammed, 116, 118
Djalasiga, 22
Djebel Aurès, 214
Djebel Chélia, 214
Djohar, Said Mohammed, 125-6
Djoussouf, Abbas, 122
Dolinchek, Martin, 130, 132, 136, 140-1, 143-5, 241
Dondo, Prime Minister Leon Kengo wa, 232
Dooreward, Pieter, 146
Drakensburg Mts, 100
du Plooy, Lieut., 41-2
Dubrovnik, 188
Duffy, Peter, 142, 146
Dukes, Charlie, 132-4, 138, 142
Dungu, 23
Durban, 81-2, 127, 132, 137-8

Edwards, L/Cpl. Trevor, 93-4
el-Yachroutu, Caabi, 126
Elizabethville, 14, 233, 234
ELNA, 58
ELP, 58
Envigado, 184-5
Escobar, Pablo Emilio, 171, 176, 178, 182-5
Española, La Legión, 218-26
Evans, Colin, 72, 73, 77, 237
Executive Outcomes, 229-30, 233

Fairburn, Nicholas, 142-3
Falcon, 194
Falkland Islands, 211
Falques, Roger, 14
FAPLA, 58, 72-3, 74, 76, 92, 95-8, 102, 110-13
Faradje, 22
Ferdinand VII, King, 213
Ferreira, Col. Deon, 93, 98
Ferrier, President, 155
Ferson, Dave, 189-91
Finch, Carl, 157
'Finny', 159-69

Fireforce operations, 38-40, 44

Fizi, 25-7

FNLA, 56, 58-9, 61-3, 65-6, 69, 75, 91-2

Foran, John, 49

Force John-John, 22, 25-6

Force Oscar, 25-6

Forsbrey, 2nd Lieut., 18

Fortuin, Cecil 'Snatch', 66, 77

'Fran', 192

Freeman, Barry, 67-8, 71, 73

FRELIMO, 34-5, 82

French Foreign Legion, 14, 62, 66, 157, 192, 213-18

French Guiana, 157, 159, 161, 166-9

Frichot, Robert, 130

Fritz, Johan, 133, 136, 241

Front for the Liberation of Mozambique, see FRELIMO

Gacha, José Gonzalo Rodríguez, 171-5, 185, 244

Gaddafi, Muammar, 124

Galan, Luis Carlos, 183

Gaudet, L/Cpl., 102, 239

Gaviria, Pablo Escobar, see Escobar, Pablo Emilio

Gawthrop, Brian, 237

Gawthrop, Vic, 75, 237

Gayoom, President Maumoon Abdul, 227-8

Gbadolite, 233

Gbenye, Christopher, 13, 20

Gearhart, Daniel, 76-7

Gemena, 18

Geneva Convention, 10

Georgiou, Costas, 58, 76
see also Callan, Tony

Geraghty, Tony, 59-60

Ghana, 227

Għargħur, 151, 153

Ghys, Roger, 240

Gillmore, Cpl. Graham 'Gilly', 110, 113

Gilmour, Cpl., 103

'Ginger', 72, 237

Giscard d'Estaing, Valéry, 118

Gizenga, Antoine, 13

Goatley, Charles, 135, 142, 146

Golu, 22

Goražde, 206, 245

Gorkha, 210

Gorogonza, 84

Grande Comore, see Comoros Islands

Grant, Richard, 226

Green, WO2, 105

Grey's Scouts, 36, 42, 84, 122

Gribbon, Barry, 127

Grillo, 'Gus', 76-7

Guevara, Che, 234

Guillame, Comdt, 240

Gulf War, 217

Gurkhas, 219-11

'Gus' (Cayenne), 169-70, 227

Habré, Hissène, 123-5

Hacienda Napoles, 176-8, 183

Hadlow, Steve, 107-10

Hall, Nick, 58-60

Hammarskjöld, Dag, 14

Hankin, Bryn, 197

Harare, 89

Hardenne, Lieut. Col. Roger, 27

Harland, Gordon, 91

Harris, Col. 'Jock', 98

Henson, Maj., 53

Hoarau, Gerard, 130, 143, 146

Hoare, Chris, 130-1

Hoare, Lieut. Col. 'Mad' Mike, 15-20, 22-8, 116, 127, 129-37, 140, 142-3, 146, 227, 241

Hod Hahanit (Spearhead), 244

Holland, see Netherlands

Honduras, 229

Hong Kong, 211-12

Horb, Roy, 155, 157

Howie (Croatia), 204

Hussey, 'Fuzz', 63, 73

Hutchinson, Robert, 83, 84

Ibrahim, Prince Said, 116

Igman, Mount, 202, 204

Ikela, 20

Ilio, Joseph, 13

Imamović, Gen. Zayim, 208

India, 209-10, 212

Indo-China, 214

Indonesia, 230

Ingle, Sue, 132, 136, 140-1, 142-3

Inkomo, 89

Inyazura, 53

Iraq, 227

Itsandra, 119

Izetbegović, President Alija, 205

Jadotville, 14

Jeffrey, Raymond, 193-5

Joe (French Foreign Legion), 218

Johannesburg, 99

John (French Foreign Legion), 218

'John' (of London), 192-3

Johnson, Mike, 62-3, 74

Johnstone, Maj. Peter, 25

Jones, Fred, 75

'Joseph', 149-50, 152

Julio, 174

Kabare, 19

Kabila, Laurent, 230-3

Kabimba, 24

Kaj, 189

Kalahari Desert, 98, 105

Kalonji, Albert, 11

Kamina, 20

Kandani, 120

Karlovac, 192, 195, 202

Kasatići, 203, 204

Kasavubu, President Joseph, 11, 15, 27

Kasimia, 27

Kasongo, 24

Katima Malilo, 85

Kavumbwe, 27

Kelly, John 'Spider', 65, 67

Kendall, Tony, 199-202

Kenge, 247

Kenya, 129-31

Kerekere, 22

Khamani, Ras-Al, 227

Kibombo, 19

Kimba, Prime Minister Evariste, 27, 234

Kindu, 19-20, 29

Kinshasa (Léopoldville), 59, 61, 64-6, 73-5, 231-3

Kirton, Pat, 17

Kisangani, 232, 247

Klein, Yair, 244

KMS, 228-9

Köhtler, 17

Kolwezi, 217

Kongolo, 19

Krajina, 188

Kraka, 163

Kruger National Park, 91

Kumrovec, 191

La Gagua, 177

Laurent, Col., 21

Lawlor, John, 73
Lebanon, 217, 227
Léopoldville, 13, 18, 20, 25, 27, 29, 234
see also Kinshasa
Lewis, Bryan, 65, 73, 74-5
Libya, 18, 124-5, 148, 157, 161
Lieberman, Senator Joseph, 173
Liegeois, Lieut. Col., 19
Likati, 24
Lima, Comdte 'Sonny', 75
Limpopo River, 87-8
Linford, Comdt Delville, 92
Lisala, 19
Lister, Thomas, 205
Ljesvojac, 199
Lokve, 202, 205
London, 58, 150-1, 154, 176
Lorient, 119
Louw, Lieut. Ben, 18
Love, John, 157, 160
Luanda, 30
Lubero, 19
Lubondja, 27
Lubumbashi, 232
Lubutu, 20
Lucas, Ken, 40
Lulimba, 25-7
Luluabourg, 15-16
Lumumba, Prime Minister Patrice, 11, 13, 234
Luqa, 153

Mabalique, 100, 101-2
McAleese, Peter, 48, 59, 61, 63, 73-4, 75, 99-101, 103-5, 171-83, 185, 236
McAndless, Jamie, 62, 65, 77
McIntyre, Malcolm, 72-3, 77
McKenzie, Andy, 71, 72, 76
MacKenzie, Maj. Bob, 41, 46, 48, 81, 229
MacPherson, Pat, 73
McPherson, Stuart, 63, 74
Madagascar, 116, 214
Madden, Brian, 196
Madrid, 219
Mahagi, 22
Mahé, 127-47
Mahmut, 202-4
Maiden, Jack, 19
Mala Bosna, 196
Málaga, 220
Malaya, 211

Maldives, 228
Malloch, Jack, 29, 46
Malloum, Gen. Félix, 123-4
Malone, John, 72
Malta, 148-54
Mambasa, 20, 21
Mancham, Prime Minister James 'Jimmy', 129-31, 141, 143, 146
Mandela, Nelson, 232
Manoel Island, 153
Maputo, 82-4
Maquela, 63-4, 66-70, 72, 73-4
Marchant, Kevin, 72, 77,
Mare, Cpl. Bates, 47
Marengo, Maj., 141
'Mario', 150-1, 242
Marsamxett, 151-3
Martinek (in Algeria), 215
Martinique, 159
Mauritania, 219
Mayotte, *see* Comoros Islands
Melilla, 219, 226
mercenary, definition, 10
Messina, 80
Mexico, 214
Meyer, Maj., 41
Mick, 159, 163, 165
Mifsud-Bonnici, Dr Karmenu, 154
'Mike', 149-54
Milošević, President Slobodan, 186
Mintoff, Prime Minister Dom, 148-9, 151-2, 154
Miran, 200-1
Mirkovci, 195-6
MNR (RENAMO), 84, 91, 123, 227
Mobutu, Lieut. Gen. Joseph Désiré, 13, 22-5, 27-31, 56, 75, 231-3, 234
Mockler, Anthony, 234, 236, 241
Moengo, 155, 160-3, 169
Moengu Tapu, 161
Mohammed (of Gambia), 204
Mohammed, Abdallah, 122
Mohammed Ahmed, 122
Mohammed Taki, 126
Moheli, *see* Comoros Islands
Moneta, Tullio, 130, 142, 146
Moore, Mike, 53-5

Morocco, 215, 218-9, 225-6, 233
Moroni, 120, 121
Morrison, Hugh, 66
Mosley, Charlie, 157
Mosta, 153
Mozambique, 34-5, 42-9, 82, 84, 86, 91, 95, 123, 227
Mozambique National Resistance, *see* MNR
MPLA, 56, 58, 60, 62-3, 76, 92, 236
MPRI, 229
Msida, 153
Mugabe, President Robert, 32, 34, 55, 80, 88
Muké, Col. Norbert, 11
Mulamba, Lieut. Col. Leonard, 27
Mulele, Pierre, 15, 234
Müller, Capt. Siegfried, 18-19
Munongo, Godéfroid, 234
Murray, Simon, 214-16
Murrayhill, 105
Muzorewa, Bishop Abel, 55
Myers, Andy, 230

N'djamena, 124
Nai, Ako Joseph, 65, 77, 236
Namibia, *see* South West Africa
Nammock, John, 77
Nash, Chris, 222-6
Naweji, 30
Negage, 58-9
Nel, Comdt Gert, 93
Nepal, 209, 212
Nestler, 17
Netherlands, The, 155, 157, 168
Neto, President Agostinho, 56, 92
Newby, Douglas 'Canada', 61, 65, 75-6, 237
Ngiva, 90
Niangara, 23
Nicaragua, 227, 229
Nickerie, 160
Nigeria, 32
Nioka, 22
Njonjo, Charles, 129-30
Nkomo, Joshua, 32, 34
Noel, Lieut. Col. Jacques, 23-4
North Korea, 148
Nustar, 202
Nyerere, President, 129

'O', Bill, 158-68
Oates, Tom, 75
Oberholtzer, Petrus, 34
Ojukwu, Col., 32
Okolongo, 110
Ollivier, Patrick, 122
Oman, Sultanate of, 228-9
Omauni, 92
Omuthiya, 110
Ondangwa, 86, 90, 104, 107
Opela, 20
Operation Askari, 97
  Daisy, 114
  Deny Flight, 206
  Dingo, 45-6
  Handsack, 114
  Hooper, 98
  Mebos, 97
  Missing Link, 114
  Modular, 98
  Phoenix, 183, 185
  Protea, 90, 91, 97, 110-11, 239
  Reindeer, 92
  Rumpunch, 13
  Savannah, 91, 92, 236
  Sceptic, 97
  Super, 97
  Vasbyt 5, 102
  Violettes Imperiales, 23
  Watch Chain, 16-17
  White Giant, 22
Organization of African Unity, 123
Os Terrivis, 91-8
Oueddeï, Goukouni, 123-4
Owen, Ned, 183

Pag, island of, 197
Papua New Guinea, 228, 230
Paraga, Doboslav, 193-4, 199
Paramaribo, 157
Park, Jim, 84
Parry, Michel, 236-7
Pathfinder Company, 98-115
Paul (in Croatia), 202
Paul (in South Africa), 84-7, 89, 91, 238
Paulis, 20-1, 23
Pavelič, Ante, 245
Payden, Dave, 68, 69-71
Pederson, Oyvind, 158, 160
Pemberton, Mike, 158, 160, 164-6, 169
People's Caretaker

Council, 34
People's Liberation Army of Namibia, *see* PLAN
Perren, Frank, 59
Perry (Cayenne), 169
Peters, Comdt John, 22, 23, 25-6, 27-8
Petrinja, 189-91
Phalaborwa, 84, 87, 89, 91
Philip, 201
Philippeville, 214, 217
Philistines, The, 98-115
Phillips, Keith, 196-7
PLAN, 92, 97, 114
Platte, 146
Poko, 24
Pomfret, 98
Port Mahagi, 22
Portugal, 35, 56, 213
Portuguese Liberation Army, 58
Potgieter, Hennie, 40
Pretoria, 84, 99-100
Prinsloo, Vernon, 135, 146
Puerto Boyaca, 173
Punia, 20, 28-9
Puren, Jerry, 13, 14-15, 27, 28-31, 130, 136, 141, 143, 145, 234

Quibocolo, 63, 67-9, 71
Quintin, Maurice, 28, 235

Ramon (interpreter), 177, 182
Rawat, Lieut. Col. Bijaykumar, 212
Rawlings, Flt. Lieut. Jerry, 228
Recce Commandos, 78-91
RENAMO (MNR), 84, 91, 123, 227
Réne, President France-Albert, 129, 141, 143-5, 147
Rennie, Mick, 63, 75
Réunion, 126, 132
Rhodesia, 30, 32-55
  see also Zimbabwe
Rhodesian Light Infantry, 36-42, 45, 53, 55, 87
Ricardo, 172, 174, 176
Richards, John, 157-8, 160, 162-9
Ridgway, Brig. Andrew, 206-7
Rio Zardi, 63
Rive Gauche, 21
Roberto, President Holden, 56-8, 61, 63, 66, 75

Robinson, Maj. Brian, 46
Roebuck, Derek, 236-7
Roger, 127, 130, 133-4, 136-41, 143-5, 241-2
Rogers, Anthony, 53-4
Ronda, 219-20
Roth, Senator William, 244
Ruys (Belgian mercenary), 234
Rwanda, 19, 30-1, 231

Sahara Liberation Army, 219
Sahnoun, Mohammed, 232
Said Ali, Sultan, 116
Said Ibrahim, Prince, 116
Said Mohammed Cheik, 116
Said Mohammed Djaffer, Prince, 116, 118
Said Mohammed Djohar, 125
Salan (in Algeria), 216
Salzmann, Cpl. Carl, 53-4
Samba, 19
Santo Antonio do Zaïre, 63, 66, 74, 236
São Salvador, 59, 61, 65-6, 70, 73-5, 237
Sarajevo, 198, 205-7, 245
Saunders, Doug, 63, 74
Savimbi, Jonas, 56
Saxema, Capt. Umesh, 135
Schramme, Jean 'Black Jack', 14, 28-31, 235
Schröder, George, 28, 129
Security Advisory Services, 59
Séko, Mobutu Sése, 31, 56, 230, 233
  see also Mobutu, Lieut. Gen. Joseph Désiré
Selous Scouts, 36, 42, 44-5, 55, 78, 80, 84, 86
Serbia, 186
Sergeanaro, 72
Seychelles, 127-47
Shah, Prithi Narain, 209
Shankar, President Ramsewak, 157-8
Sierra Leone, 229-30
Simbas, 15, 18, 20-4
Sims, Bob, 130, 132, 136, 140-1, 143-4
Singh, Paul Chow, 143
Singirok, Brig. Gen. Jerry, 228
Sipaliwini, 157
Sisak, 189-91
Sithole, Revd Ndabaningi,

INDEX

32, 34
Slavonia, 188, 195, 207
Slovenia, 186, 193, 198
Smith, Prime Minister Ian, 34
Soames, Nicholas, 212
Soilih, Ali, 118, 121-2
Sollaiman, 202
South West Africa (SWA), 85-7, 92, 98, 106, 107, 114
South West Africa People's Organization, *see* SWAPO
Spanish Civil War, 213
Spanish Legion, The, 218-26
Special Air Service, 18, 34-5, 36, 41, 45-8, 55, 228-29
Spicer, Tim, 228
Srebrenica, 205, 207, 245
Sri Lanka, 229
Stanleyville (Kisangani), 13, 19, 20-1, 23, 29-30, 232
Steiner, Rolf, 32
Stirling, Col. David, 228
Stolkertsijvew, 157
Sudan, 23, 32, 124, 214
Surinam, 155-70
Suttil, Ian, 84
SWAPO, 86, 92, 95, 97-8, 102, 105-6, 113

Ta'Xbiex, 152
Tacujana Indians, 160-2
Tagney, Terry, 176, 183
Taki, Mohammed, 126
Tanzania, 24, 34, 129
Tappie, Hugues de, 118-19, 121, 124
Tavernier, Comdt Christian, 14, 22, 231
Taylor, Colin, 58-9
Tel Aviv, 244
Tembue, 45, 48
Tempe, 98
Terreros, Lieut. Col. José Millán, 218
Thapa, Gen. Amarsing, 219
Theo (in Algeria), 215
Thomas, Commander, 162
Tibet, 209
Tickler, Peter, 237
'Tiger', 177, 179-80, 183
Tilsey, John, 63, 74
Tim, 94
Tito, Josip Broz, 186
Tombalbaye, President

François, 123
Tômboco, 70, 74, 75, 236, 237
Tomkins, Dave (Angola), 59, 62-6, 74-5, 171-84
Tomkins, Dave (Croatia), 197
'Tony', 149-54, 152
Topusko, 193
Toyco, 177, 182
Travnik, 205
Treskavica, 207-8
Tripoli, 124
Trnovo, 207
Trujillo, President César Gaviria, 183
Tshiksekedi, Etienne, 232
Tshombe, Moise, 11, 13-15, 19, 24, 27, 28-9, 31, 234, 235
Tuđman, President, 193
Turanj, 202
Tuzla, 245

UDI, 34-5
Uganda, 22, 231
UNITA, 56, 92, 97-8, 247
United Arab Emirates, 227
Uvira, 19, 231
Ustaše, 245

Valentine, Neil, 195-6
van Oppens, Capt. Hugh, 25
Veldhuizen, Capt., 112
Venter, Al, 239
Victoria (Mahé), 130-1, 136, 141
Viljoen, Col. Eddie, 98
Villepin, Dominique, 247
'Vincent', 150-2
Vinkovci, 195-6
Vlasić, Mount, 207
Voidjou, 120
Von Rosen, Count Carl Gustav, 32
Vozuća, 206
Vukovar, 188, 195

W, Cpl. Nigel, 51-2, 94-6,
W, Tim, 114, 220, 222, 225
Wainhouse, Mick, 58-9, 61-2, 74, 75-6
Walker, Reg, 195
Walters, Lieut., 53-4
Wamba, 21
Wanie Rukulu, 21
'Ward, John', 193-5
Watsa, 22-3
Webb, Mike, 127, 146

Weinberg, Samantha, 240
Wessels, Sgt John, 115
Whirity, Kevin, 67-9, 71
Whitburn, Karl, 192
Wibaux, Fernand, 247
Wicks, Maj. Alastair, 22, 25-7
Wileman David, 237
Wileman, Michael, 237
Williams, 'Taffy', 32
Willis, Maj. Colin, 81
Wilson, 2nd Lieut. Gary, 18
Wilson, Terry, 69, 70
Wiseman, Mike, 73, 77
Woodley, Philip, 59
Wright, Robin, 74
Wyatt, Sean, 99-100

Xangongo, 90-1, 111, 112

Y, Tony, 50
Yakusu, 21
Yemen, 32, 228
Yugoslavia, 186-208, 218, 230
Yumbi, 20
Yungu, 27

Zadar, 205
Zagreb, 188, 189, 191, 193, 197
Zaïre, 31, 217, 229, 230-3, 247
see also Belgian Congo
Zambia, 35, 56, 86
ZANLA, 34-5, 42, 45-8
ZANU, 32, 34, 89
ZAPU, 32, 34
Žepa, 245
Zeralda, 218
Zimbabwe, 55, 80, 82, 87-8, 114
see also Rhodesia
Zimbabwe African National Liberation Army, *see* ZANLA
Zimbabwe African National Union, *see* ZANU
Zimbabwe African People's Union, *see* ZAPU
Zimbabwe People's Revolutionary Party, *see* ZIPRA
ZIPRA, 35, 114
Zuć, 205
Zulu Force, 92